COOPERATIVE VOCATIONAL EDUCATION

COOPERATIVE VOCATIONAL EDUCATION

A Successful Education Concept

How to Initiate, Conduct and Maintain
a Quality Cooperative Vocational Education Program

By

JOHN A. WANAT, M.A.

Director, Cooperative Vocational Technical Education
Division of Vocational Education and Career Preparation
New Jersey Department of Education
Trenton, New Jersey

and

MARGARET A. SNELL, Ed.D.

Assistant Professor
Vocational-Technical Education
Rutgers—The State University
New Brunswick, New Jersey

With a Foreword By

William Wenzel, Ed.D.

Assistant Commissioner of Education
Division of Vocational Education and Career Preparation
New Jersey State Department of Education
Trenton, New Jersey

CHARLES C THOMAS • PUBLISHER
Springfield • Illinois • U.S.A.

Published and Distributed Throughout the World by
CHARLES C THOMAS • PUBLISHER
BANNERSTONE HOUSE
301-327 East Lawrence Avenue, Springfield, Illinois, U.S.A.

© *1980 by* CHARLES C THOMAS • PUBLISHER
ISBN 0-398-03948-8
Library of Congress Catalog Card Number: 79-16576

Printed in the United States of America
N-11

Library of Congress Cataloging in Publication Data

Wanat, John A.
   Cooperative vocational education.

   Bibliography: p.
   Includes index.
      1. Education, Cooperative.   2. Vocational education.
I. Snell, Margaret A., joint author.   II. Title.
LB1029.C6W36   373.2'7   79-16576
ISBN 0-398-03948-8

FOREWORD

COOPERATIVE VOCATIONAL EDUCATION has been in existence for a long time; it is not new; it is no longer experimental. It has a long and proud history as a method of instruction that links the school's classrooms to the community classrooms in the shops, stores, offices, factories, and service agencies. Cooperative vocational education holds as its basic goal the preparation of students for useful and gainful employment in occupations of their choice.

The success of this program is demonstrated by the success of its graduates. Cooperative employers around the country have attested to the value of this program. A key indicator of the program's success can be gleaned from the growth cooperative education has experienced across the nation. It had a very modest beginning in the early 1960s. The growth since then has increased at an accelerated pace. According to the Annual State Report submitted to the U.S. Office of Education, there were 186,953 students enrolled in cooperative vocational education programs in 1968. By 1972 enrollments reached the half million mark. The three-quarter million mark was reached by 1977. It is forecasted that two million enrollments in cooperative vocational education will be reached by 1985.

Business people can appreciate the fact that cooperative vocational education students are the best source of trained manpower in our business/industrial community. Cooperative vocational education students have not fallen into the business/industrial world; they have chosen to enter it. These students are interested in a career not just a job. They are eager and enthusiastic young people who are anxious to try out the theories and skills they have been taught in the classroom.

In addition to the opportunity the cooperative vocational education program can provide to the business-industrial commun-

v

ity, it offers a tremendous service to the youth of our country. It is a workable approach to the challenge of overcoming unemployment among our youth. It is a most effective method of conveying an appreciation for and an understanding of a free enterprise system.

I believe the cooperative vocational education programs will continue to grow as more and more employers and students become involved in this educational process. I further believe we can find five clues to the future success of cooperative vocational-technical education throughout the country:

1. It is a popular program with "good vibrations" when it comes to public relations.
2. It is a highly versatile program.
3. It requires a special kind of leadership.
4. Thorough and efficient education demands its accountability and growth.
5. Public Law 94-482, the Vocational Education Amendments of 1976, provides for both continuation and improvement of cooperative vocational education.

WILLIAM WENZEL, ED.D.

PREFACE

THIS BOOK IS CONCERNED with how to plan and conduct cooperative vocational education programs. It is written to orient the beginning teacher-coordinator to the co-op program, while providing the experienced teacher-coordinator with a handy reference guide. This text, then, is a practical, workable, and up-to-date guide for vocational educators interested in the field of cooperative education.

There are fifteen chapters in the text. Each chapter is related to an aspect of cooperative vocational education and is presented in the sequential order normally encountered in initiating, conducting and maintaining a cooperative education program. Sample forms are used extensively throughout the text.

Unique features of this book include—

1. a chapter on safety as it relates to the total cooperative education program.
2. a chapter on management techniques to assist coordinators in maximizing time and communication techniques.
3. evaluation techniques used throughout the text in the form of self-evaluation spot checks along with a chapter concerned with the formal evaluation process of a cooperative education program.
4. numerous and various helpful hints and samples on how to involve cooperating employers in the total training function of cooperative education.
5. the latest information on labor regulations as it affects student-learners at their training stations.
6. the cocurricular features of the vocational youth organizations as they are used in cooperative education.
7. a chapter on special education populations.

ACKNOWLEDGMENTS

THIS BOOK is dedicated with deep appreciation to our spouses, Arlene and Arthur. We are especially grateful to the following individuals for their editorial and technical assistance: Meredith C. Hentschel, Mary Reece, Richard Van Gulik, Nancy Moore, and Joan Birchenall. We also wish to acknowledge Jack V. McGuigan, Ronald C. Flood, and Mike Mitchell for their contributions.

Finally, we express our sincere gratitude to all those who have assisted us with their advice and efforts in preparing this text, and a special thanks to Arlene Wanat, Deborah Makarski, and Alfreda Obornik for their typing and productive clerical skills.

CONTENTS

COOPERATIVE VOCATIONAL EDUCATION

Chapter 1

A HISTORY AND OVERVIEW OF COOPERATIVE VOCATIONAL EDUCATION

WHAT IS COOPERATIVE VOCATIONAL EDUCATION?

Eₗₑₘₑₙₜₛ of cooperative vocational education can be found in education for over a hundred years. As early as 1824, an orphanage at Potsdam encouraged boys to learn trades in the community. It was quite common in England during the nineteenth century for children to work in factories part of the day while attending school. Early in this century college students were supervised by school personnel while they worked on their jobs in the community.

Vocational education legislation served as an incentive to many schools to start cooperative education programs. Although some school systems offered programs much earlier, most schools began their cooperative education programs in the 1960s. One major reason is that legislation provided funds, which acted as an incentive to start programs. The Vocational Education Amendments of 1968, in particular, contained funding provisions for cooperative education. Part G of the Act contained a definition that spelled out policies relating to the nature of the training experiences, the type of related instruction, and the extent of student supervision required in cooperative education programs:

> A program of vocational education for persons who, through a cooperative arrangement between the school and employers, receive instruction, including required academic courses and related vocational instruction by alternation of study in school with a job in (any) occupational field. The two experiences, related vocational instruction and job, must be planned and supervised by school and employers, so that each contributes to the student's education. Work periods

3

and school attendance may be on alternate half days, full days, weeks, or other periods of time.[1]

MILESTONES IN COOPERATIVE VOCATIONAL EDUCATION[2]

1906   Cooperative vocational education inaugurated at the University of Cincinnati by Dean Herman Schneider. The first "cooperative" program combined work and study as an integral part of the educational process.

1909   High school work experience programs established at Fitchburg, Massachusetts, in cooperation with the General Electric Company.

1910   High school cooperative courses established in the Cincinnati, Ohio, public schools.

1911   Experimental high school cooperative program established at York, Pennsylvania.

1912   First RETAIL SELLING Cooperative Training Program in Boston, Massachusetts, high schools organized by Mrs. Lucinda Wyman Prince.

1914   Dayton Cooperative High School, Dayton, Ohio, established cooperative programs.

1915   High school cooperative programs established in ten New York City schools.

1917   Smith-Hughes Act (Public Law 347, 64th Congress). Approved February 23, 1917, a month and a half before the United States entered World War I. Provided approximately 7 million dollars annually as a permanent appropriation for vocational education in the areas of agriculture, trades and industry, home economics, and teacher training. The Federal Board for Vocational Education recognized cooperative courses and encouraged schools to establish these courses.

---

[1]90th Congress, H.R. 18366: '*An Act to Amend the Vocational Education Act of 1963, and for Other Purposes*,' Public Law 90-576, 82 STAT 1064. Washington, D.C., U.S. Government Printing Office, October 16, 1968, p. 23.

[2]*A Report of Research Findings Regarding Cooperative Vocational Education as Identified Through the ERIC System*, Guide for Cooperative Vocational Education. Denver, Colorado State Board for Community Colleges and Occupational Education, *and* Public Law 94-482, October 12, 1976, 90 STAT 2145.

Antioch College, Yellow Spring, Ohio, initiated a plan for alternating study and work periods.

1921 Wilmington, Delaware, organized an office cooperative program in 1921.

1929 Murray-Wright High School in the Detroit Public School System designed a cooperative office education program.

George-Reed Act (Public Law 702, 70th Congress). Approved February 5, 1929. A temporary measure that authorized an increase of 1 million dollars annually for four years (1930–1934) to expand vocational education in agriculture and home economics.

1931 Federal Board for Vocational Education modified policy for part-time cooperative courses.

1933 Conference at Biloxi, Mississippi, arranged by C. E. Rakestraw. Plans emerged from this conference for expanding part-time cooperative education programs.

1934 George Elizey Act (Public Law 347, 73rd Congress). Replaced the George-Reed Act of 1929. Approved May 21, 1934. Authorized an appropriation of 3 million dollars annually for three years. Funds were apportioned equally for training in agriculture, home economics, and trade and industry.

1936 George-Deen Act (Public Law 673, 74th Congress). Approved June 8, 1936. Authorized on a continuing basis an annual appropriation of approximately 14 million dollars for vocational education in agriculture, home economics, trade and industry, and for the first time, distributive occupations.

1946 George-Barden Act (Public Law 586, 79th Congress). Amended and superceded the George-Deen Act of 1936. Approved August 1, 1946. Authorized 29 million dollars annually for vocational education and extended provisions of the Smith-Hughes Act and authorized increased annual appropriations to the states. Funds for vocational education were authorized for agriculture, home economics, trade and industry, and distributive occupations.

1957 Conference on Cooperative Education and the Impending

Educational Crisis held at Dayton, Ohio, on May 23–24. Conference was sponsored by the Thomas Alva Edison Foundation.

1963   Vocational Education Act (Public Law 82-210, 88th Congress). The central purposes of the Act were as follows:

1. To assist states to maintain, extend, and improve existing programs of vocational education.
2. To develop new programs of vocational education.
3. To provide part-time employment for youths who need such employment in order to continue their vocational training on a full-time basis.
4. To provide instruction so that persons of *all* ages in *all* communities will have ready access to vocational training or retraining that is of high quality, realistic in relation to employment, and suited to the needs, interests, and ability of the persons concerned. Such persons were identified as—
  a. those in high school; and
  b. those who have completed or discontinued formal education.

1968   Vocational Education Amendments of 1968. This Act received unanimous approval of both the House and the Senate. The main feature of the Act included:

1. Greatly increased authorizations of money.
2. Earmarked funds for the disadvantaged, postsecondary, and handicapped.
3. Work study and cooperative programs were given increased visibility and support.
4. Consumer education was authorized as a legitimate vocational expenditure.
5. Certain programs (disadvantaged) have waived the matching fund concept.
6. Earmarked funds for new and expanded cooperative vocational education programs.

1970   National Advisory Council on Vocational Education—a twenty-one-member body appointed by the President to advise the Commission of Education, the Secretary of HEW, and the Congress on the progress of vocational education in the country as required by the Vocational Education Amendments of 1968. The Council published five reports, which identified vocational education concerns, problems, and recommendations.

1971   Colorado Vocational Education Act of 1970 (Senate Bill 78, the 47th Colorado General Assembly) became effective July 1, 1970. This act provided financial assistance to school districts conducting approved vocational education programs.

1976   Public Law 94-482 "Educational Amendments of 1976" enabled the Commissioner to make grants to higher education institutions. The grants were for planning, establishing, and expanding cooperative education programs.

OVERVIEW OF EDUCATIONAL PROGRAMS USING THE WORK ENVIRONMENT

There are other educational programs, besides cooperative vocational education, that use the work environment. Some discussion of these alternative programs is deemed appropriate in order to avoid confusion.

Career Education and the Work Environment

With the advent of career education, many school districts encourage their students to explore career possibilities by observing and working in the work environment. Observation-type programs generally last from one day to a few weeks. Other programs encourage students to perform simple job tasks. These programs last from a few days to several months. The school's involvement, in terms of supervision and follow-up with career counseling, varies depending on each school's commitment to its program. The major purpose of these programs using the work environment is to provide general career information.

In 1974 a federal law dealing with education and known as the "Educational Amendments of 1974" included a section dealing with career education. Section 406 (d) states that—

The term "Career Education" means an education process designed:

(1) to increase the relationship between schools and society as a whole; (2) to provide opportunities for counseling, guidance and career development for all children; (3) to relate the subject matter of the curriculum of schools to the needs of persons to function in society; (4) to extend the concept of the education process beyond the school into the area of employment and the community; (5) to foster flexibility in attitudes, skills, and knowledge in order to enable persons to cope with accelerating change and obsolescence; (6) to make education more relevant to employment and functioning in society; and (7) to eliminate any distinction between education for vocational purposes and general or academic education.

A typical example of a career education model using the business/industry community for career choices other than vocational preparation is the Experience-Based Career Education Program (EBCE). This model was piloted through Part D Exemplary funds, through the Educational Amendments of 1968, Public Law 90-576.

Experience-Based Career Education (EBCE)

A concept that can result in numerous program forms, EBCE is a community and experience-based educational option for all students during the last two years of high school that maximizes the value of direct student experience and the unique capabilities of community institutions in helping young people prepare for adult responsibilities.[3]

Job Placement

Job placement is an integral part of career education. It is a work experience program on a part-time basis with a possibility of some released time from school. The primary purposes are to earn money and to explore career avenues. Very little effort is made to coordinate the work experience with the school studies.

Vocational Uses of the Work Environment

Work study programs use the world of work to encourage students to complete their formal education. While there are several reasons why students quit school, one of the major reasons

---

[3]Hagan, Rex W.: *Illinois Career Educational Journal,* What is experience-based career education? *33*:6-7.

is to earn money. Work study programs offer students a chance to work at a job and earn money. Though this program uses the work environment, the jobs generally are unrelated to the students' career goals.

Cooperative vocational education requires that students be placed in a job related to their career interest. Each phase of the program is designed to help students achieve their career goals, from selecting the training station to the training plan and related instruction. Students receive pay for their work experience as well as credit toward graduation. Upon graduation from high school and completion of the cooperative education program, they have developed entry level job skills and the technical knowledge of the occupation of their choice.

THE TYPES OF
COOPERATIVE VOCATIONAL EDUCATION

Cooperative education programs are offered in various fields of vocational education. These fields are agricultural education, business and office education, distributive education, health occupations, home economics, trade and industrial education, diversified occupations, and work experience career exploration.

Cooperative Agricultural Education

The need for increased agricultural education became evident around the beginning of this century. Soil erosion caused a decrease in the national food supply and the population growth resulted in an increasing demand for food. Besides those two considerations, the development of power-driven farm machinery required people to learn new skills. A means of improving food production also was needed. A solution was to improve agricultural education.

An increased interest in ecology created another dimension in agricultural education. As the need for additional food supplies continues and the population increases along with the new interest in ecology, numerous career opportunities will become available for students in cooperative agricultural programs.

Additional opportunities for students are available in the

off-farm occupations that include agribusiness/natural resources occupations. The total spectrum of cooperative education experiences include such training stations as milk plants, food processing plants, farm supply companies, greenhouses, nurseries, farm agencies, livestock sales, outdoor recreational areas, and wildlife conservation agencies.

Cooperative Business and Office Education

Business and office occupations have changed over the past fifty years. Skills that were formerly taught in commercial courses are offered now in business education courses. Students learn skills such as typing for their personal use in general business education courses, while in vocational business education courses students develop skills for employment purposes. In cooperative business education programs, students work in a variety of settings associated with the business world that include the following broad categories:

* Accounting and Computing Occupations
* Business Data Processing Systems Occupations
* Filing, Office Machines, and General Office and Clerical Occupations
* Information Communication Occupations
* Materials Support Occupations: Transporting, Storing, and Recording
* Personnel, Training, and Related Occupations
* Stenographic, Secretarial, and Related Occupations
* Supervisory and Administrative Management Occupations

Cooperative Distributive Education

As this country changed from an agricultural economy to an industrial one, distributive education became increasingly important. This field of service includes occupations that prepare individuals for gainful employment or advancement in jobs concerned with merchandising, marketing, management, and service operations.

Cooperative Health Occupations

In comparison to some fields of service, health occupations programs have developed slowly. At the turn of this century, the physician and nurse comprised a health team. That team now includes over ten members. With increasing technology, the health team will continue to grow. Another factor influencing the growth of this field is that health care is no longer reserved for the well-to-do but is regarded as the right of all people.

Several factors will insure job opportunities for cooperative education students in this field of service. Among them are increased insurance coverage, the increased life expectancy of people, and the advances of technology. These employment possibilities include hospitals, extended health care facilities and health professional's offices, pharmaceutical companies, drug stores, and community health agencies.

Cooperative Home Economics Education

Home economics education also has changed since the start of this century. Initially, home economics prepared students in the skills required for home management. While high schools still offer that type of program, vocational home economics programs train students to fill wage-earning jobs outside the home. Cooperative education students are placed in such general occupational areas as consumer education; child care and development; food and nutrition; textiles, clothing, and fashion careers; institutional, hospitality, industry, and home service careers.

Cooperative Trade and Industrial Education

Trade and industrial education is the field of service that includes the design, production, processing, assembly, maintenance, servicing, and repair of products. Cooperative education programs in this field of service generally are called cooperative industrial programs. In an industrial society the opportunities for employment are numerous. As a result, students find employment in a variety of businesses and industry.

Cooperative industrial education usually encompasses two basic models. One involves a program where the students are assigned to a daily block of periods in a given shop area for specific in-school instruction. These students are placed directly from their shop class to an on-the-job experience for which they were specifically trained.

The other model consists of a period each day of related class instruction for a group of students who are employed in a variety of diversified occupations. These students receive their specific training on the job and are released from school on either a half day basis or a week about arrangement. The instruction in this program is individualized to the unique needs of each student.

Cooperative industrial education students in either model are placed in the following trade and industrial occupational clusters:

* Temperature Control Cluster
* Visual Arts and Design Cluster
* Textiles and Leather Cluster
* Maritime Cluster
* Repair Cluster
* Service Occupations Cluster
* Quantity Food Occupations
* Industrial Energy Cluster
* Electric—Electronic Cluster
* Aviation Occupations Cluster
* Material Processing Cluster
* Construction and Maintenance Cluster
* Mechanics and Maintenance Cluster

Diversified Programs

At times it is neither feasible nor desirable to offer a specialized cooperative education program. Interdisciplinary or diversified programs combine the occupational fields of business and office education, distributive education, agricultural/agribusiness/natural resources education, consumer and home economics education, and trade and industrial occupations. This type of cooperative program is known as diversified cooperative programs in some states and cooperative occupational education in other states and is best suited to small rural high schools that have neither sufficient students nor quantity training stations in one occupational area available to justify a program in one field of service.

Work Experience Career Exploration Program (WECEP)

Educators have expressed concern for those students who develop a feeling of frustration or failure in academic achievement and wait for their sixteenth birthday in order to quit school. In this regard, educators in several states, in cooperation with the Bureau of Labor Standards, have developed a program that would permit youngsters fourteen and fifteen years of age to explore career possibilities while they earn credits toward graduation.

The WECEP program was developed in accordance with the concepts of action-oriented research recommended by the workshop on research techniques conducted by the Office of Education (U.S.O.E) for implementing the 1968 Amendments to the Vocational Education Act. This legislation was prompted by a vast amount of educational research that indicated that in order to help school-alienated or disadvantaged youth see purpose and value in their education it must include school-supervised work experience and training and exposure to real jobs and careers as a vital core of the educational program. This type of a program in many states is used as a precooperative education program.

Employment is restricted to three hours per day in nonhazardous occupations. Typical areas of training include, but are not limited to, entry level skills in food distribution, custodial services, general office clerks, and automotive services.

VOCATIONAL DELIVERY SYSTEMS

Several delivery systems offer cooperative education programs. Among them are comprehensive high schools, shared-time vocational schools, self-contained vocational schools, technical institutes, and community colleges. The format of cooperative education is essentially the same regardless of which delivery system offers the program.

Comprehensive High School

While comprehensive high schools may contain some vocational shops, they often do not have adequate facilities to train all of their students who are interested in learning the skills of various occupations. Then, too, some comprehensive high school shops offer only general training. The skills learned there frequently are inadequate for employment purposes. Cooperative education provides an answer to the dilemma of how to serve all those who desire to gain entry level skills for employment purposes, to make a comprehensive high school truly comprehensive, and keep the school budget within the acceptable limits.

Area Vocational Schools

Two types of vocational schools use cooperative education. The shared-time vocational school serves several communities. Students attend their local high school for academic education and spend the remainder of their school day at the vocational school. The self-contained vocational school differs from the shared-time school in that students receive both academic and vocational education at the same institution. In both cases, students receive their vocational training in shops that teach them the skills and knowledge they will need for employment. Then, students demonstrate their proficiency in a skilled area in an on-the-job experience.

Other Vocational Delivery Systems

Technical institutes and community colleges serve postsecondary students. Technical institutes have vocational shops and labs and many community colleges have laboratory type experiences for their students. These delivery systems offer cooperative education programs as a part of their training curriculum.

The postsecondary cooperative education programs are different from secondary level programs in three major ways. Secondary programs require regularly scheduled related class instruction. The postsecondary programs are more inclined to provide weekly or periodic seminars where the students have an opportunity to discuss their on-the-job experiences.

High school students are usually released from school on a half-day basis for part-time employment for an entire year. Postsecondary students usually serve a full-time internship ranging from a semester to an entire year.

Supervision at the high school level averages one visitation approximately once every two weeks. Postsecondary students may be visited from one to four times a semester.

THE VALUES OF COOPERATIVE EDUCATION

Cooperative education provides substantial benefits to students, schools, the business community, and the general community.

Values to the Student-Learner

Cooperative education offers students a chance to learn the technical knowledge and vocational skills of their career choice while attending high school. They learn from craftsmen working in the field about the most up-to-date methods and they work on equipment reflecting current technology. Besides on-the-job learning, students receive high school credit and earn wages for their work experiences. Often students who have been nonproductive in school find school more interesting when they are in a cooperative education program. Subject matter takes on a relevance that heretofore had little meaning to many in-school youth. The on-the-job experiences in the work environment provide the graduating high school student with that first job when applying for "with experience only" positions.

Values to the Schools

Schools benefit from cooperative education because the program enables schools to offer a greater variety of educational opportunities to students. Schools could not possibly afford to budget for all the equipment and facilities used by cooperative education students, nor could they afford to pay for the skills and experiences of community experts who share in the training of student-learners. Other values to the schools include utilizing the services of community leaders as advisory committee members; securing trade journals, materials, and equipment for classroom use; developing a list of experts in the field who are willing to make presentations to small groups or to entire school assemblies; and bridging the communication gap between the school and business community.

Schools are up-to-date on changes that are planned, or are occurring, in the business community. Is a business planning an expansion program? Is a business considering moving out of the area? Is a lay-off coming? Has a big new contract been received, which will result in people being hired? Is the company shifting from a manual operation to an automated operation? The answers to these and other questions affect the school's programs and especially cooperative education programs.

Schools who work closely with their business community have an opportunity to share in these changes. For example, in a tight labor market, alternatives can be found for students who cannot be placed in part-time training stations. On the other hand, additional training stations will "open up" to the schools as the business community prepares to expand their operation. The most important value to the school is that the business community shares their concerns and needs with the school. Once expressed, the schools have an opportunity to modify their curriculum to meet those needs.

Values to the Business Community

An important benefit realized from working with the schools in a cooperative education program is that the business establishment has very important input into how students are trained. The student's on-the-job training plan is developed by the coordinator with the cooperation of the training station employer or supervisor. While some general training plans exist, the outline must be individualized for each student. Input from the employer is needed to insure that the student will be able to accomplish all of the activities listed in the training plan.

In cooperative education, employers are under no obligation to hire the student-learner after graduation from high school. The employers have a chance to observe their cooperative education students in action and consider whether or not they want to employ them after graduation.

Another benefit to business is the development of a labor pool. With several people to select from, employers can hire the best qualified workers for their particular purpose. Many people feel that the quality of workmanship improves when there is a pool of workers in a particular occupation. At least by training high school students in different trades, businesses should be able to locate trained personnel when they need them.

Lastly, businesses have an opportunity to perform a community service by working with the schools to educate the youth of that community. The general public tends to be supportive of such activities and respects any organization working with students. Businesses that participate in cooperative programs often receive plaques or certificates stating that they worked with the school system as a training sponsor. Many businesses place the award on their reception room wall and regard it with considerable pride.

BIBLIOGRAPHY

Armsby, Henry H.: *Cooperative Education in the United States*, Bulletin No. 11. Washington, D.C., U.S. Office of Education, 1954.

Auld, Robert B.: Cooperative education: The case for the name. *Journal of Cooperative Education*, 1-5, November 1971.

Barbeau, J.E.: *Cooperative Education in America: Its Historical Development, 1906–1971*. Boston, Northeastern University, Ph.D. dissertation, 1971.

Crumley, Marguerite: Cooperative part-time programs — weaknesses of the past and present. *National Business Education Yearbook*, 6:205-216, 1968.

Canjar, Lawrence N.: Making co-op a truly educational experience. *Journal of Cooperative Education*, 6-8, November 1971.

Dilenschneider, R.L.: Ohio seminar stresses cooperative education. *American Vocational Journal*, 41-43, October 1966.

Evans, Rupert N.: Cooperative programs: Advantages, disadvantages, and development. *Contemporary Concepts in Vocational Education*, 282-290, 1971.

———: Cooperative programs. In *Foundations of Vocational Education*. Columbus, Merrill, 1971.

———: Expansion of cooperative education work-study plan. *School and Society*. February 1963.

Fitzwater, I.W.: Co-op education fills a gap in today's curriculum. *National Association of Secondary School Principals Bulletin*, 52, 80-99, February 1968.

Funk, J.C. and Windle, A.G.: Cooperative planning. *American Vocationaal Journal*, October 1955.

A Guide for Cooperative Vocational Education. University of Minneapolis,

College of Education, Division of Vocational Technical Education, September 1969.

Hagan, Rex W.: What is experience based career education? *Illinois Career Education Journal, 33*:6-7.

Huffman, Harry: Cooperative Vocational Education: Unique among learn and work programs. *American Vocational Journal*, 16-18, May 1969.

———: Is cooperative vocational education unique? *Contemporary Concepts in Vocational Education*, 300-306, 1971.

Keller, Louise: The teaching and coordination of cooperative office education. *National Business Education Yearbook*, 114-130, 1971.

Kramer, Rex and Boegli, Robert: Project and cooperative methods team up. *DE Today*, 4, Fall 1971.

Lanham, Frank W.: Cooperative part-time programs — projections for the future. *National Business Education Yearbook, 6*:217-226, 1968.

——— and Weber, Edwin J.: Cooperative occupational training programs need quality control. *Business Education Forum*, 11-13, May 1970.

Law, G.F.: *Cooperative Education Handbook for Teacher-Coordinators.* Chicago, American Technical Society, 1970.

Mason, Ralph E.: The effective use of cooperative work experience. *Business Education Forum,* 9-10, May 1970.

Parsons, Cynthia: Community involvement: An essential element. *Contemporary Concepts in Vocational Education,* 296-300, 1971.

Patrick, Paul: A work experience program meets two needs. *Agricultural Education,* 61, September 1966.

Pettebone, E.R.: Co-op as a basis for credit. *Journal of Cooperative Education,* 8-10, November 1971.

Public Law 94-482, October 12, 1976, 90 STAT 2145.

A Report of Research Findings Regarding Cooperative Vocational Education as Identified Through the ERIC System, Guide for Cooperative Vocational Education. Denver, State Board for Community Colleges and Occupational Education.

Robinson, Max B.: Some reflections on early cooperative education. *Journal of Cooperative Education,* 1-5, May 1969.

Rymell, Robert G.: Unique features and fringe benefits in co-op programs. *Journal of Cooperative Education,* 15-20, November 1971.

Silvius, G. Harold and Wolansky, William: Co-op program trains craftsmen and technicians to teach. *Industrial Arts and Vocational Education,* 58, 89-95, February 1968.

Smith, Farmer S. and Corbett, Julius D.: Industrial cooperative training. *American Vocational Journal,* 30-31, May 1969.

Sredl, H.J.: Cincinnati's CCST success: Cincinnati cooperative school of technology. *School Shop, 26*:34-35, June 1967.

Swenson, Leroy H.: Are co-op programs possible in small schools? *American Vocational Journal,* 22-23, May 1969.

Thomas, Lowell G.: Service is our business — Midland's 25 years in cooperative education. *Journal of Business Education,* 153-154, January 1966.

Thorne, Marian H.: Maximum benefits from the cooperative work experience program. *Journal of Business Education,* 327-329, May 1964.

Trapnell, Gail: A cooperative approach with DE setting peace. *American
Vocational Journal,* 31-32, September 1965.

Wanat, John A.: *Success Route for Your Students—Cooperative Vocational
Education.* Trenton, New Jersey Department of Education, Division of
Vocational Education and Career Preparation, 1978.

———, Cooper, Samuel and Klavon, Michael K.: *Cooperative Industrial Education: All Purpose Manual.* Jersey City State College, The Center for
Occupational Education, 1973, ERIC, ED096-387.

Zimmer, Kenneth: Cooperative part-time programs — strengths of the past
and present. *National Business Education Yearbook,* 6:195-204, 1968.

90th Congress, H.R. 18366: An Act to Amend the Vocational Education Act
of 1963, and for other Purposes. Public Law 90-576, 82 STAT 1064.
Washington, D.C., U.S. Government Printing Office, October 16, 1968,
p. 23.

Chapter 2

DETERMINING THE NEED FOR
AND STARTING A COOPERATIVE
VOCATIONAL EDUCATION PROGRAM

HOW DOES A COOPERATIVE EDUCATION PROGRAM
GET STARTED?

THE NEED for a cooperative education program becomes apparent in many ways and the decision to start a program involves several steps. One reason why schools initiate a co-op program is that the school usually does not have multiple facilities for its students to learn extensive vocational skills. Where schools have vocational shops, such as area vocational schools and comprehensive high schools, they may wish to implement a cooperative education program to act as a "capstone" program. This type of program affords students the opportunity to practice the skills they learned in school on jobs in the community. Guidance counselors, teachers, and administrators can feel a cooperative program would be a worthwhile addition to the school's current offerings.

Although interest in a cooperative program may come from several sources, the steps in starting a program are similar. First, a feasibility study is conducted. This is accomplished by establishing a steering committee and conducting a community survey. The community survey will determine if there are sufficient opportunities for on-the-job learning experiences in the business/industry community. It would consider current and projected employment trends as well as other pertinent employment and demographic data. Upon completion of the survey, the school administration evaluates the findings and considers the recommendations from the steering committee. If the decision is made to have a cooperative education program, the school administration seeks approval from the state department of education. Upon receiving approval from the state department, information about the program is disseminated to interested persons. Students then are selected for the program.

THE STEERING COMMITTEE

The steering committee has a limited existence because it serves only one particular function. A steering committee represents the community and gives advice about whether or not a cooperative education program should be established. A few weeks of investigation will often provide sufficient information for the committee to make its recommendation. Once the recommendation is made, the need for the committee ceases to exist.

Selecting The Steering Committee

The school administration selects the steering committee. Names of potential committee members are suggested by various people in the school system, such as guidance personnel, teachers, and administrators. When a qualified coordinator works in a school district that is considering a cooperative program, that person might be asked to prepare a list of potential candidates. The names would then be checked and approved by the school administration. Regardless of who has the initial responsibility for suggesting steering committee members, the chief school administrator makes the final decision.

The committee should represent the various groups in the community. Some of the groups are large and small businesses, different trade and professional organizations, community service organizations, the Chamber of Commerce, the communications media, community action groups, and parent groups. School personnel should also be represented, such as administration, guidance, and teachers. Students might also be included. Consideration should be given to current school students as well as alumni. While a committee may not contain representation from all of those groups, a cross section should be included.

Inviting People to Serve on a Steering Committee

Although various individuals may be involved in suggesting people in the community who should be invited to serve on a steering committee, the invitational letter should be sent from the chief school administrator. This procedure will not only give the members the feeling of being important and needed by the school, it will also minimize any apprehensions the administrators might have about its authority being usurped.

The Invitational Letter

The invitational letter should include several items. Among them are the purpose of the letter and why that particular person was chosen. If available, also include a listing of other members. Only a few well-constructed sentences of the letter should be devoted to explaining the cooperative education concept. Correspondence containing detailed information is often not read by busy people. Instead, a person from the school should visit or call each potential member of the steering committee and explain the cooperative education program and the function of the committee. The name of the school representative who will call the individual should be included in the letter. A final statement should address the extent of the obligation requested.

Sending a letter serves at least three purposes. First, it introduces the cooperative education program concept. Second, the introductory letter provides the recipient with a chance to talk to their associates about the program. While some people might decline to be on the committee when asked for their immediate decision, they might be more willing to serve after thinking about the idea for a few days. Finally, the letter sets the stage for a school representative to contact the proposed member within a few days to explain in detail the cooperative education program.

THE BUSINESS COMMUNITY SURVEY

Before the school administration can make their decision to establish a cooperative education program, they need information from various sources. The steering committee will supply some in its report. The business community survey will provide other considerations.   The general economic outlook of the area is another factor.   Once the various reports have been evaluated, the school administration can decide whether or not to seek approval from the state department of education to start a cooperative education program.

Recording Information from a Business Community Survey

Information learned on a community survey should be recorded on a form.   Although some of the information collected about potential training stations will vary from one field of service to another, much will be the same.   Demographic data should include the following: the name, address, and telephone number of the business, the name and title of the person interviewed, and the date of the visit.

Information About a Training Station

Training station information should include some data that will be helpful to the coordinator at a later time.   Many coordinators want to know how many full-time and part-time employees work for the company, the seasonal needs of the business, and the prospective employment needs.   That information indicates to coordinators where jobs are available at various times during the year.

Questions should be asked of the business representative about the business's hiring practices of teenagers.   It is important to know whether or not students have ever been employed by the business.   Other questions should pertain to the number of students employed and how satisfied the company is with their work.   The school representative should inquire about the willingness of the business to cooperate with the school in this education program, including some indication of the number of students needed and for what positions.

Figure 1*

COMMUNITY SURVEY

Name of Establishment _____ Date_____

Type of Business _____

Address _____

(1) Number of employees working at this establishment? _____

Full-Time _____   Part-Time _____

(2) Do you currently hire high school students for part-time work? _____yes _____no

(2b) If the answer to above is yes, how many? _____. Are you satisfied
with their work? _____yes _____no.

(3) If the answer to question #2 is no, would you consider hiring high school students
for part-time employment in a joint school/industry cooperative education learning
experience? _____yes _____no

(3b) If yes, in what areas?
Distribution and Marketing _____
Agribusiness/Natural Resources _____.____
Trade and Industrial _____
Business and Office _____
Food Service and Clothing _____
Health Care _____
Other _____

(4) Are temporary employees needed by your establishment during any of the follow-
ing times?
Holiday seasons _____   Summer _____   Weekends _____
Other _____

(5) Would you be interested in contributing learning material to the school? _____yes
_____no

(5b) If yes, what materials? _____

Name of person completing this survey _____

Position _____   Telephone # _____

General Comments:

_____

*The North Dakota Guide for Cooperative Vocational Office Education Programs.

OBTAINING OCCUPATIONAL DATA

Cooperative vocational programs should be designed to prepare students for those occupations that need additional workers.
Reliable data on occupational needs for the area served by the
program should be utilized. The following information should
be used:

1. Unemployment and employment rates in a geographic area
   and by occupational categories.
2. The availability of suitable work training stations in a
   geographic area that may extend beyond the local community or local school district.
3. Quantitative data on typical manpower needs including—
   a. Youth unemployment rate in the school district.
   b. Current job openings in the labor market area.
   c. Labor turnover and employment expansion rates.
   d. Five-year projections for employment growth.
   e. Job qualifications in occupational categories.
   f. Hazardous occupations for which student-learners may
      be exempt.
   g. New and emerging occupations.

Sources of Information

1. Government publications
   a. *Occupational Outlook Handbook* (published biennially)
      and the *Occupational Outlook Quarterly.*
   b. Manpower Report of the President (published annually)
   c. Census of Business (published every five years)
2. Local Public Employment Service
3. Comprehensive Area Manpower Planning Systems (CAMPS)

THE SCHOOL SURVEY

A school survey provides information helpful for the school
administrator to decide whether or not to offer a cooperative education program. The student body and the physical plant are
investigated. The students are checked to determine their needs
and interest in a cooperative program. The school plant is

checked to see that adequate facilities are available for a program. This information coupled with the community survey will determine the steering committee's recommendation to the school administration.

Survey of the Current Student Body

School administrators need to know the number of students interested in a cooperative education program in order to make an intelligent decision about whether or not to start such a program. When conducting an interest and need survey, the committee should check several grade levels. The reason is to provide an estimate of potential cooperative education students for an on-going program.

The student survey, however, should be just one indicator in arriving at a decision to implement a cooperative education program. Although students might indicate an interest in participating in a program, there is no guarantee that they will elect to participate in the program after it is established.

Surveying Former Students

Follow-up studies of former high school students who graduated one, five, or ten years earlier could be helpful in identifying the need for establishing a cooperative education program. The data could indicate unmet needs of graduates that could have been met through a cooperative education program. Factors to be considered in such a follow-up could include, but not be limited to—

1. The current status of the high school graduate.
2. Periods of unemployment after graduation.
3. Expressed needs for training that could have been met through a cooperative education program.
4. Identification of occupations best learned through on-the-job learning experiences.
5. The graduate's perception of readiness for the world of work.

Figure 2*

STUDENT INTEREST SURVEY FORM
COOPERATIVE OFFICE EDUCATION PROGRAM

Name _____ Date _____

Grade Level _____ Date of Birth _____ Male _____ Female _____

Homeroom Teacher _____

Do you plan to:

(1) Attend college?   Yes_____   No_____

(2) Attend junior college?   Yes_____. No_____

(3) Attend private business school?   Yes_____   No_____

(4) Seek employment?   Yes_____   No_____

        Name of school or college you plan to attend _____

What field or vocation would you like to enter?   Rank in order of preference your top three choices.

_____ Office Work (Secretarial, Clerical, Receptionist, etc.)

_____ Selling

_____ Store Management

_____ Office Management

_____ Mechanic

_____ Nursing (Registered, Licensed Practical Nurse, Nurses' Aides)

_____ Printing

_____ Church Work (Parish Secretary)

_____ Photography

_____ Service Station Owner or Attendant

_____ Military

_____ Data Processing

_____ Medical Technology

_____ Accounting

_____ Other _____

_____ Other _____

_____ Other _____

*The North Dakota Guide for Cooperative Vocational Office Education Programs.

Cooperative Vocational Education

Figure 3*

STUDENT INTEREST SURVEY FORM

Name of Student _____ Date _____

School Year _____ Grade Level _____

I am employed part-time. Yes_____ No_____
(If yes, answer no. 1, 2, and 3. If no, answer no. 4.)

(1) Occupation _____

(2) Name of Employer _____

(3) Address of Employer _____

(4) I am not currently working but am interested in pursuing a cooperative education program. Yes_____ No_____

I am now working and feel I would benefit from classroom training that would help me do a better job. Yes_____ No_____

I am undecided. Please give me additional information. _____

Signature_____

(Copy sent to Guidance Department.)

_____

*The North Dakota Guide for Cooperative Vocational Office Education Programs.

Survey of Professional Staff

Classroom teachers should be surveyed as well as guidance counselors. They might verify the names on the existing potential co-op student list or supply names of other students who they feel would benefit from a cooperative education program. Because teachers see students in different settings, the person conducting the school survey should check with many of the school's supportive staff. Among those people interviewed should be guidance counselors, teachers, school nurse, and members of the child study team.

Figure 4*

COOPERATIVE EDUCATION PROGRAM
TEACHER RECOMMENDATION

Dear Fellow Teacher:

_____ has applied for admission into the
Diversified Occupational Education Program. As you know, many factors other than
grades must be considered in order to select deserving, sincere, capable young people
who can best benefit by the training this program can offer. Having previously taught
this student, you are in a position to help me greatly in making a wise decision in this
case.

_____

Circle the word after each characteristic listed below that best describes the above-named
student and return the completed form to me at your earliest convenience.

1 Ability to learn	Quick	Fair	Slow	
2. Capacity for work	Unusual	Industrious	Average	Poor
3. Judgment	Uncanny	Sound	Average	Poor
4. Initiative	Exceptional	High	Fair	None
5. Appearance	Very neat	Neat	Careless	Slovenly
6. Leadership quality	Outstanding	Noticeable	Low	
7. Desire to make good	Pronounced	High	Average	Low
8. Ability to take orders	Outstanding	High	Average	Low
9. Reliable	Very	Ordinarily	Unreliable	
10. Perseverance	Unlimited	Ample	Moderate	Weak
11. General conduct	Courteous	Discourteous	Rude	
12. Accepts criticism	Readily	Indifferently	Reluctantly	
13. Ability to mix	Natural	Fairly good	Doubtful	

14. Would you want this person working for you? _____Yes _____No

15. Grade earned to this point: _____

Remarks: _____

_____

Return to: _____

_____ Signed _____
      Teacher-Coordinator   Teacher

---

*Work Education: **Diversified Occupations Cooperative Education Guidelines.** Arizona Department of Education, August 1975, p. 36.

Additional Information Needed in a School Survey

In addition to determining the nature and extent of student interest in a cooperative education program, the school survey seeks answers to several questions.

Are other schools in the immediate area offering similar cooperative education programs? The proximity of other programs is important because there is usually a limited number of training stations in the area. Of course, a factor would be the number of training stations located in the area served by several school districts. There are some instances, however, where two nearby school districts can offer the same cooperative education program without adversely affecting either program.

UTILIZING SUPPORT PERSONNEL FOR COOPERATIVE EDUCATION PROGRAMS

In addition to the teacher-coordinator, the training station employer, and the advisory committee, there are several groups of people in the school who contribute to making a cooperative education program successful. Sometimes they provide acceptance and endorsement for the coordinator and the program, and other times they actually provide some support service. The service might be given on an occasional basis or it may be an ongoing activity lasting from several weeks to several months.

The coordinator must work closely with the support personnel in the school. In many instances the coordinator has to identify the person needed, interest the person in the program, and then request the desired support. Among those people who are apt to be invited to provide some service for the students are guidance personnel, members of the teaching faculty, and on occasions, the child study team. The coordinator also works closely with members of the administrative staff.

Guidance Personnel

Guidance counselors provide a very important service for a cooperative education program. They might even be considered the front line in interesting students in cooperative education. The various members of the guidance department see all of the students in the school at one time or another during the school year. As a result, they are able to make a preliminary identification of potential candidates for the cooperative education program.

In order to make guidance counselors informed and supportive members of cooperative education, the program coordinator must share information with them about the program. It must be an ongoing process. By establishing and encouraging communication with the guidance personnel, a coordinator usually receives input from them about potential candidates for the cooperative education program.

The relationship between the guidance department and program coordinator depends in part on the way students are accepted into the cooperative education program. Some coordinators have no say regarding which students become cooperative education students. Others have varying degrees of approval over candidates. Still others have varying degrees of input about which students should be accepted. Finally, there are coordinators who have complete authority over which students are accepted.

When the guidance department has the responsibility of selecting the cooperative education students, the program coordinator must provide the counselors with information regarding what type of students achieve the greatest success in the program and what type of educational background the students should have. The relationship between the counselors and the coordinator is understandably affected by the students recruited by the guidance personnel.

In addition to the recruitment of students for the program, the guidance department also provides some testing services for the students. Such tests are in addition to the usual battery of tests routinely given to the student body.

Once students are accepted into the cooperative education program, the counselors continue to see them periodically. Sometimes they see the students regarding their cooperative education program. At other times they discuss the students' other classes and activities at school. Good communication is important between the coordinator and counselors so that the counselors will report any problems that seem to be developing with a cooperative education student.

Teaching Faculty

Teachers also provide assistance to cooperative education co-ordinators. In order to engage in a worthwhile working relationship with teachers, a coordinator must do considerable public relations work. Many teachers fail to understand or appreciate the work schedule of a coordinator as compared to their own. They see that some coordinators have no extra duties, or homeroom, teach only one or two related classes in the morning, and are routinely seen leaving the school premises about halfway through the usual school day.

One of the services provided by teachers for the program coordinators is information about students who are applying to the program. Teachers are aware of students' peer relationships as well as the students' interest in and ability to do school work. In addition, they can provide insight into the students' personal habits.

While many teachers are reluctant to write a review about their students, they are willing to verbally express their feelings to the coordinator. The verbal response can be time-consuming, but it often is advantageous in that it permits a discussion to occur about some detail that might pass unnoticed on a checksheet evaluation.

In addition to providing initial information about students who apply to the program, many teachers continue to apprise the coordinator about the continued productivity of cooperative education students. By having such a working relationship, many coordinators are able to maintain a continual evaluation of their students' educational progress and keep problems from developing.

Besides providing information for the coordinator, teachers also give cooperative education students special help with their studies. Some students need review help for concepts they failed to learn fully or properly. Others need additional help of a temporary nature about some specific problem they are experiencing. The coordinator usually identifies the problem and then seeks a teacher who is willing to help the student on a temporary basis. Arrangements of a more permanent nature must be approved and arranged through the accepted channels.

The Administration

While the school administration provides support and endorsement for the program in terms of public relations, it also reinforces that support and endorsement by its policies and practices.

A successful cooperative education program needs a supportive scheduling process for the coordinator and students. It is essential that the students' required subjects be scheduled in a block of time so that part of the school day can be spent at the work station. It also is essential that the coordinator be free to supervise those students and to attend to those other duties commonly found in a coordinator's job description.

The school administration also shows support for the cooperative education program by the professional arrangements it makes with the teacher-coordinator. Some administrators provide an eleven or twelve month contract for the coordinator. Other administrators encourage their coordinator to attend professional conferences and meetings. Still others make no arrangements for their coordinators beyond the travel allowance for the required supervisory visits that must be made to observe the students in the program.

Child Study Team

Most schools have a child study team, which provides specialized help for students with unusual types of problems. Among the members of the team are a school psychologist, social worker, reading and speech specialists, the school nurse, and representatives from the guidance department. The usual route for a student to receive help from the team is through the guidance personnel or, at times, the school nurse. As each member of the team has responsibilities relatively well known to most people, only the particular help the school nurse can provide to the cooperative education teacher-coordinator is discussed here.

Students are seen by a school nurse on several occasions during their high school years. There are routine screening procedures that must be conducted and physical examinations and immunizations that have to be documented. In addition, students are sent to the nurse when they are injured or are sick at school.

The school nurse can provide information to the teacher-coordinator regarding candidates for the cooperative education program and then follow-up information, as indicated, about students in the program. Sometimes students fail to remember their corrective glasses, or refuse to tell people that they have a hearing loss. Some students disregard a major weight loss or hide a skin rash or allergy. Those problems and others, such as students who frequently come to the medical department with vague ailments, should be brought to the teacher-coordinator's attention.

Besides physical problems and complaints, the school nurse follows up on injuries and accidents. Accident forms must be completed within a prescribed period, and many students tend to be casual about notifying the appropriate people when they are injured. Good communication between the teacher-coordinator and the school nurse can insure that proper procedures are followed.

INITIATING AND ORGANIZING A COOPERATIVE VOCATIONAL EDUCATION PROGRAM[1]

1. Notify the state department of education, division of vocational education, of your intent to explore the possibility of setting up a part-time cooperative program and request their assistance.
2. Meet with representatives of business, labor, and management to (a) establish the general need and (b) explain the nature of the program, its purposes and objectives.
3. Survey the community to determine occupational and training opportunities. Special attention must be given to safety factors, working conditions, wages, and all federal and state labor laws. Employers should be approached to discover their willingness to employ cooperative education students and participate in the program.
4. Select a qualified teacher-coordinator on the basis of the duties and functions to be performed and the candidate's ability to meet the state certification requirements. Often,

---

[1]Wanat, John A.: *Success Route For Your Students — Cooperative Vocational Education.* New Jersey State Department of Education, 1978, p. 10.

a teacher-coordinator is selected as the first step in the process. He or she then becomes the principal investigator and prime mover in carrying out these thirteen steps.

5. Acquaint the school staff with the program.
6. Form a representative advisory committee to—
   a. Set minimum standards for training stations
   b. Help set standards for selection of students
   c. Make suggestions for course content
   d. Assist in placing students
   e. Help procure training materials
7. Consider the training qualifications of prospective employers.
8. Check the employers' facilities to determine their suitability for training students.
9. Obtain local and state board of education approvals of the program.
10. Acquaint all students with the program and determine their interests in enrolling. The process for application and selection should be widely announced.
11. Arrange for students to be interviewed by approved employers. Placement of students should follow only after a "co-op" training agreement has been signed by all parties and after working certificates for students have been obtained.
12. Provide adequate school classroom facilities and resources for the related technical instruction, which will be conducted by the teacher-coordinator.
13. Arrange "in-school" and "out-of-school" schedules for students.

Figure 5

A CHECKLIST FOR THE TEACHER-COORDINATOR IN UTILIZING SUPPORT PERSONNEL
FOR COOPERATIVE EDUCATION PROGRAMS

Yes   No

——— ———   1. I work closely with support personnel in the school.

——— ———   2. I supply guidance personnel with criteria for selecting student-learners into the program.

——— ———   3. I maintain an open communication link with the guidance department.

——— ———   4. I utilize the guidance department to administer and interpret a series of tests given to cooperative education student-learners.

——— ———   5. I discuss potential solutions to student-learner problems with guidance counselors.

——— ———   6. I utilize the teaching faculty to obtain referrals to the cooperative education program.

——— ———   7. I coordinate learning activities with other teachers.

——— ———   8. I solicit advice and assistance from the teaching faculty in preparing individualized student-learner assignments.

——— ———   9. I utilize the expertise of other teachers to provide remedial assistance, where needed, for student-learners.

——— ——— 10. I assist the administration in solving scheduling problems.

——— ——— 11. I keep the administration completely abreast of cooperative education activities, successes, and problems.

——— ——— 12. I supply the administration with a summary report of all professional conferences and meetings I attend.

——— ——— 13. I maintain a schedule of supervisory visits for my administration's information.

——— ——— 14. I effectively utilize the child study team to provide specialized assistance for students with unusual types of problems.

——— ——— 15. I maintain a system of communication with the school nurse, especially in following up injuries and accidents.

BIBLIOGRAPHY

Crum, Dwight R.: Implications for planning vocational education resources. *American Vocational Journal,* April 1971.

Evans, Rupert N.: *Foundations of Vocational Education.* Columbus, Ohio, Merrill, 1971.

Feirer, John L.: Let's get our content organized and our teachers cooperating. *Industrial Arts and Vocational Education,* 15, December 1964.

Goodwin, Robert C.: Locating manpower needs. *American Vocational Journal,* 19-21, September 1968.

A Guide for Cooperative Vocational Education. University of Minneapolis, College of Education, Division of Vocational and Technical Education, 1969.

Hill, Joseph E. and Nunney, Derek M.: Career mobility through personalized occupational education. *American Vocational Journal,* 36-42, October 1971.

Hoover, N.K.: Guidelines for successful supervised occupational experience programs. *Agricultural Education Magazine,* 41:132-133, December 1968.

Hopkins, Charles R.: A Feasibility Study of a Cooperative Office Education Work Experience at Mounds View High School. University of Minnesota, Master's Thesis, 1966.

Juergenson, E.M.: Some guidelines — planning work experience. *Agricultural Education,* 257, May 1967.

McGorman, George B.: Project 70001: New route for cooperative DE. *American Vocational Journal,* 60-61, April 1970.

Ristan, Robert A.: Manpower planning and vocational education. *Delta Pi Epsilon Journal,* 17-26, August 1968.

Rosenburg, Jerry: *New Conceptions of Vocational and Technical Education.* New York, Teachers College Press, Teachers College, Columbia University, 1970.

U.S. Department of Labor: *The 1978 Employment and Training Report of the President: A Report on Manpower Requirements, Resources, Utilization and Training.* Washington, D.C., Superintendent of Documents, 1978.

Wanat, John A., Van Gulik, Richard, Pfeiffer, E. Weston, and Mintz, Florence C.: *Cooperative Industrial Education — Administrative Handbook.* New Brunswick, New Jersey, Vocational-Technical Curriculum Laboratory, Rutgers University, April 1978.

Williams, David L.: Factors influencing the adoption of cooperative experience programs. *Agricultural Education,* 180, January 1970.

Winer, Ellen N.: Work experience education in secondary schools — a Massachussetts study. *The Journal of Cooperative Education,* 46-59, May 1978.

Chapter 3

SELECTION AND PLACEMENT
OF STUDENT-LEARNERS

SELECTION OF STUDENTS

COOPERATIVE education is for those students who need, want, and can profit from a program of this nature. Students should be selected "into" and not "out of" the program. Where there is an in-school vocational program, the cooperative educational program can be used as a capstone to their training by providing students with an opportunity to demonstrate their skills on the job in the world of work. For other students who have no specific vocational training, or limited training, selection into cooperative vocational programs should be based upon the criteria of student need and desire to enter the program, plus the teacher-coordinator's ability to place the students in meaningful, realistic learning experiences. The selection of students into the cooperative education program should not be used as reward or punishment. Students should not be selected into the cooperative education program because they are good, quiet, straight "A" students. Students must be interested in learning a skill and they must be able to benefit from the on-the-job training in a work situation. On the other hand, the program should not be used as a dumping ground for disciplinary problem students.

Application to Participate

The application form for a student wishing to enter a cooperative education program should contain information such as—What is the student's career goal? How old are they? Do they have a valid driver's license? Do they have their own means of trans-

38

portation? What hours can they work? What limitations, if any, would they impose upon themselves when seeking employment? What is their academic standing in school? Are they passing all of their courses?

Following the preliminary application, students should be interviewed. The teacher-coordinator should endeavor to learn more about the student's aspirations, skills, abilities, and personality.

SOURCES OF PROSPECTIVE STUDENTS

Recruitment of vocational students into cooperative educational programs is accomplished by teacher-coordinator visits to shop classes. The coordinator usually visits the students in their junior year. Shop teachers often refer exceptional students to the teacher-coordinator. The capstone experience gives the student an edge on the employment market by allowing the student to begin work in the latter part of the student's senior year.

In the case of the comprehensive high school, the teacher-coordinator usually visits students in sophomore English classes. Another approach is to assemble sophomores for a slide presentation on cooperative education, followed by short presentations from former students on the benefits of participating in the program.

Success is always a selling factor. The best and most effective recruiting device is a successful program. Students currently enrolled in a successful program will convey by word of mouth the benefits of participating in the co-op program. Peer involvement is one of your best selling tools. Cooperative education student participation in vocational youth activities will also bring recognition to the program.

SOME PROBLEMS

The teacher-coordinator must constantly keep in mind that the cooperative education program is an integral part of the total school program. Cooperative education is not job placement. Students who have existing jobs will often come to a coordinator to explore the possibility of entering the program while maintaining their part-time job. Students can come into the co-op program with a job in hand. However, the job must be approved by the teacher-coordinator. It is the coordinator who is responsible for developing a training prescription with the cooperating employer for the student. It is also the coordinator's responsibility to supervise the student on the job. If the student comes to the coordinator with a job that is not acceptable (the job does not meet the educational objectives of a cooperative education program) then that student should be told that he/she will have to forgo that particular job. If the student is reluctant to switch jobs, the coordinator should not select that student into the program.

Another problem arises when cooperating employers wish to have students for part-time work experience without providing a planned educational training program. If realistic on-the-job training, with rotation from simple tasks to more complex tasks, cannot take place, then the job training station should not be considered.

Another problem may occur when the parent is reluctant to have the student participate in the program. This problem can be eliminated, or minimized, by having the teacher-coordinator describe in detail to the parents the benefits to be derived from participation in the cooperative program and the specific job training station.

Final say in the selection process should rest with the teacher-coordinator. If the student wishes to pursue an occupational objective that cannot be secured in the immediate employment community, then the student should be placed in some elective course(s) within the school that would better serve the student's long-range goals.

INFORMATION BROCHURES FOR STUDENTS

A successful recruiting device is a simple but carefully considered brochure that describes the benefits of participating in a cooperative vocational education program. The brochures could be used as "handouts" accompanying teacher-coordinator presentations to assembly groups. They can be placed in career resource libraries. They can be left with guidance counselors.

Figure 6
HOW CAN A SENIOR QUALIFY FOR CIE?

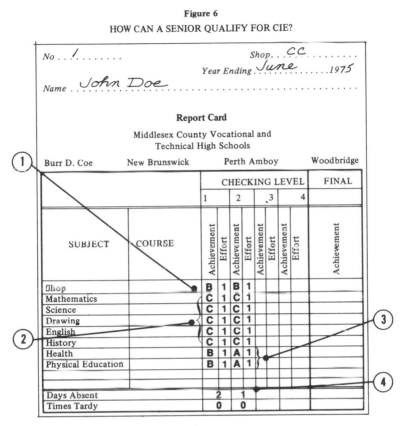

No. . . *1*. . . . . . .   Shop. . . *C.C.* . . . .

Year Ending . *June* 1975

Name . . *John Doe* . . . .

Report Card

Middlesex County Vocational and
Technical High Schools

Burr D. Coe   New Brunswick   Perth Amboy   Woodbridge

SUBJECT	COURSE	1 Achievement	1 Effort	2 Achievement	2 Effort	3 Achievement	3 Effort	4 Achievement	4 Effort	FINAL Achievement
Shop		B	1	B	1					
Mathematics		C	1	C	1					
Science		C	1	C	1					
Drawing		C	1	C	1					
English		C	1	C	1					
History		C	1	C	1					
Health		B	1	A	1					
Physical Education		B	1	A	1					
Days Absent		2		1						
Times Tardy		0		0						

1. A. Be recommended by shop teacher
   B. Have a grade of "B" or better in shop
   C. Be clean in appearance
   D. Have a good attitude
   E. Show initiative in seeking employment on his or her own, or through CIE coordinator

2. A. Have a grade of "C", or better, in all academic classes
   B. Be recommended by all academic teachers

3. A. Be physically able to work
   B. Have very few absences from school due to illness
   C. Show ability to care for one's physical and mental well-being

4. A. Excellent attendance during each marking level with each absence officially verified
   B. No cuts

5. A. Must carry necessary health insurance plan through family or school
   B. Supply own transportation to and from job
   C. Ability to make decisions on his or her own
   D. Maintain good grades and attendance after obtaining employment

If you meet the above requirements, contact your CIE coordinator or your guidance counselor.

Students can take brochures home to their parents to provide a preliminary overview of what the co-op program is all about.

The co-op brochure should briefly describe the purposes of the program, should describe the benefits of the program, should outline some of the program's rules and regulations, should highlight some of the successes of former students, and should provide information for the student on how to apply for entrance into the program.

WHY STUDENTS ELECT COOPERATIVE VOCATIONAL EDUCATION

There are multiple reasons why students elect, or are selected for, a cooperative vocational education program. Some students in their early high school years have a career goal in mind when they choose a particular curriculum of study. For example, a student entering high school makes a tentative choice to enter the field of electronics. That student then enters a curriculum track that will lead to skill development within the electronics field. Let us assume that the student entered a four-year vocational program. For the first three years that student receives a heavy concentration of electronic theory and lab experiments. In the senior year, the student is placed in the cooperative education program to relate what was learned in the classroom on the job. This on-the-job experience normally provides the student with the opportunity of demonstrating what was already learned in school, but more importantly, the student has the opportunity to learn new skills and techniques on the job in an industrialized setting. Accountability on the job does not merely rest with a grade, but rather with a standard that meets the specifications of the industry.

Some students enter a cooperative vocational education program to obtain skills in the business and industrial community that are not offered through in-school curriculum offerings. Through the cooperative vocational education program, the high school's curriculum offerings expand a hundredfold. Students can specialize on a one-to-one basis in any number of occupational fields. Very few high school students have the opportunity to have the individualized instruction that is afforded the cooperative education student-learner on the job.

Other students enter a co-op program in order to acquire an entry level skill. These students, for the most part, have pursued a high school curriculum in a general track that prepared them neither for college nor for the world of work. These students enter a cooperative education program in the senior year, and some enter as early as the junior year.

Still others are guided into the cooperative education program by teachers and counselors as a means of helping the students find themselves and as a means of keeping the students from dropping out of school. For many students, especially those who are very bright but unmotivated or unchallenged by the formal classroom approaches to learning, cooperative education becomes an alternative approach to achieving a high school diploma. The relevance of related subject matter becomes quite evident to the student who discovers that basic skills are needed on the job in order to be successful in a career choice. It is not uncommon for the student-learner, with prior poor academic grades, to considerably improve their academic standing after entering a cooperative education program.

Still, there are other students who elect a cooperative education program not for the immediate academic benefits of the program but for the instantaneous financial benefits of the program. Many high school students are finding themselves in adult roles with pressing financial obligations. Often, cooperative education is the partial answer to earning money and staying in high school. Frequently, this group of students are living on their own, married and in school, trying to raise their family's low income, trying to earn sufficient funds to further their education, or merely desiring to earn some extra spending money. Whatever their monetary reasons, these students soon discover that the business and industrial community has a lot more to offer than merely providing a paycheck at the end of the *work/study* week.

OBTAINING JOB TRAINING STATIONS

One of the most difficult tasks facing a teacher-coordinator is obtaining educationally sound job training stations for their stu-

dents.   Even more difficult is finding suitable training stations
during the month of September, especially if the teacher-coordinator does not have the opportunity to locate training stations during the summer periods.   For this reason, it is most advantageous
and advisable to have teacher-coordinators placed on extended
contracts over the summer so that they can canvas the area, from
door to door, looking for realistic job training stations.   Rarely
do job training stations come to the coordinator.   Most often, the
coordinator must seek out job training stations.   Of course, there
are referrals by other cooperating employers.   Fellow businessmen
often talk to associates about their participation in the program.
This often results in the interested party requesting to train a
student or two.   This procedure, however, is the exception rather
than the rule.   Much of the teacher-coordinator's time is spent
locating job training stations that are willing to rotate the students from simple tasks to more complicated tasks in the learning
process.

How Does One Canvas the Employment Area
for Job Training Stations?

A canvasing recruitment procedure that has proven successful
is to prepare a short letter describing cooperative education.   It
should explain why employers should participate in the program.
This letter, often accompanied by a brochure, can be mailed to
the business/industrial community serving the school district.   It
should be addressed to personnel managers and company presi-
dents.   There should be room at the bottom of the letter, or an
accompanying post card, that the reader can return to the teacher-
coordinator expressing interest in learning more about the program.   Irrespective of whether a return card is forwarded or not,
this letter should provide the coordinator with entry into the
establishment.   A follow-up telephone call to the company asking
if they had reviewed the letter often affords the coordinator the
opportunity to further discuss the program.

The co-op program cannot succeed unless the teacher-coordinator literally knocks on doors to "sell" the program.   Teacher-
coordinators must be convinced that the program works.   They

must show enthusiasm. They must develop a presentation that will entice employers to participate in the program. The coordinator, however, should not resort to high pressure sales tactics. This, above all else, can turn a potential employer off to the program.

Leads to Potential Employers

Teacher-coordinators should try to adopt real estate agency procedures when seeking potential employers. An effective real estate agent makes telephone calls to potential buyers and/or sellers. Irrespective of how they make their contacts for a potential client, they keep an up-to-date file on potential leads. Likewise, a teacher-coordinator should have a file containing information such as name of company; person to contact; number of personnel employed; do they hire young people; have they had a co-op student in the past; and if there was a previous bad experience and the cooperative employer no longer participates, what was that experience and how can it be rectified? Teacher-coordinators often fail to follow-up on employers who previously trained cooperative education students. Sometimes a cooperating employer will take a student for a year and not take another student the subsequent year. A reason for not hiring a student the second year could be that the cooperating employer retained the graduated co-op student and did not have need for an additional part-time worker. The coordinator should not eliminate this training station from the files. The coordinator should make a note on an index card to follow-up the training station in a few months to see if the cooperating employer's needs have changed. A telephone call to the employer may result in a continuation of that employer in the program.

The public libraries contain bound copies of industrial indexes on major companies located in the state. The Chamber of Commerce usually has a listing of its members that gives statistical data on the size of the company, the number of employees, hourly wage rates, and types of positions offered. Teacher-coordinators should make use of this information in canvassing for leads for potential training stations.

Figure 7*

COMPANY _____

Address _____

Town _____

Phone _____ Date _____

Dear _____

This will introduce _____

from _____ High School,

who wishes to apply for a _____

position with your company.

Time available for work _____

Comments/Experience _____

_____

_____

_____

Teacher/Coordinator

Phone

Teacher/Coord. _____

Dear Employer:

Please complete and mail at the conclusion of the interview. Thank you.

Co-op Student _____

1. Has been accepted _____

2. Has not been accepted _____

3. Is under consideration _____

Starting date _____

Work Schedule _____

Comments: _____

_____

Personnel Representative

_____

Company

*BOCES III, Division of Occupational Education, Diversified Cooperative Education Program. The reverse of the form is preprinted with the school's mailing address. The form is to be folded, stapled, and returned to the school.

Figure 8*

EMPLOYER RECORD

Job Title _____ Date _____

Update File _____ CO-OP _____ Developed by _____

Send Letter _____ WECEP _____ Referred to _____

FULLTIME _____ Date _____

NAME OF FIRM _____ TYPE OF BUSINESS _____

ADDRESS _____ PHONE _____

CONTACT PERSON _____ HOURS _____ WAGES _____

JOB DESCRIPTION _____

QUALIFICATIONS _____

Student referred _____ Date _____ Results _____

*BOCES III, Division of Occupational Education, Diversified Cooperative Education Program.

Figure 9

MIDDLESEX COUNTY

VOCATIONAL AND TECHNICAL HIGH SCHOOLS

COOPERATIVE INDUSTRIAL EDUCATION   1 - 2 - 3

STUDENT RECORD

_____   YEAR _____
SCHOOL   SHOP _____
                       TRADE_____

NAME _____
ADDRESS_____
CITY & STATE _____
ZIP CODE_____PHONE _____

Submitted voluntarily

1. Placement date _____
2. Place of employment   OWN _____CIE _____
    1. Name _____ 2. Name _____
       Address_____   Address _____
       City & State _____   City & State _____
       Zip Code_____ Phone _____ Zip Code_____Phone_____
3. Hours worked _____
4. Salary: Beginning $_____hour   End $_____ hour
5. C.I.E. awards received _____
6. Graduation date_____
7. School honor roll_____
8. Extra curricular activities _____
    _____
9. Successful completion of program_____
    _____
10. Coordinator's comments _____
    _____

A coordinator should not overlook the opportunity to make presentations to civic groups, Chamber of Commerce, professional business organizations, and parent/teacher organizations.   Presentations can consist of prepared talks about the benefits of participating in the cooperative education program. These presentations can be accompanied by a slide/tape presentation of students and cooperating employers. Presentations should be followed up with handout material on the program including the teacher-coordinator's name and telephone number so that interested employers know who to contact for additional information or to offer a training station. Ideally, the cooperative employer will take on a student each and every year.

In order to keep a cooperating employer content and in order to live up to training agreement arrangements, it is necessary for the teacher-coordinator to communicate with them by follow-up visitations to the community on a regularly scheduled basis. Supervisory visits are essential to a co-op program. Cooperating employers must feel that they are part of the educational team. If cooperating employers do not feel they are part of the educational team, they will find very little relevance in continued participation in the program.

Another very important source of potential training stations is an active advisory committee. Frequently, advisory committee members will help find employment for co-op students. Frequently advisory committee members hire students in their place of employment. Advisory committee members also sell the program to other potential employers in the community.

Utilizing the State's Employment Centers

A source for potential job training stations is the state's employment centers. They receive, on a daily basis, employment opportunities from all over the business/industrial community. The agency reduces the pertinent employment data onto microfiche for easy access and dissemination to their regional offices. Contacts with the state employment agency can provide the teacher-coordinator with sources of available positions as they are received in the regional offices.

Another very important source of potential job training stations is the local newspaper want ads. Teachers and students should review the want ads for leads to job training stations.

Wherever the source of job training station leads to, the actual selling depends on the teacher-coordinator's ability to furnish the employer with a reliable employee and to furnish the student with a realistic on-the-job learning experience.

SUPERVISING STUDENTS ON THE JOB

Once the students are placed in a job training station, it becomes the responsibility of the teacher-coordinator to supervise these students on the job, preferably once every two weeks. During the initial employment stage it might be necessary to supervise the students more frequently. Many students will have attitudinal adjustment periods that will require more supervisory time. The supervisory process is more than merely "popping in" to see a student or cooperating employer. It requires that the teacher-coordinator observe the student on the job to see that the student is involved in job rotation as outlined in the training agreement. The coordinator should schedule visits to coincide with the students' training schedule as changes are made from one phase of the job to another. The supervision of students should take place over the entire spectrum of the students' workload. There is no fixed time that the teacher-coordinator should visit the student on the job. The coordinator should stagger the visits and the hours so that the student can be observed in all facets of the on-the-job work experience. A coordinator should not overlook the geographic location of the various training stations, which can assist the coordinator in mapping out a visitation route for various periods of the month.

The teacher-coordinator should allow at least one-half hour per training visit. This one-half hour of time should, on an average, include the travel to the training station and the actual visitation. A coordinator's schedule should be arranged in such a way that ample time is provided for on-the-job supervision as well as time for canvasing new training stations for cooperative education student-learners. The coordinator's schedule should be flexible enough to allow the visitation to begin as soon as the students are released to go to the job training station. Because students work part-time, over a period of time that normally exceeds the school's closing time, the teacher-coordinator's day is unlike other teachers since the coordinator must visit the student over the entire spectrum of the on-the-job placement.

It is of the utmost importance that the teacher-coordinator, as well as the cooperating employer, understand the rules and regulations established by the state department of education and the department of labor and industry. It is the coordinator's responsibility to inform the cooperating employer of the school's and the department of education's regulation governing cooperative education programs. It is also often necessary for the teacher-coordinator to remind the cooperating employer about the Child Labor Laws and the provisions contained therein. Since the cooperating employer is, in fact, co-teaching the cooperative education student, it becomes necessary for the teacher-coordinator to provide the cooperating employer with a set of regulations and some helpful hints on how to assist the student-learner on the job. In providing this information, the teacher-coordinator should be careful not to insult the cooperating employer but to offer suggestions and guidance to make the cooperating employer feel as though they are an integral part of the educational team. If time and circumstances permit, it is advantageous to call together all the cooperating employers for a few hours during an evening. The teacher-coordinator, in cooperation with the advisory committee, should provide a formal presentation to assist the cooperating employer in understanding the program's concepts, as well as how to deal with on-the-job training for the students they are going to serve. One of the greatest dangers that can befall a cooperative education program is to have the cooperating employer feel that he or she is not part of the educational team. When this happens, the cooperating employer begins to treat the student-learner as any other employee. The student-learner's training is reduced to repetitive tasks, day in and day out. The student-learner would not be considered a student-learner but an employee who contributes to the profitability of the employer. On the other hand, if the cooperating employer feels part of the educational team, the student-learner will receive a varied background of on-the-job experiences in harmony with the student's career goals and objectives. It is up to the teacher-coordinator to assist the cooperating employer to be an effective teacher on the job.

Utilizing Information Secured
Through Coordinator's Visitations

Coordinator's visits have no meaning unless the coordinator makes use of the information secured through the visit. The purpose of the visitation is to observe the student so that information gathered at the job site can be used to provide the student with individualized instruction back in the related class. It is wise for the teacher-coordinator to make a memorandum of the points observed while visiting the training station. If a teacher-coordinator observes the student engaged in an unsafe act, the coordinator should immediately correct the situation and then reinforce the proper safety procedures with the student back in the related classroom. The observation might also lead to a unit lesson that would benefit all students in the class.

Conversations with the cooperating employer and the student-learner could result in providing some individualized instruction to the student-learner that will assist the student-learner on the job. For example, during a visitation to a distributive education student at a retail outlet, the cooperating employer might indicate to the teacher-coordinator that the student needs assistance in calculating "mark-ups." The teacher can provide the student-learner with individualized instruction on "mark-up" during related instruction.

The coordinator should utilize this visitation time to ask the cooperating employer for assistance in obtaining reading literature that the student-learner can use back in the classroom. Employers can provide programmed instruction texts, periodicals, publications, schematic drawings, and technical material associated with the occupation the student is learning.

Summary Points to Observe When Making Visitations
  • The student-learner is being provided on-the-job supervision and instruction by the cooperating employer.

Figure 10*

TEACHER-COORDINATOR'S CALL REPORT

Business _____ Trainee _____

Person Contacted _____ Position _____

Date _____ Time _____

Points to Observe: Comments:

1. Conditions surrounding place
   of business.   _____

2. Attitude and interest of
   employer toward student learner.   _____

3. Specific operations in which
   student-learner is engaged.   _____

4. Immediate related subject
   matter needed.   _____

5. Personal appearance of the
   student-learner.   _____

6. Apparent interest of the
   student-learner in work.   _____

7. Miscellaneous information
   and comments.   _____

_____

_____

_____

_____

_____

_____

_____

*From Irvington High School, Irvington, New Jersey.

- The student-learner is being rotated in a multitude of on-the-job learning experiences.
- The student-learner is working in a safe environment.

Conversations with cooperating employers should indicate the student's progress on the job, the student's willingness to cooperate with fellow employees, the student's progress in meeting the

Figure 11

THE TRAINING STATION VISIT REPORT

Training Location	Student Visited	Supervisor's Name	Date/Time of visit	Mileage	Remarks & Outcomes
B&S Garage	Mary Smith	Rick Blake	11/1/78 3:45 P.M.	10	Mary was working on a carburetor at the time of my visit. She has received a good evaluation from her supervisor
Amazing Auto	Bob Gray	Jim Richter	11/2/78 2:15 P.M.	5	Bob was completing an automotive tune-up at the time of my visit. He appears to be doing a good job and received a very good evaluation from Mr. Richter.
Bamberger's	Steve Camp	Robert Burns	11/3/78 6:15 P.M.	20	Steve was completing a display during my visit. His supervisor indicated he needed additional help in calculating "mark-ups" and discounts.
The First Bank	Mary Ellen Wiley	Mrs. Fay	11/4/78 1:15 P.M.	3	Mary Ellen was typing mortgage notices at the time of my visit. She is doing a very good job and received an excellent evaluation. Mrs. Fay said Mary Ellen could use additional instruction in telephone techniques.
Presswell Records	Dan Brown	Sal Joseph	11/5/78 5:20 P.M.	15	Dan was drilling record blanks during my visit. I cautioned him about safety glasses, which he must wear. Dan is doing a very good job.

training outline schedule, the related instruction as suggested by the cooperating employer, and the student's and the employer's understanding of the intent and the objectives of the program.

How to Observe Students On The Job

The coordinator must remember that the cooperating employer's time is valuable. They are providing a service to the school system by training a student-learner on the job. The coordinator's responsibility is to observe this mode of training. Their observations are to be made as inconspicuously as possible and, occasionally, as unexpectedly as possible. The coordinator should not, however, interrupt the cooperating employer's work schedule. The normal work of the agency should continue uninterrupted.

The coordinator should make the observations and conferences as businesslike as possible. The coordinator's purpose for being there is to observe the student in operation and to discuss with the cooperating employer the student's progress on the job. The coordinator should, therefore, not waste the cooperating employer's time by talking about irrelevant activities. This does not mean that the coordinator should not be sociable and pleasant in the dealings with the cooperating employer. The conference and the visitation should be maintained at a professional level. If the professionalism is lost, it could jeopardize the entire training program.

How to Cope with Special Problems

A teacher-coordinator can often prevent certain problems from occurring if he or she takes the necessary precautions ahead of time. Utmost in importance is for the coordinator to determine the sincerity of the employer in regard to training the student-learner. During the initial canvasing for the training station, the coordinator should be able to ascertain whether the employer is looking merely for a part-time employee or whether the employer is truly interested in providing a true on-the-job learning experience. The employer's eagerness to review or work out a training plan with the teacher-coordinator is a sure indicator that the employer is willing to cooperate with the school. Training plans ensure that the progression of training agreed by the employer is carried out.

The student-learner must be interested in the job that they are going to undertake. If the student is mismatched to the job, both the employer and the student-learner are losers. The purpose of a cooperative vocational education program is to provide the student with a learning experience that matches their career goals and objectives. The job, therefore, should be one that can enhance the student's opportunity to reach that objective. A student who is interested in working in a particular job will show enthusiasm. The student who is not interested in that particular occupation will generate negativism. Employers pick up negativism and are reluctant to take on future students.

Even if the students like and want the job that they are engaged in, they will become dissatisfied if supervision is not provided by the cooperating employer. It is important, therefore, that student-learners be placed under supervision by a qualified person while on the job. The supervisory person should show enthusiasm and interest in the student-learner.

Employers often expect too much from the beginning trainee. This problem can be alleviated if the teacher-coordinator reviews the purposes and objectives of the program with the cooperating employer before the student begins to work. Employers who are given pretraining and/or direction are more than willing to cooperate.

The student-learner should be given a set of rules and instructions at the beginning of their participation in the program. Student-learners should understand that they are expected to fulfill the following responsibilities to the school and to their training sponsor:

1. to start and quit work on time each day.
2. to call the training sponsor and the school by 10 A.M. of the day they expect to be absent due to illness or other emergencies.
3. to be honest in all undertakings on the job.
4. to not entertain friends at the place of employment.
5. to not sever connections with the training sponsor without the consent of the teacher-coordinator.
6. to conform to the dress code of their place of employment.
7. to complete all wage and hour report forms.
8. to follow all safety rules and regulations on the job.
9. to leave the school premises promptly at the end of their regular class day.

Figure 12

A SELF-INVENTORY CHECKLIST FOR SELECTING AND PLACING STUDENTS
ON THE JOB

Yes   No

_____ _____   1. I select students into the program and not out of the program.

_____ _____   2. I have developed criteria for selecting students into the program based on the student's needs and career objective; the needs of the community and the student's readiness for entrance into the program.

_____ _____   3. I consult multiple individuals for student referrals into the program, e.g. guidance counselors, teachers, etc.

_____ _____   4. I utilize a well-prepared brochure that describes the benefits of participating in a cooperative education program.

_____ _____   5. I interview each student before accepting them into the program.

_____ _____   6. I make presentations on the benefits of participating in the program to civic groups, chamber of commerce, professional business organizations, and parent-teacher organizations.

_____ _____   7. I only select training stations in the community that are respected firms.

_____ _____   8. I select only employers who are interested in training the student.

_____ _____   9. I provide the training sponsor with an understanding of the objectives of the program.

_____ _____   10. I develop the training plan in consultation with the cooperating employer.

_____ _____   11. I select training stations that comply with all safety regulations.

_____ _____   12. I maintain an up-to-date filing system on training stations and potential training stations.

_____ _____   13. I endeavor to supervise the student-learner on the job at least once every two weeks.

_____ _____   14. I supervise the student-learner over the entire spectrum of the training schedule, including evenings, weekends, and holidays where applicable.

_____ _____   15. I avoid making unnecessary interruptions to the cooperating employer work schedule.

_____ _____   16. I maintain a progress chart on each student-learner.

_____ _____   17. I maintain a professional level in all my dealings with the cooperating employer.

BIBLIOGRAPHY

Brown, Bill Wesley: How adequate are our selection techniques?   *American Vocational Journal,* 44-46, November 1966.

Cottrell, J.:   Recruitment of training stations.   *Business Education Forum,* 22, December 1962.

Herr, Edwin, L.:   Decision making and employability skills and the role of cooperative work experience.   *Technical Education News,* 9-11, May-June 1977.

Kalugin, Lloyd: Marketing the student worker.   *Cooperative Education Quarterly,* 5-13, August 1978.

Kjeldsen, Christian C.:   Seeking that first job.   *Cooperative Education Quarterly,* 6-7, August 1978.

Klaurens, Mary: Co-op plan or "Cop-out" plan?   *DE Today,* 1, Fall 1971.

Lee, C.:   Cooperative office education and the low average student.   *Balance Sheet, 50:*204-205, January 1969.

Meyer, Robert H.:   The local community — a general business laboratory.   *Journal of Business Education,* 333-349, May 1964.

McMillion, Martin: Supervision and co-op education.   *Agricultural Education,* 276, June 1967.

Nunnery, Michael L. and Sharp, Bert L.:   Assisting students in making vocational choices.   *American Vocational Journal,* 21-22, November 1963.

——— and ———:   Nature of vocational choice.   *American Vocational Journal,* 9-10, October 1963.

Occupational Work Experience.   Columbus, Trade and Industrial Education, State Department of Education, Division of Vocational Education, 1970.

Olszewski, Lydia H.:   Are we preparing our students for job competence?   *Journal of Business Education,* 96-97, December 1967.

Partners in Education — Teachers Manual.   Fort Worth, Texas, Fort Worth Public Schools, 1971.

Pender, Albert R.:   Selection and placement of students in cooperative programs.   *Business Education Forum,* 21-22, April 1970.

Ritz, Frances Jean: Teach students how to obtain jobs.   *Journal of Business Education,* 287-288, April 1968.

Vanetta, Nick: The role of the students in cooperative education, 14-18, May 1969.

Wanat, John A.:   The learning exchange program: A cooperative venture for realistic job training.   *Technical Education News,* 12-13, May-June 1977.

Chapter 4

COOPERATIVE VOCATIONAL EDUCATION FOR SPECIAL EDUCATION POPULATIONS

COOPERATIVE vocational education serves as a highly effective means of providing a realistic educational experience for special education students. Special education students who are educationally disadvantaged and/or handicapped learn more quickly by doing with a "hands-on" approach rather than by abstractions.

Cooperative vocational education programs are designed for students who can benefit more by spending a portion of their school day in the community in an on-the-job work experience. The student-learner receives individualized instruction, both in and out of school, that prepares them with a saleable skill while developing their self-awareness.

Disadvantaged Students

The 1968 Amendments to the Vocational Education Act categorically identified the educationally disadvantaged. In it, 15 percent of the funds were earmarked for—

> Vocational education for persons (other than handicapped persons . . .) who have academic, socio-economic, or other handicaps that prevent them from succeeding in the regular vocational education program.

Public Law 94-482, the Educational Amendments of 1976, mandated additional funding for vocational education and training for educationally disadvantaged persons, including those with limited English-speaking ability, those subject to sex discrimination in job training and employment, and sex stereotyping in vocational education.

EDUCATIONALLY DISADVANTAGED STUDENTS

Educationally disadvantaged students are not necessarily socio-economically disadvantaged students, although there might be a high correlation of educationally disadvantaged students who are socioeconomically disadvantaged. The fact remains that there are students who are not succeeding in the traditional academic settings for a variety of reasons. The following characteristics are usually associated with educationally disadvantaged students.

- They have poor grades and are below grade level for their age.
- They are deficient in communication and computation skills.
- They are frequently tardy.
- They have poor attendance records.
- They generally have poor study habits.
- They lack motivation for learning.
- They have behavioral problems.
- They may be disrespectful.
- They have a short attention span.
- They may be in poor health.
- They have poor comprehension.
- They may have parents who demonstrate no concern.
- They are potential dropouts.
- They are unable to form responsible relations with the school and/or community environment.
- They demonstrate other evidence of failure.

Cooperative education holds much promise for educationally disadvantaged students. Experiences on the job often provide rewards they never experienced in the traditional classroom setting:

- A pat on the back by the boss for a job well done.
- A sense of accomplishment.
- A feeling of being part of the team.
- A foot into the adult world.
- A paycheck at the end of the week.
- A true sense of responsibility.

* A challenge.
* An awareness of being trusted.
* A boost in their self-respect.

Because the disadvantaged students experience success in a co-op program their grades, attendance, and attitudes often significantly improve. In order to improve their performance on the job, they find meaning for improving their computational and reading skills. Cooperative vocational education often makes the difference between success and failure for many disadvantaged students who were not succeeding in the conventional academic atmosphere.

HANDICAPPED STUDENTS

The Vocational Amendments of 1968 defined the handicapped as "mentally retarded, hard of hearing, deaf, speech impaired, visually handicapped, seriously emotionally disturbed, crippled or other health impaired persons who by reason thereof require special education and related services."

Cooperative vocational education has proven to be an effective means to serve this specific population. Cooperative vocational education, coupled with a specialized in-school curriculum, can and does serve the handicapped students throughout the country.

Who Are They?[1]

Who are the handicapped persons? Handicapped pupils are formally identified by child study teams in the local educational agencies.

Once a child with learning handicaps is identified and diagnosed by the local child study team, he/she is then classified, if necessary, into one of the following categories.

MENTALLY RETARDED EDUCABLE: That child whose capacities for abstract thinking are limited to a low level; he/she also gives evidence of less ability to function socially without direction than that displayed by his/her intellectually average peers.

---

[1]*Bureau Briefs*, Vo. 5, November, 1973, Division of Curriculum and Instruction, Branch of Special Education and Pupil Personnel Services, New Jersey State Department of Education.

NEUROLOGICALLY IMPAIRED: That child whose central nervous system shows a specific and definable disorder upon neurological examination.

PERCEPTUALLY IMPAIRED: That child who exhibits a learning disability in one or more of the perceptual areas involved in listening, thinking, speaking, reading, writing, spelling, and arithmetic. This disability must have a perceptual etiology and not be primarily due to sensory disorders, motor handicaps, mental retardation, emotional disturbance, or environmental disadvantage.

EMOTIONALLY DISTURBED: That child whose pattern of behavior is characterized by an inappropriate pattern of functioning that severely limits the child from profiting from regular classroom learning experiences. The emotionally disturbed child experiences difficulty in the area of interpersonal relationships, and often expresses emotion inappropriate to the situation, in matter of degree and quality.

SOCIALLY MALADJUSTED: That child whose pattern of interaction is characterized by conflicts he/she cannot resolve adequately without the assistance of authority figures. The child exhibits his/her maladjustment chiefly in his/her persistent inability to abide by the rules and regulations of a social structure.

VISUALLY HANDICAPPED: That child whose visual acuity with correction is 20/70 or poorer, or who, as a result of some other factors involved in visual functioning, cannot function in a learning environment without a special education program. A child whose visual acuity with correction is 20/200 or poorer in the better eye and requires a knowledge and skill in the use of Braille is legally "blind."

AUDITORILY HANDICAPPED: A. *Deaf:* That child whose residual hearing is not sufficient to enable him/her to understand speech and develop language successfully, even with a hearing aid. B. *Hard of hearing:* That child whose sense of hearing, although defective, is functional with or without a hearing aid but whose hearing loss renders him/her unable to make full use of regular school experiences without special education.

COMMUNICATION HANDICAPPED: That child whose native speech is severely impaired to the extent that it seriously interferes with his/her ability to use oral language to communicate, and this disability is not due primarily to a hearing impairment.

ORTHOPEDICALLY HANDICAPPED: That child who, because of malformation, malfunction, or loss of bones, muscle, or body tissue, needs a special educational program, special equipment, or special facilities to permit normal learning processes to function.

CHRONICALLY ILL: That child who, because of illness such as tuberculosis, epilepsy, cardiac condition, leukemia, asthma, malnutrition, pregnancy, or other physical disabilities that are otherwise uncategorized, cannot easily receive adequate instruction through the regular school program.

MULTIPLY HANDICAPPED: That child who exhibits handicaps in any two or more categories. These handicaps shall be independent of one another and shall be identified as primary and secondary for classification purposes.

A PROGRAM MODEL

There are many program models that utilize the cooperative vocational education concept. The model presented here is just one based on key elements frequently found in operation throughout the country.

- Individualized counseling is essential. A child study team should evaluate the student and prescribe an individualized learning package for the student.
- Following intensive counseling, the student should be cycled through a series of exploratory occupational experiences (pre-training). These experiences will help determine an area of study best suited to the student, such as assembly line production, automotive tune-up, commercial foods and baking, drafting, flower arranging, dry cleaning and pressing, maintenance, small engine repair, and woodworking.
- Simulated work experiences provide all the elements of real work. It develops an understanding of work requirements as well as an understanding of human relations. It helps to build proper attitudes toward work, to train students in working with others, and to develop a sense of personal responsibility.

- Students should undergo a job analysis consisting of the following items: a. aptitude profile, b. physical requirements, c. interest rating, d. job description, e. task analysis, f. temperment conditions, and g. working conditions.
- On-the-job, supervised work experience(s) should enable students to be placed in local business and industry that will provide them with the necessary work habits and skills to enable them to become employable. The program should be based on a philosophy of providing the "optimum" to the handicapped students. Placement should be realistic in terms of meeting the student's needs, interests, and abilities.
- The teacher-coordinator must conduct frequent observations and must spend considerable time outside of school in frequent supervisory visits to students in the establishment when they are working. Close coordination between the cooperating employer and teacher-coordinator are essential if the program is to be a success.

School work scheduling patterns may vary so as to provide sufficient flexibility to achieve the objectives of the program. The key factor in the length of the program will be based on the individual student's needs. Greater flexibility should be permitted with regard to hours and amount of work than is required in other cooperative vocational education programs.

Ideally, the teacher-coordinator of the cooperative vocational education program serving the handicapped student should be competent in the fields of cooperative vocational education and special education. Where states require coordinators to be certified, the teacher-coordinator of the special education program should be dually certified. Where a certified teacher-coordinator does not have the special education certification, arrangements should be made with the special education teacher for a team approach in conducting the program.

Figure 13

A CHECKLIST FOR TEACHER-COORDINATORS OF SPECIAL EDUCATION POPULATIONS

Yes	No	
_____	_____	1. I am familiar with the problems of special education students.
_____	_____	2. I understand and utilize effective methods of communication with the educationally disadvantaged.
_____	_____	3. I develop and implement programs based on the needs, interests, and abilities of students.
_____	_____	4. I work closely with the Child Study Team.
_____	_____	5. I am eager to increase my knowledge in the area of the educationally disadvantaged and handicapped.
_____	_____	6. I am able to provide assistance to other teachers who must provide additional educational services for special education students.
_____	_____	7. I am thoroughly familiar with methods and techniques used in motivating special education students.
_____	_____	8. I place students in training stations at a level of competency which matches the student's capabilities.
_____	_____	9. I place students in training stations which can prepare them with a saleable skill.
_____	_____	10. I provide academic teachers with information about the academic needs of the special education student-learners.
_____	_____	11. I conduct frequent on-the-job supervision to insure the student's success in the employment world.
_____	_____	12. I correlate the student-learner's on-the-job learning experiences with related classroom learning activities.
_____	_____	13. I provide extensive individualized counseling.
_____	_____	14. I provide for flexible scheduling patterns to assist the special education student to achieve the objectives of the program.
_____	_____	15. I keep abreast of the latest developments in the field of special education.

BIBLIOGRAPHY

Guidelines for Employment Orientation Programs for Special Needs Students, A Broad Base Curriculum. New Brunswick, New Jersey, Vocational-Technical Curriculum Laboratory, Rutgers—The State University, May, 1973.

Helping Educationally Disadvantaged Students Through Vocational Education. Trenton, New Jersey State Department of Education, Division of Vocational Education and Career Preparation, 1978.

Meers, Gary D.: Bridging the gap, *Cooperative Education Quarterly,* 11-12, February, 1979.

A Plan for a Cooperative Employment Orientation Program for Retarded Pupils in Public Schools in New Jersey. Trenton, New Jersey State Department of Education, November, 1965.

A Report to the Nation on Vocational Education. Flagstaff, Arizona, Project Baseline, Northern Arizona University, 1975.

A Resource Guide for Cooperative Work Experience Programs. Providence, Rhode Island Department of Education, Division of Development and Operations, Bureau of Technical Assistance, 1975.

A Sample Course Outline for Employment Orientation. Trenton, New Jersey State Department of Education, Division of Vocational Education and Career Preparation, 1975.

Schmitt, Henry E. and Woodin, Ralph S.: Strategies for preparing teachers to reach and teach the disadvantaged. *American Vocational Journal, XXXXV*:24-25, 81, November, 1970.

Schwartz, Louis: An integrated teacher education program for special education — a new approach. *Exceptional Children, XXXIII*:411-416, February, 1967.

Selected Career Education Programs for the Handicapped, DHEW Publication No. (OE) 7305501. Washington, D.C., U.S Department of Health, Education and Welfare, Education Division, December, 1972.

Siegal, Herbert and Haug, Eugene: Skill development for the handicapped. *Industrial Arts and Vocational Education, LIX*:24, 26, September, 1970.

Smith, Robert M.: Preparing competent special education teachers. *Education Canada, IX*:31-36, December, 1969.

Smith, William L.: Ending the isolation of the handicapped. *American Education, VII*:29-33, November, 1971.

Sparks, Howard L and Younie, William J.: Adult adjustment of the mentally retarded: Implications for teacher education. *Exceptional Children, XXXVI*:13-15, September, 1969.

"Vocational Education for the Handicapped, Special Paper. Trenton, State of New Jersey, Department of Education, September, 1974.

Work Experience and Career Exploration Program. Washington, D.C., United States Bureau of Labor Standards, no date.

Wyllie, John R.: *Sequence of Vocational and Occupational Training Programs for Handicapped Students.* Trenton, New Jersey, Department of Education, Division of Vocational Education, no date.

Chapter 5

THE ROLE
OF THE TEACHER-COORDINATOR

THE FUNCTIONS OF A COOPERATIVE
EDUCATION COORDINATOR

IN MANY WAYS, coordinators set the standards and goals for cooperative education programs. They do so within established
guidelines for cooperative education and with consideration to
the philosophy of the school in which they are employed. It
would not be overstating the importance of a teacher-coordinator
to say they can "make or break" a program. It becomes extremely
important that those individuals who are seeking employment as
teacher-coordinators know in advance the duties and responsibilities associated with the position.

Coordinator's Responsibilities

Coordinators have many responsibilities that can be identified
according to the following aspects of cooperative education: starting a program, selecting and placing students in training stations,
establishing and maintaining training stations, teaching related
instruction; and providing a public relations program. These
responsibilities can be grouped into three major types of activities:

a. Starting a program
b. Coordinating a program
c. Maintaining a program

In order to fulfill these activities, a coordinator's job description would have some similarities to several careers: investigators,
salesman, administrator, teacher, guidance counselor, social worker, personnel officer, supervisor, and public relations officer.

Duties and Tasks Performed by Teacher-Coordinator[1]

1. GUIDANCE AND SELECTION OF STUDENTS
   Describing the program to students
   Working with guidance personnel
   Providing occupational information
   Counseling students about entering the program
   Gathering information on students
   Programming and scheduling
   Helping enrollees with career planning
2. PLACING STUDENTS IN TRAINING JOBS
   Enlisting participation of cooperative employers
   Selecting suitable training stations for each student
   Orienting employers, training supervisors, and co-workers
   Preparing students for job interviews
   Placing students on the job
3. ASSISTING STUDENTS IN ADJUSTING TO THEIR WORK ENVIRONMENT
   Helping students on their jobs
   Dealing with job problems
   Planning personnel development with training supervisors
      and students
   Evaluating job progress
4. IMPROVING TRAINING DONE ON THE JOB
   Establishing responsibilities on the job
   Developing training plans
   Consulting and assisting training supervisors
   Maintaining training emphasis
5. CORRELATING CLASSROOM INSTRUCTION WITH ON-THE-JOB TRAINING
   Determining needed instruction
   Assembling instructional materials
   Preparing for instruction
   Teaching classes
   Directing individual projects and study

---

[1] *A Guide for Cooperative Vocational Education.* Minneapolis, University of Minnesota, September 1969, pp. 93-94.

Obtaining assistance from other teachers

Advising training supervisors concerning applications of classroom instruction to be made on the job

Evaluating learning outcomes

6. ASSISTING STUDENTS IN MAKING PERSONAL ADJUSTMENTS

Aiding students in correcting poor personal habits

Counseling students with personal and socioeconomic problems

Assisting students with educational problems

Resolving behavioral problems

7. DIRECTING VOCATIONAL YOUTH ORGANIZATION

Advising youth group

Guiding students in organization of activities

Participating in group activities

8. PROVIDING SERVICES TO GRADUATES AND ADULTS

Providing guidance and placement services for graduates

Participating in the planning and operation of adult education programs

9. ADMINISTRATION ACTIVITIES

Planning program objectives

Research and planning surveys

Organizing and working with advisory committee

Planning curriculums

Communicating school policy

Preparing reports

Budgeting and purchasing

Participating in professional meetings

Consulting with manpower agencies such as employment services and CAMPS

10. MAINTAINING GOOD PUBLIC RELATIONS

Planning a publicity program

Preparing printed publicity

Constructing displays and exhibits

Maintaining communication with faculty, parents, community, employers, school administrators, and student body

Responsibilities in Starting a Program

Coordinators frequently are responsible for behind-the-scenes activities necessary to start a cooperative education program. They have to know the steps to take to invite people to serve on a steering committee. They have to be enthusiastic about cooperative education and be able to instill that attitude in others. They must know how to survey the area for employment opportunities and how to record the survey information for immediate and future use.

After the survey is completed, coordinators must publicize the program, arrange for classroom facilities, and select students. In those activities, coordinators work with a variety of people. They must know what to do and how to do it, as well as how to establish rapport with various groups of people. Students and their parents could have different purposes for choosing a cooperative education program. School administrators could view the importance of cooperative education differently from students or their parents. A coordinator must understand how students, their parents, and the school administrators view cooperative education and work with them accordingly.

Additional Responsibilities in Starting a Program

In order to qualify for funding for cooperative education programs, school administrators and program coordinators must supply certain information to their state department of education. Among the requirements are such things as specifications for the classroom facilities, program materials, and equipment. The applicant for funding must show that they have adequate facilities for the particular type of program they want. As might be expected, the requirements will vary from one type of program to another. The applicant must specify what they need for supplies and equipment. They also must prepare a course of related instruction. In most of these activities, coordinators should be aware of their state requirements. At times, coordinators may even initiate the paperwork necessary to receive funding for a program. Even if funding is not a consideration to starting a program, coordinators should have a role in the planning process.

When selecting students, coordinators should check with a variety of people. Some of the people are guidance counselors, pupil personnel team members, and classroom teachers. Possibly the most important person to discuss the program with is the potential students. Coordinators have to be able to evaluate whether or not a student can benefit from a cooperative education program. The student should then be counseled accordingly.

Responsibilities in Coordinating the Program

Coordinators have other responsibilities once the cooperative education program is established. The responsibilities can be grouped into activities within the school and activities in the community.

Responsibilities within the School

The school responsibilities include teaching related instruction and arranging special help for students who need it. Some students have weaknesses in their educational background. Coordinators provide individualized instruction as well as arrange for help for students with other teachers within the school system.

The related class instruction will normally consist of general information needed by all entry level employees such as how to get a job, preparing for an interview, maintaining a job, getting along with fellow employees, etc. The other portion of the related class will be specific to the student-learner and the training station, such as how to figure percentages, how to read blueprints and schematics, etc. The coordinators, therefore, have to prepare curriculum materials that are both general in nature, common to all students, as well as specific in nature, on a one-to-one basis. Furthermore, they must be familiar with the total school curriculum in order to provide meaningful vocational guidance to student-learners.

Some students need career counseling and others need counseling regarding what is considered appropriate behavior in the world of work. Some of their problems can be personal and unrelated to the cooperative education program. Coordinators should still try to help their students because anything that troubles their students will keep them from doing their best work in the cooperative education program.

Responsibilities in the Community

Coordinator's responsibilities within the community include working with the business community and publicizing information about their program. Both represent important features of a cooperative education program. A large part of the coordinator's responsibility involves working with training stations in the community. They locate and investigate potential work stations for suitability. They do a safety check of that station before placing a student at the site. They must be able to select or reject training stations without antagonizing people. Once a training station is accepted, coordinators work with employers to develop a training plan for the student who will work there. They also arrange the student's work schedule and develop a reporting system to measure the student's work progress.

Publicizing information about the cooperative education program may not seem as productive as working with training stations. Nevertheless, it is a very important part of any coordinator's responsibilities. Coordinators must be able to meet with a variety of people, talk knowledgeably and enthusiastically about cooperative education, and even prepare copy for publication. Coordinators must be able to sell their program and keep students, the school, business, and the community aware of the many values derived from cooperative education. In this way, positive support is built and maintained for cooperative education.

Maintaining a Program

Even though cooperative education programs are started successfully and coordinators perform the various functions described earlier in this chapter, there are still other activities necessary to insure that the program will continue successfully.

A teacher-coordinator should supervise each student on the job at least once every two weeks in order to ascertain how the student is progressing and to determine from the cooperating employer what specific information should be emphasized back in the classroom. Failure to carry out this function by the coordinator will alienate the cooperating employer, reduce the program to a mere job, and possibly involve the school in a heavy lawsuit should a student become injured on the job.

Coordinators should maintain relationships with former students and employers in the community. Coordinators can learn about the effectiveness of their programs by conducting both student follow-up surveys and employer follow-up surveys. The findings of the follow-up instruments would then be a means for helping the coordinator to update, expand, and improve the program.

These, then, are some of the major responsibilities of cooperative education coordinators. In order to assume responsibility for a cooperative education program, coordinators should be well prepared for the position. The legal implications of incorrect or inappropriate behavior in cooperative education are such that coordinators cannot only fail the various groups of people they serve but could end up in considerable legal difficulties. Coordinators, therefore, owe it to themselves, as well as to those they serve, to be well prepared.

THE ROLE OF THE TEACHER-COORDINATOR

At the beginning of this chapter it was stated that a teacher-coordinator's job description often has many similarities to several careers. It is not uncommon for a teacher-coordinator to function in five distinct roles in one day. A typical example illustrating the many roles of a teacher-coordinator can be seen in the work day schedule (Fig. 14).

The Arizona Cooperative Education Guidelines (p. 49) lists the role of the teacher-coordinator under five headings, with activities associated with each one of those functions.

Teaching

Prepares and revises teaching materials
Teaches co-op high school students
Teaches adults

Figure 14

WORK DAY SCHEDULE

Role	Time	Activity
Teacher	9:00 A.M.	Teach Related Class Begin the unit on job interviews.
Guidance Counselor	11:00 A.M.	Conduct student counseling sessions on "postsecondary schools" on a individualized basis.
Coordinator	1:00 P.M.	On-the-Job Supervision. Review the training plan for the student-learner and his/her cooperating employer.
Administrator	3:00 P.M.	Advisory Committee Meeting. Establish a scholarship fund and report on the five year follow-up study of cooperative education graduates.
Public Relations	7:30 P.M.	Chamber of Commerce Meeting. Make a presentation to the members on the advantages of providing training opportunities for cooperative education students.

Evaluates the results of his/her teaching

Maintains teaching content resource files

Provides for classroom participation experiences for students

Plans yearly, monthly, and weekly teaching calendars as well as daily lesson plans for classroom activities

May teach a prerequisite class to the cooperative program

Guidance

Explains co-op programs to students, parents, and school officials

Selects students for co-op program

Places high school co-op students in appropriate training stations
Counsels with high school students
Acts as a training consultant to business and industry
Offers information on students
Follows up on student progress
Works cooperatively with school guidance counselors

Coordination Activities

Selects appropriate training agencies
Prepares a training agreement and plans a profile for each student
Coordinates classroom activities with on-the-job training
Makes on-the-job coordination and home visits
Gives needed information and training to the training sponsors of
    the students
Enlists participation of cooperating employers
Assists students in adjusting to their work environment

Operation and Administration

Plans a well-rounded program of work
Arranges for adequate classroom facilities
Makes a community survey
May organize and supervise a vocational student organization
Works with advisory committees
Prepares necessary reports
Conducts practical research
Supervises student teachers

Public Relations

Explains co-op program to business, labor, civic, and school groups
Participates in local community functions
Plans and prepares publicity
Takes part in extracurricular activities and other school duties
Keeps in direct contact with school principal, superintendent, par-
    ents, business, industry, labor, and community
Arranges and directs programs for vocational youth organizations.

SELECTION OF THE TEACHER-COORDINATOR

Competencies Needed by the Teacher-Coordinator

The selection of a teacher-coordinator is a very crucial one. The varied duties and tasks of a teacher-coordinator necessitate an individual who can demonstrate competencies in—

1. Assisting students to attain entry level skills in their chosen field;
2. Recruiting and effectively utilizing cooperating employers;
3. Providing individualized instruction;
4. Maintaining effective communications up and down the chain of command in the school system as well as in the employment community;
5. Maintaining good public relations;
6. Knowing federal, state, and local laws and regulations pertaining to the employment of minors;
7. Directing vocational student organization activities;
8. Dealing with the educational and personal problems of student-learners.

Personal Characteristics of the Teacher-Coordinator[2]

The qualified cooperative vocational education teacher-coordinator should possess the physical stamina, emotional traits, and personal traits necessary to organize the resources of the school and the employment community in preparing students for occupations. The following traits and habits of the teacher-coordinator are considered essential to effective program operation:

1. Pleasing, neat appearance
2. Warm, outgoing personality
3. Strong commitment to helping young people
4. Systematic and orderly habits in organizing work
5. Self-confidence and positive attitude in dealing with problems
6. Good judgment

---

[2]*A Guide for Cooperative Vocational Education,* Minneapolis, Minnesota: University of Minnesota, 1969. pp. 97-98.

7. Empathy with students, employers, and others
8. Self-motivation

The coordinator must be the kind of person who relates well with students, employers, parents, other faculty members, administrators, and interested people in the community in order to enlist their cooperation and help. The time and efforts of individuals who have the necessary qualifications are also in great demand by business, industry, and other institutions and government agencies. Salaries must be adequate to attract individuals with the capabilities the positions require. The teacher-coordinator is the key factor in the success of a cooperative education program.

Professional Growth

No educator can stagnate but must continue to grow and learn to be successful in the field. As futuristic planners, teacher-coordinators deal with the needs of today, while preparing their students for the world of tomorrow.

Teacher-coordinators must constantly be aware of changes taking place in the world of work. They have to be thoroughly familiar with new and pending legislation that affects employees, specifically youth under the age of eighteen. They must be able to forecast future employment needs as well as be aware of those occupations that are vanishing from the employment sector. Teacher-coordinators, therefore, must be constantly engaged in the self-improvement process.

Continual improvement of cooperative vocational education programs rests with the teacher-coordinator. Continued professional growth, therefore, is the key to this improvement. The following guidelines[3] suggest various methods. The teacher-coordinator should—

1. Become an active member in local, state, and national teacher associations.
2. Become an active member in occupational associations.

---

[3]*Management Systems for Cooperative Education*, Wyoming State Department of Education, Second edition, 1976, pgs. 3-15/16.

3. Participate in organized workshops conducted by local, state, or national associations or agencies.
4. Become involved in the community. Join social and civic organizations, and take part in community projects.
5. Subscribe to and read professional publications and keep abreast of current events and conditions.
6. Become acquainted and work closely with the state department of education. Know their policies and objectives.
7. Whenever possible, work in a field of employment related to the area being taught.
8. Develop, and participate in, local in-service training programs.
9. Work for advanced degrees in specific teaching areas.
10. Be willing to take a professional leave to observe other cooperative vocational education programs in the region.
11. Communicate with fellow teachers, business, and industry within the state and across the country, in order to keep abreast of latest developments.
12. Become familiar with the teacher-education institutions within the area.
13. Continually critique and evaluate the cooperative vocational education program, with the assistance of other professionals.
14. Work closely with faculty and community to ascertain their perspective and ideas.
15. Attend school board meetings and be familiar with school district policies and procedures.

Educational and Work Experience Preparation

There is a definite need to provide all teacher-coordinators with the necessary information they need concerning the organization and implementation of a quality cooperative education program. The information that a coordinator needs concerning child labor laws, legal restrictions, federal and state minimum wages, training agreements, training plans, individualized instruction, and a whole host of rules, regulations, and methods associated with cooperative education programs should not be learned by trial and error on the job, but rather beforehand in a formal educational program where questions can be asked and answers given. The coordinator's role and responsibility, therefore, should be thoroughly understood before an individual is placed in a cooperative education program.

Although there are no mandated uniform standards to which all states subscribe in the preparation of teacher-coordinators, there are generally recognized standards. In addition to meeting certification standards required of all secondary teachers, the teacher-coordinator should have specific course work in the following areas:

a. Organization and administration of a part-time cooperative education program.
b. Vocational curriculum construction—with an emphasis on individualized learning.
c. Principles and philosophy of vocational education.
d. Vocational guidance.

A review of most state department of education's guidelines reveals that the above four course areas are frequently listed as requirements or suggested courses for their teacher-coordinators. Course titles change from state to state, and often from college to college within a given state. In addition, the number of courses required differ from state to state. Some states combine the above areas into two or three courses, while others divide the subject areas into four or five courses. For example, the subject area of organizing and administrating a part-time cooperative education program can be covered in one course with the same title or in two courses such as organizing a cooperative education program and coordinating a cooperative education program.

Occupational Work Experience

Teacher-coordinators should have work experience, other than teaching, in the area they are going to coordinate. For example, an individual who is going to coordinate an industrial education co-op program should have some relevant on-the-job work experience in an industrial setting using power driven tools and equipment.

Similarly, a person who is to coordinate a cooperative health education program should have on-the-job experience in a health occupation field. Coordinators who conduct homogenous programs, therefore, should have appropriate on-the-job work experience in their respective discipline.

The work experience should also be sufficiently diversified within their respective field so as to provide the teacher-coordinator with the necessary skills and job awareness to help enable their students to progress in the classroom and on the job.

In addition to the quality of the work experience, the recency of the occupational experience should be considered. It is desirable for teacher-coordinators to have recent experiences in the occupational field in order to be aware of technological advances made within the field. It is not uncommon for teacher-coordinators to engage in short business/industry internships. These internships provide the teacher-coordinator with relevant information that can be used in the related class instruction phase.

The length of time required for the occupational work experience usually ranges from one to three years, or from 2,000 to 6,000 hours. Many states have provisions to enable teacher-coordinators to participate in a directed work experience internship supervised through a college program. The length of time for the directed internship is of shorter duration than the self-obtained occupational experience. The recognized ratio is one hour of directed work experience for each four hours of self-obtained work experience.

The rational for the shorter length of experience is based on the assumption that the directed internship provides a quality experience that may not be obtained through the normal unsupervised college process. It is conceivable that a year of self-obtained experience might have been nothing more than a repetition of one experience multiple times, while the directed experience should be multiple experiences on a planned sequential program basis.

Figure 15

A SELF-INVENTORY FOR TEACHER-COORDINATORS

Yes   No

____ ____ 1. I set realistic goals for myself, my students, and the program in general.

____ ____ 2. I provide individualized instruction to meet the needs of the student-learners on the job.

____ ____ 3. I supervise each student on the job at least once every two weeks.

____ ____ 4. I conduct follow-up surveys on students and employers.

____ ____ 5. I make an effort to attend and participate in professional development meetings and seminars.

____ ____ 6. I maintain effective communications up and down the chain of command in the school system as well as in the employment community.

____ ____ 7. I keep abreast of the latest developments in the employment field for which I train students.

____ ____ 8. I work closely with the training sponsors to provide the best possible training to the student-learners.

____ ____ 9. I seek assistance and guidance from my advisory committee.

____ ____ 10. I counsel each student regarding their career choice.

____ ____ 11. I develop a training plan for each student to meet their individual needs on the job.

____ ____ 12. I am familiar with the federal, state, and local labor laws as they affect students I place on the job.

____ ____ 13. I maintain a close working relationship with unions and other community agencies.

____ ____ 14. I endeavor to maintain positive public relations with the administration, faculty, parents, employers, and community organizations concerning all aspects of the cooperative education program.

____ ____ 15. I maintain adequate records concerning all aspects of the program.

____ ____ 16. I maintain a training profile on the student-learner's on-the-job progress as it relates to his or her training plan.

____ ____ 17. I operate the program in accordance with established state operational procedures for a Cooperative Education program.

____ ____ 18. I correlate the related class instruction with the student-learner's on-the-job training.

____ ____ 19. I place student-learners in bona fide training stations.

BIBLIOGRAPHY

Ashmun, Richard D. and Klaurens, Mary K: Essentials in educating the teacher-coordinator. *American Vocational Journal,* 28-29, May 1969.

Ellis, William G.: Work experience for business teachers. *National Business Education Quarterly,* 42-45, Winter 1969.

Gooch, Bill G.: The key to success. *Cooperative Education Quarterly,* 8-19, November 1978.

Grovom, Dorothy C.: Simulated coordination experience for teacher-coordinators. *Journal of Business Education,* 197-198, February 1969.

A Guide for Cooperative Vocational Education. Minneapolis, University of Minnesota, September 1969.

Malkan, John L.: How to be a successful cooperating teacher. *Industrial Arts and Vocational Education,* 26-27, January 1963.

Management Systems for Cooperative Education, 2nd ed. Wyoming State Department of Education, 1976.

Mitchell, Mike: What vocational cooperative teacher-coordinators do in their jobs in secondary schools in Texas. Texas Education Agency, Contract #78230027, May 1978.

Muncy, Hugh E.: Put specificity in coordination. *American Business Education,* December 1961.

Neel, Binnie L.: A study of how coordinators of cooperative education perceive their role. *Journal of Cooperative Education,* 21-29, May 1969.

Plachta, Leonard: The role of the teacher in cooperative education. *Journal of Cooperative Education,* 18-20, May 1969.

Winer, Ellen N.: The identification of training needs of secondary school cooperative work experience education. *Cooperative Education Quarterly,* 8-12, August 1978.

Work Education: Diversified Occupations Cooperative Education Guidelines. Arizona Department of Education, August 1975.

Chapter 6

THE ROLE OF ADVISORY COMMITTEES IN COOPERATIVE EDUCATION

ADVISORY COMMITTEES PROVIDE an essential component in the development and management of local cooperative education programs. Their composition, organization, role, and function are discussed in this chapter.

FUNCTIONS OF AN ADVISORY COMMITTEE

The Vocational Education Amendments of 1976 stipulated that all states desiring federal funding for their programs *must* have a state advisory council as well as local advisory councils. As a result of that mandate, advisory committees have several functions:

1. Communicate information to the general and professional communities about the nature and purposes of a school's cooperative education program.
2. Assist the program coordinator and school administrator in short- and long-term planning for that program by keeping them aware of the needs and trends in business and industry.
3. Provide assistance to the program coordinator by helping to clarify thinking when there is inaccurate or insufficient information available.

Advantages to Having an Advisory Committee

Besides complying with the federal regulations, there are many advantages to having an advisory committee for everyone involved with the program, both inside and outside the school. The business and industrial communities and the community in general benefit from the advisory committee's recommendations for the occupational skills that the students should develop and the technical knowledges that the students should be taught. The public also knows that the advisory committee works to keep the cooperative education program relevant to the current needs of the business and industrial communities.

The school and the cooperative education program benefit from having an advisory committee in several ways. The committee provides prestige for the cooperative education program to people within and outside of the school. In its liaison capacity, it publicizes that the school is trying to serve the needs of the community, how it is being accomplished, and why it is important. In addition, it assists the school to modify the cooperative education program to reflect the current changes in business and industry and to anticipate trends that are occurring.

DUTIES AND RESPONSIBILITIES
OF AN ADVISORY COMMITTEE

The duties and responsibilities of an advisory committee are numerous and varied. They can be divided into activities generally related to the program, those providing advice and support to the coordinator, and those bringing the committee into contact with the students in the program.

The committee provides assistance and support to the coordinator in several ways:

1. Reviews the instructional material and suggests additions and revisions.
2. Suggests standards for the students in the program, sometimes identifying what aptitudes and attitudes the students should have and at other times specifying the nature and extent of skills and technical knowledge the students should acquire.
3. Helps to prepare training plan outlines, which will be the basis for the work experience at the training stations.
4. Provides support and assistance by identifying potential

problems, suggesting solutions for them, and helping to solve problems brought to its attention by the coordinator.

The advisory committee offers advice and support for the cooperative education students either as a group or as individual members:

1. Simulates interview situations for students so that they can experience typical questions they might be asked and receives feedback of what type of impression they made during that process.
2. Acts as guest speakers or suggests other persons that might be interesting and informative speakers for the students.
3. Recommends field trips that might be educationally worthwhile.
4. Promotes and supports the various student organization activities associated with the program.

Besides those functions closely associated with helping the program coordinator and the students, advisory committee members also serve other functions that are of a more general nature:

1. Help with the acquisition of equipment and materials for the program.
2. Assess the local training needs based on their experience, background, and professional contacts, and make recommendations concerning them as those needs relate to the program.
3. Help to determine training station standards based on the objectives of the program.
4. Assist in locating and developing new training stations.
5. Support the program by helping to prepare promotional materials.
6. Help in publicizing the cooperative education program to their peers and to the general public.

TYPICAL ADVISORY COMMITTEE MEMBERS

Most advisory committees are composed of eight to ten members, as a larger number often slows committee action and limits their constructive help. The type of committee determines the representation from the general community and the business and industrial community. Craft advisory committees usually have a large number of business and industrial representatives. Generally, these representatives are selected from people in positions of authority so that they will be aware of trends and changes in the world of work and in a position to make decisions pertaining to the business and industry they represent. These people are selected from organizations of various sizes, companies that are part of a national chain, cooperating businesses, or subsidiary industries.

In addition to representatives from the business and industrial world, advisory committee members are recruited from the employment service, the Chamber of Commerce, the Parent Teachers Association, sometimes legal and banking representatives, as well as trade association and trade union representatives. Some advisory committees have representatives from the school administration and guidance department as well as current and former cooperative education students.

Selection of Advisory Committee Members

The selection of advisory committee members often determines how successful the committee will be in assisting and supporting the cooperative education program. Some of the items to consider in selecting committee members follow:

1. What is the nature and extent of their interest in education? If the person is not supportive of education in general, he or she may be more of a detriment to the committee and the program than a help.
2. Is the person a respected authority in the field he or she represents? If the recommendations made by this person are to be regarded as significant, then the person should be as well informed and knowledgeable as his or her peers.
3. Does the person have sufficient time to devote to fulfilling the obligations of an advisory committee member? While it is impressive to have some people's names on an advisory committee, their contribution is limited unless they are available for meetings and periodic assistance to the pro-

gram. Thus, a person selected should be one whose appointment schedule permits attending occasional advisory committee meetings.

4. Does the person represent the general business-industrial community in terms of ethnic considerations?

The Appointment Procedure

The appointment procedure includes several people in the school system and on several levels of authority. The cooperative education coordinator usually starts the procedure and involves the school principal, superintendent, or designated representative, and occasionally the board of education. The sequence is as follows:

1. The cooperative education coordinator prepares a list of prospective members that represents all areas of the community where students in the program might be employed. A few sentences of descriptive information are included about each person.

2. The vocational director, supervisor or principal reviews the list.

3. The superintendent or designated representative identifies those people on the list who shall compose the advisory committee. One or two alternates are added to cover the eventuality that someone on the list might be unable or unwilling to serve as an advisory committee member.

4. The board of education reviews and approves the list.

5. Concurrent with preparing the list of candidates for the advisory committee, the coordinator drafts a letter of invitation to be sent by the superintendent. It should contain a brief overview of the program and invite the person to become an advisory committee member. The letter should also state that the coordinator will contact the person within a few weeks of receipt of the letter to further discuss the program and to answer questions. In addition, the letter should contain information about the first meeting.

Figure 16*

1 September 19___

Mr. John Jones, President
Blank City Stores, Inc.
Blank City, New Jersey   07095

Dear Mr. Jones:

You have been recommended by our distributive education teacher-coordinator, Mr. Joseph Smith, and his principal, Mr. Ralph Brown, as being very interested in the success of the distributive education program in our community. The distributive education program, being a cooperative-type program in which the students learn on the job as well as in the classroom, requires the cooperation of business leaders such as yourself in order to accomplish its purpose. The Board of education has approved the establishment of an advisory committee to the distributive education program. This committee will be composed of business and civic leaders engaged in or interested in distribution and the distributive education program. The advisory committee will act in the capacity of advisors to the coordinator, Mr. Smith, seeking to facilitate his work and to pursue the growth and development of distributive education.

The Board of Education invites you to join with other interested business leaders in serving on the advisory committee. The first formal meeting of the group will be held at 2:00 p.m. at Blank High School. Mr. Smith will provide you with an agenda and further information prior to the meeting.

I would like to express my appreciation and that of the Board of Education for your service to the youth and to the school programs of Blank City.

Sincerely,

Superintendent of Schools

---

*Morton Shenker: **Advisory Committees for Cooperative Education Programs.** Trenton, NJ, Trenton State College, 1968, p. 18.

Length of Service

In order to avoid problems or confusion at a later time, it is important to insure that advisory committee members know the length of their term of service. Once a new member has agreed to be on an advisory committee, a letter specifying the length of the appointment should be sent. Appointments for new advisory committees are equally divided between one, two, and three year terms. Once the committee is established, the usual appointment is for three years. By doing so, the committee always has some experienced members and some new ones.

The steering committee can form the pool from which advisory committee members are selected. By using their services, the program coordinator has the advantage of working with people who are somewhat familiar with cooperative education. A staggered system of appointments should be made if the entire committee is to be composed of former steering committee members. An alternate possibility is to select some of the outstanding steering committee members and ask that they serve for the first year. Second and third year appointments would be given to new members.

The practice of reappointing advisory committee members of successive terms should be limited to outstanding members and, even then, used with caution. People that serve for an extended period of time on an advisory committee tend to take a proprietary interest in the program and sometimes cease to be objective about certain aspects of it. Certainly there should be consideration regarding whether or not the contributions of the person to be suggested for reappointment can equal or surpass those of a new member who can bring new ideas and contacts to the program.

The suggestion is frequently made to increase the size of the advisory committee by reappointing existing members and adding new members. It is unadvisable to do so because the size of the committee can become unmanageable.

While some advisory committee members may be relieved that their term of office is completed, others may have wished to continue with their duties and thus feel unappreciated, perhaps even somewhat antagonistic. In order to avoid such complications, the school can recognize the service provided by the advisory committee in such a way that the person's service is publicly acknowledged. This can be accomplished at a board of education meeting, in the communications media, by a certificate or plaque specifying the person's name and length of service, or at the annual banquet of the program.

THE ADVISORY COMMITTEE MANUAL

An advisory committee manual will answer many of the questions that new members have, while acting as a source of reference for other members. It should be prepared by the program coordinator and reviewed by the school administration before it is distributed to the advisory committee.

Among the items that might be included in an advisory committee manual are the following:

1. A letter of welcome from a school representative regarding the importance of their advice and support for the program.
2. A listing of current advisory committee members, their term of office and the part of the community the person represents.
3. A listing of former advisory committee members, including company affiliation and their term of office.
4. The duties and responsibilities of various officers and members of the committee, including the responsibilities of the teacher-coordinator relative to the advisory committee.
5. The ways in which advisory committee members can serve the program.
6. A general and brief description about the cooperative education program, including the philosophy and objectives of the program.
7. A course of study.
8. A floor plan of the school and the room where the related subject material is taught.
9. The equipment inventory list including the date of purchase and an assessment of its condition.
10. The materials inventory list.
11. Information about the student organization activities including the names of the officers.
12. A list of all the students in the program.
13. Information about graduates of the program in terms of their job selection or educational pursuits following high school graduation.

14. A listing of the training stations that have cooperated with the school.
15. The names of members of the board of education and the school administration.

In order to insure that the manual contains correct information, the teacher-coordinator must review and update it periodically. A loose-leaf notebook has the flexibility of adding to or deleting information from it, as compared to the inflexibility of a stapled or bound version of that information.

The Responsibilities of the Teacher-Coordinator To the Advisory Committee

A cooperative education coordinator has several functions relating to the advisory committee. Among those responsibilities are the following:

1. Assist in selecting new advisory committee members and informing them about their duties and responsibilities.
2. Prepare and update the advisory committee manual and distribute the manual to new committee members.
3. Assume responsibility for the first advisory committee meeting by acting as the temporary chairperson of the committee.
4. Advise the elected chairperson of the need for a meeting and help to prepare the agenda for that meeting.
5. Assume the role of secretary.
6. Report back to the committee the disposition of their recommendations.

Responsibilities of the Advisory Committee Chairperson, Vice Chairperson, and Secretary

The advisory committee officers consist of a chairperson, a vice chairperson, and a secretary. The chairperson and vice chairperson should be representatives from the community. The secretary could be the teacher-coordinator or a community representative.

The chairperson conducts the meetings and, in cooperation

with the program coordinator, determines the need for an advisory committee meeting and its agenda.

The vice chairperson assists the chairperson and conducts the advisory committee meeting in the absence of the chairperson. In addition, this person makes suggestions regarding the meeting agenda. On occasion, the vice chairperson also assists the secretary if that person is unable to perform a particular responsibility.

The secretary takes minutes of the meeting and prepares announcements and meeting reminders. Minutes of the meeting should be mailed a week after the meeting was held. Minutes of the meetings should be retained for five years.

Subcommittees of the Advisory Committee

Subcommittees give each member of the advisory committee some responsibility. Members usually serve on a committee for a minimum of a year. Their activities may include investigating various considerations, reviewing certain materials, and specifying standards. Their findings are shared with the committee and usually result in the committee making recommendations regarding their investigation. These recommendations are made to the coordinator in writing and the recommendations become part of the written record of the advisory committee.

While the number and type of subcommittees vary from one program to another, most cooperative education programs have many of the following subcommittees.

1. *Course of Study Subcommittee.* Committee members review the course of study and make suggestions regarding information that should be added or deleted. This review reinforces the coordinator's decision about what skills and technical knowledge should be taught to the cooperative education students.

2. *Student Selection Subcommittee.* Based on their experience in business and industry, committee members identify the characteristics and aptitudes they feel students should have in order to obtain employment.

3. *Training Station Subcommittee.* Committee members help to identify potential training stations. They also help

specify standards for those stations.

4. *Training Plan Subcommittee.*   While training plan development is the teacher-coordinator's responsibility, committee members help to develop a realistic training outline for students by reviewing the draft plan before it is formalized.

5. *Public Relations Subcommittee.*   This committee shares the responsibility with the coordinator regarding providing the community with information about the cooperative education program.   The two parties may operate independently of each other, but their efforts are coordinated.

6. *Planning Subcommittee.*   Members of this committee try to determine what the advisory committee can do to enhance the cooperative education program.   Their suggestions may be for their action or for the program coordinator.

ADVISORY COMMITTEE CONTITUTION AND BY-LAWS

An advisory committee should have a constitution and by-laws to give it a formal and meaningful basis.   There are several ways that the constitution and by-laws can be developed.   Some states have samples, sometimes other program coordinators will share a copy of the one used by their advisory committee, and at other times, models can be found in textbooks or manuals.   Having obtained a sample constitution and by-laws, the document can be tailored to the particular cooperative education program that will use it.   The document can be prepared by the teacher-coordinator and the school administration, a committee composed of steering committee members, or a sub-committee of the advisory committee.   Once drafted the document should be reviewed and approved by the school superintendent and the board of education.

Even though the constitution and by-laws will be designed for a particular cooperative education program, most documents contain many of the same items.   The name of the committee and its objectives are listed.   Membership is discussed in terms of the number of members, their qualifications, and their term of office including the rotation schedule and the process of obtaining new members.　In addition, an attendance requirement usually is specified.

Other items regulated by the constitution and by-laws are the officers of the advisory committee with respect to who they are, what their responsibilities include, and how vacancies are filled. The procedure for nominating the officers also is discussed. Other information includes specifications about the subcommittees, special committees, and reports of the advisory committee. Finally, the document tells how changes can be made in the by-laws.

Figure 17*

CONSTITUTION AND BY-LAWS
COOPERATIVE EDUCATION ADVISORY COMMITTEE

ARTICLE I — NAME
The name of this committee shall be the Advisory Committee for the C.I.E. (Cooperative Industrial Education) Programs.

ARTICLE II — OBJECTIVES
The purpose of the committee shall be to act in an advisory capacity to the Board of Education with respect to the following functions related to the Cooperative Industrial Education Programs:
　　Be a sounding board on new ideas.
　　Aid in determining standards for student selection.
　　Help to achieve the objectives of the employment programs.
　　Support the need of the programs to the employment community.
　　Act as a diplomatic corps for program expansion.
　　Create goodwill in the community.
　　Give prestige to the school, programs, and community.
　　Guide solutions to wage and hour problems.
　　Help to evaluate the programs and establish standards making the programs realistic.
　　Aid in publicizing the programs.
　　Serve as a coordinating body for C.I.E. Programs.

ARTICLE III — MEMBERSHIP
Section I — Number of Members
The committee shall consist of five to seven members, some of whom should be from the lay community (former and present employers, or Union representatives), and seven members of ex-officio status (Superintendent of Schools, High School Principals, Coordinator of Instruction, Vocational Guidance Counselor, Coordinator of Cooperative Office Education Program, Coordinator of Cooperative Industrial Education Program).

*Wanat, John A., Samuel Cooper and Michael K. Klavon (Eds.): **Cooperative Industrial Education: All Purpose Manual.** Jersey City, The Center for Occupational Education, Jersey City State College, 1974, ED096-387 (ERIC), pg. 102-104.

Section II — Qualifications for Membership

The lay members of the committee should represent diverse occupations and businesses in the Cooperative Employment Programs and should reflect a sincere interest in advancing cooperative employment programs at the high school level.

Section III — Term of Membership for Other Than Ex-Officio Members

Members will be appointed to the committee for a term of three years. No member may serve more than two consecutive terms. One and one-half year or longer shall be considered a term of office when determining eligibility for re-appointment.

Section IV — Rotation of Membership

One third of lay members shall be replaced each year.

Section V — Appointment of Members

Appointment of new members shall be made by the Board of Education upon recommendation of the Advisory Committee.

Section VI — Attendance

Each member is expected to attend at least 60 percent of the meetings. In the event such absenteeism is exceeded, the Chairperson will report the circumstances and the committee will consider whether there should be a replacement nomination.

ARTICLE IV — OFFICERS

Section I — Elective Officers

The elective officers of this committee shall be:

    Chairperson

    Vice Chairperson

    Recording Secretary

Section II — Chairperson

The Chairperson of the Committee must be a member of the lay group and must have served on the committee at least one year.

The term of office for the chairperson is one year, and the chairperson may succeed himself/herself.

The duties of the chairperson will include: conducting regular meetings, calling special meetings, and appointing committees as the needs arise.

Section III — Vice Chairperson

The vice chairperson must be a member of the lay group. The vice chairperson shall serve in the absence of the chairperson.

Section IV — Recording Secretary

The recording secretary shall record the proceedings of the meetings and shall distribute them to the membership and members of the Board of Education.

The recording secretary shall maintain an up-to-date roster of membership of the Advisory Committee.

Section V — Vacancies

In the event of a vacancy in an office, the chairperson shall appoint a nominating committee to nominate a replacement to be approved by a majority of those in attendance.

ARTICLE V — NOMINATIONS

Section I — Appointment of Nominating Committee

As need arises, the chairperson shall appoint a nominating committee consisting of three or four members, two representing the lay group, and two representatives from the school group.

Section II — Nominating Committees
Nominating committees will serve either of two functions:
    To nominate replacements to the committee
    To nominate officers

Section III — Nominations for Officers
The nominating committee for annual election of officers shall be appointed in March and shall present its report at the April meeting. Nominations may be accepted from the floor.

ARTICLE VI — ELECTIONS
The officers shall be elected at the May meeting and installed at the following meeting.

ARTICLE VII — MEETINGS
A minimum of six meetings shall be held during the school year. Special meetings may be called by the chairperson. A two-thirds attendance of members shall constitute a quorum.

ARTICLE VIII — COMMITTEES

Section I — Standing Committees
There shall be no standing committee.

Section II — Special Committees
Special committees shall be appointed by the chairperson as the need arises.

Section III — Reports
All chairpersons of special committees shall report on their activities at each monthly meeting.

ARTICLE IX — CHANGES IN OPERATING GUIDELINES
When proposals for changes in the Operating Guidelines are suggested, such proposals shall be voted upon at the meeting following such introduction, and must be approved by a majority of the members present.

This set of by-laws may be adapted for any phase of cooperative education.

ADVISORY COMMITTEE MEETINGS

The First Advisory Committee Meeting

The first meeting of the advisory committee is a very important one because it sets the pattern for future meetings. It should be well organized, start at the scheduled time, progress in an orderly fashion, and be over by the time specified in the meeting announcement.

In addition, the meeting should be formal as opposed to informal. All items on the agenda should be discussed. The cooperative education coordinator is responsible for planning the first meeting and attending to the numerous details associated with having such a meeting. Even if some members have indicated that they plan to attend the meeting, they should receive a reminder about it. This can be done quite easily by sending the new members a map showing the location of the building where the meeting will be held, directions regarding where to park, and specific information about how to find the meeting room once inside the building. Those directions can be accompanied by a short letter from the coordinator stating that he or she looks forward to seeing the advisory committee member at the meeting with the time, date, and location included as part of the statement.

Figure 18

October 1, 19___

Mr. Red E. Cash, Vice President
County Savings & Trust Company
121 Currency Boulevard
Anytown, OH   00000

Dear Mr. Cash:

Welcome to the Good High School Clerical Program Advisory Committee. Our first meeting is planned for Wednesday, October 15, at 4 p.m. in Room 544 at the high school, 75 Opportunity Street.

As you will notice on the enclosed agenda, two of the items we are planning to discuss are curriculum and equipment needs for the clerical program. We want to provide a program that will satisfy the requirements of our employers in Anytown, and your recommendations are needed. A copy of our existing course outline is enclosed.

I am looking forward to meeting with you on October 15. In order that final arrangements may be made, please return the enclosed reply card by October 10.

Sincerely yours,

Myrtle Robbin
Senior Clerical Instructor

Enclosures: Agenda
              Course Outline
              Reply Card

On the Effective Use of Advisory Committees: A Manual for Business and Office Education Teachers, Business and Office Education Bulletin #20. Columbus, Kent State University, Ohio State Department of Education, 1975, pg. 53.

The coordinator is responsible for the many housekeeping duties associated with the meeting. There should be an adequate number of chairs, ashtrays, pitchers of ice water, glasses, paper and pencils, agendas and advisory committee manuals. Name plates and name tags should be available to acquaint all members with each other. Audiovisual equipment should be checked to insure it is functioning properly and ready to use.

A refreshment period before the meeting will enable the various people to meet each other informally. The social period also allows those who have lost their way or who are late in arriving for some reason to be present at the start of the meeting.

The coordinator is responsible for preparing the agenda for the meeting. An example agenda is as follows:

1. *Introduction of Committee Members.* Even though the members have an opportunity to meet each other during the social period before the start of the meeting, it is appropriate for the coordinator to introduce each person and specify the person's title and place of employment.

2. *Appointment of Temporary Chairperson.* The teacher-coordinator should preside over the meeting until a chairperson is elected. The chairperson, however, should be a voting member of the advisory committee and not a member of the school system. The advisory committee should elect the chairperson from its own ranks.

3. *Overview of the Program.* The coordinator should explain the program, making sure that the members understand the differences between the various cooperative education programs, on-the-job training, work study programs, and apprenticeship training. The need and importance for an advisory committee also should be discussed.

4. *Discussion of the Advisory Committee Manual.* While the members can read the manual at their leisure, the coordinator should discuss the responsibilities of an advisory committee member and the function of an advisory committee. In addition, the rationale for different terms of appointment should be explained.

5. *Discussion about Future Meetings.* There should be dis-

cussion and selection of the time and location for future committee meetings. Some people prefer early morning meetings while others find late afternoons more convenient. Frequently, Mondays and Fridays are busy days for business people.

6. *Election of the Advisory Committee Chairperson and Vice-Chairperson.* Usually the term of office for these officers is a year. A longer term of office often will result in a member declining the office. If there is more than one person nominated for an office, the balloting should be secret for obvious reasons.

7. *Appointment of Subcommittees.* In order to expedite the work of the advisory committee, subcommittees can be given certain charges. Their reports at the advisory committee meetings can provide the basis for committee discussion and action. By dividing the responsibilities in this way, the committee can accomplish a great deal more than if they all worked on each item.

Advisory Committee Meetings

The entire advisory committee should meet at least four times a year. If this is not possible, the committee should meet in the fall shortly after the semester starts, and in the spring just before school closes. They should meet more frequently when a problem arises and, of course, various subcommittees should meet periodically through the calendar year.

The coordinator has the responsibility to make all the arrangements for the meeting including sending a reminder memo to the committee membership. The agenda is determined in advance of the meeting and is sent to the members.

CAUTIONS AND CONSIDERATIONS

An advisory committee can provide considerable help and support for the cooperative education teacher-coordinator. In order to insure their contributions are maximized, a coordinator should remember the following:

1. Advisory committee members are busy and involved people and have little time for or interest in trivia.
2. All members should have some responsibility to the program in terms of subcommittee involvement so every member feels a sense of commitment.
3. When their help or advice is requested, it should be used. In addition, the coordinator should report back to the committee the disposition of the recommendations they made and the rationale for the action taken.
4. Advisory committee members should be aware that they serve an important purpose. They should not get the feeling that they are being manipulated. They are important and influential members of the community and their help and recommendations should be treated with respect and appreciation. Periodically, they should be accorded public and private thanks for their interest and cooperation.

Figure 19 Courtesy, New Jersey Curriculum Laboratory.

Certificate of Appreciation

WE HEREBY EXPRESS
OUR SINCERE APPRECIATION TO

fo Providing Professional Service
as an Advisory Committee Member to

The Cooperative Vocational Education Program

Awarded at _____

This _____ day of _____ 19_____

Chief School Administrator   Teacher/Coordinator

Figure 20*

ASSESSING THE EFFECTIVENESS OF YOUR ADVISORY COMMITTEE

(This instrument can provide for the self-evaluation of advisory committees for career and vocational education in terms of functions they typically fulfill. It also can assist in the setting of future goals, looking toward future assessment.)

	ESTIMATED PERCENT OF UTILIZATION				
Typical Functions	0	25	50	75	100

A. Represents a broad selection of appropriate advisors:

    Workers now on the job _____

    Educators _____

    Community organizations and groups _____

    Business and industry _____

    Labor groups _____

    Students _____

    Recent graduates _____

    Local and State government _____

    Senior citizens _____

B. Assists in short and long range planning:

    Assessment of student needs, interests, and abilities

    Assessment of labor market needs and conditions __

    Assessment of community resources _____

    Assessment of local educational agency priorities and policies _____

    Responsive to regional, state, and national conditions, goals, and objectives _____

    Recommends priorities _____

C. Communicates important information to the community:

    Newsletters _____

    Radio _____

    Television _____

    Publications, such as pamphlets, posters, reports ___

    Press releases _____

    Recommendations to key agencies _____

    Speakers' bureau _____

    Formal events such as luncheons and dinners _____

    Workshops _____

    Exhibits _____

    Personal communication _____

Figure 20 — (Cont'd.)

	ESTIMATED PERCENT OF UTILIZATION				
	0	25	50	75	100

Program information widely disseminated to prospective students _____ _____

D. Communicates important work-related information to the school:

Provides information on the labor market _____ _____

Makes appropriate recommendations concerning course objectives (including needed worker competencies, content, and procedures). _____ _____

E. Recommends competent personnel to meet program needs:

Maintains an inventory of capable instructors ____ _____

Personal contacts with potential instructors _____ _____

Personal contacts with present instructors to discover the currency and relevancy of their instruction ____ _____

Recommends a screening policy for new instructors _ _____

F. Assists with evaluation of the instructional program:
Facilitates follow-up activity _____ _____

Studies placement results _____ _____

Makes recommendations for increased relevancy of program _____ _____

Visits some programs for first-hand assessment ____ _____

Assures compliance with necessary regulations (e.g., affirmative action) _____ _____

G. Other functions:

_____ _____ _____

_____ _____ _____

_____ _____ _____

*Buontempo, Gregory and Klavon, Michael: **Making the Most of Your Advisory Committee.** Trenton, New Jersey Department of Education.

Figure 21

A CHECKLIST FOR THE TEACHER-COORDINATOR IN ORGANIZING AND CONDUCTING
AN ADVISORY COMMITTEE

Yes   No

_____ _____   1. I have familarized the Committee with all facets of the program.

_____ _____   2. I have provided all members with an updated Advisory Committee Manual.

_____ _____   3. I seek out potential Advisory Committee members who are interested and willing to serve on the Committee.

_____ _____   4. I involve at least one co-op graduate to serve on the Advisory Committee.

_____ _____   5. I solicit the advice and assistance of the Committee.

_____ _____   6. I acquaint the members with the purpose and the duties of the Committee and insure that the Committee acts accordingly.

_____ _____   7. I anticipate the problems and needs of the program by planning Advisory Committee meetings for specific purposes directed toward promoting and developing the cooperative education program.

_____ _____   8. I avoid meetings for the sake of meetings.

_____ _____   9. I avoid asking the Advisory Committee to assist me in matters that can better be made by individuals on the school staff.

_____ _____   10. I avoid compromises that are not productive or adequate to the problem faced.

_____ _____   11. I encourage Advisory Committee members to participate in youth organization activities as advisors, contest judges, and speakers.

_____ _____   12. I submit the cooperative education program to an evaluation by the Advisory Committee.

_____ _____   13. I serve as the Secretary to the Advisory Committee in a non-voting member capacity.

_____ _____   14. I avoid alienating those with unpopular opinions.

_____ _____   15. I avoid having a chairperson who unduly dominates the group.

_____ _____   16. I notify the members and the delegated school authority of the meeting date, time, and place.

_____ _____   17. I avoid manipulating members at meetings.

_____   18. I provide the Advisory Committee members with an agenda of the subsequent meetings, preferably one week in advance.

_____ _____   19. I avoid a complacent attitude in relation to the Advisory Committee.

_____ _____   20. I provide recognition of the Advisory Committee members through press releases, certificates of appreciation, invitations to employer-employee banquets, etc.

BIBLIOGRAPHY

The Advisory Committee and Vocational Education. Washington, D.C., American Vocational Association, Inc., August, 1969.

Annual Report on the New Jersey Advisory Council on Vocational Education. Trenton, New Jersey Advisory Council on Vocational Education, December, 1974.

Annual Report on the New Jersey Advisory Council on Vocational Education. Trenton, New Jersey Advisory Council on Vocational Education, December, 1973.

Apprenticeship in New Jersey. Trenton, State of New Jersey, Department of Education, Division of Vocational Education and Career Preparation, September, 1975.

Basaulso, Eugenio R.: *Advisory Committees in Vocational Technical Programs.* February, 1976.

Buontempo, Gregory and Klavon, Michael: *Making the Most of your Advisory Committee.* Trenton, New Jersey State Department of Education, Division of Vocational Education and Career Preparation, November, 1975.

Cooperative Education Training Youth for Future Employment. West Long Branch, New Jersey, Shore Regional High School, March, 1974.

Department of Health, Education and Welfare, Office of Education: *Federal Register, 42(67):43,* April 7, 1977.

Ely, Ron H.: How to organize and maintain a productive advisory committee. *American Vocational Journal,* 37-39, March 1977.

A guide for advisory committees in business education. In *Vocational Office Training,* Monograph 70. New York, South-Western Publishing Co., May 1948.

A Guide for Planning, Organizing, and Utilizing Advisory Councils. Springfield, Division of Vocational and Technical Education, Illinois Office of Education.

Highlights . . . of the Vocational Education Section (Title II) of the Education Amendments of 1976 (P.L. 94-482). Trenton, Department of Education, Division of Vocational Education and Career Preparation.

The National Apprenticeship Program. Washington, D.C., U.S. Department of Labor, 1972.

Nerden, Joseph T.: Advisory committees in vocational education, a powerful incentive to program improvement. *American Vocational Journal. 52(1):27-29,* January 1977.

On the Effective Use of Advisory Committees: A manual for business and teachers, Bulletin 20. Columbus, Ohio State Department of Education, 1975.

Public Law 90-976. 90th Congress, H.R. 18366. October 16, 1968.

Public Law 94-482. 94th Congress. October 12, 1976.

Riendeau, Albert J.: *Advisory Committees for Occupational Education. A Guide to Organization and Operation.* New York, McGraw, 1977.

The Role of Advisory Committees in Vocational-Technical Education. Trenton, State of New Jersey, Department of Education and Career Preparation.

Shenker, Morton: *Advisory Committees for Cooperative Education Programs.* Trenton, Trenton State College.

Wanat, John A.: *Leadership Functions Relating to Curriculum and Instruction, Advisory Committees and Staffing.* Unpublished, March 1972.

Chapter 7

EFFECTIVELY UTILIZING TRAINING
AGREEMENTS AND TRAINING PLANS

MANAGEMENT TOOLS

TRAINING AGREEMENTS and plans are an integral part of the cooperative education strategy. Both instruments, the agreement and the plan, are management tools for an effective cooperative education program operation. These instruments will be dealt with separately to highlight the importance of each.

The Vocational Education Amendments of 1968, Public Law 90-576, required all funded programs under Part G of that Act to utilize a training agreement. The Vocational Education Amendments of 1976 continue to require this provision for all funded programs. Irrespective of the funding source, however, individual states and the federal government encourage teacher-coordinators to effectively utilize training agreements in their everyday operation of the program for the following reasons:

1. As a planning document, it serves as a vehicle for directing and evaluating learning experiences.
2. As an information document, it helps employers to appreciate their teaching role and to understand the purposes of cooperative vocational education.
3. As a permanent record, it is useful for subsequent placement services and follow-up studies.
4. As a career decision-making document, it builds student satisfaction in fulfilling a prevailing career interest.[1]

[1]U.S. Department of Health, Education and Welfare, Office of Education: *Zero In On Cooperative Vocational Education-Training Agreements.* Washington, D.C., HEW, January, 1974, page 1.

What then is a training agreement? The training agreement is the instrument by which the school and the cooperating employer delineate, on paper, the responsibilities of each participant to the others. The training agreement is an understanding between the employer or his agent, the student learner, the student's parents, and the coordinator.

CHILD LABOR PROVISIONS, BULLETIN 101

Cooperative vocational education student-learners are specifically granted limited exclusions from the "Child Labor Provisions" of the Fair Labor Standards Act provided that the student-learner enter into a written contract with the employer. For clarification, the following excerpt from the *Child Labor Provisions, Bulletin 101,* is provided.

> *Student-learners: (1) The student-learner is enrolled in a course of study and training in a cooperative vocational training program under a recognized State or local educational authority or in a course of study in a substantially similar program conducted by a private school; and (2) such student-learner is employed under a written agreement which provides: (i) that the work of the student-learner in the occupations declared particularly hazardous shall be incidental to his training; (ii) that such work shall be intermittent and for short periods of time and under the direct and close supervision of a qualified and experienced person; (iii) that safety instructions shall be given by the school and correlated by the employer with on-the-job training; and (iv) that a schedule of organized and progressive work processes to be performed on the job shall have been prepared. Each such written agreement shall contain the name of the student-learner, and shall be signed by the employer and the school coordinator or principal. Copies of each agreement shall be kept on file by both the school and the employer. This exemption for the employment of student-learners may be revoked in any individual situation where it is found that reasonable precautions have not been observed for the safety of minors employed thereunder.*

PREPARATION OF TRAINING AGREEMENTS

The training agreement is discussed and completed before the student is employed. It outlines the responsibilities of all the individuals involved in the program. The training agreement is not a legal document. Many states prefer to refer to the training agreement as a memorandum of understanding in order to avoid the legal connotation of a formal contract. Regardless of the terminology, the training agreement is the means by which the cooperative method is emphasized. Generally, the following standard information is included in a training agreement:

    A.   Date
    B.   Name of school and program
    C.   Name of student-learner, including age
    D.   Career objective of the student-learner
    E.   Job title for the student-learner, including USOE instructional code
    F.   Length of training, including scheduled hours
    G.   Wage rates and working conditions
    H.   Student-learner status, part-time worker that does not displace the normal work force
    I.   Detailed responsibilities of the cooperating employer, student-learner, teacher-coordinator, and/or parent or guardian are delineated.
    J.   Training plans are often incorporated into the body of the training agreement or are attached to the training agreement.
    K.   Signatures of the cooperating employer, teacher-coordinator, student-learner, and parent or guardian are often requested. Additional signatures of chief school administrators, advisory committee members, and union representatives are also included in some of the training agreements.

Additional features that can be highlighted in the training agreement include the following:

    A.   Emphasis on safety instruction
    B.   Direction of learning experiences
    C.   Compliance with state and federal labor laws
    D.   Approval of state board of education and state bureau of labor and industry
    E.   Specific job activities
    F.   Hours or percentage of time spent on specific job activities

G. School credits
H. Study assignments
I. Wage adjustments
J. Local advisory committee review
K. Job rotation
L. Check points for program coordination and supervision
M. Union participation
N. Provisions for Workmen's Compensation Insurance
O. Age and health verification
P. Detailed employment schedule
Q. Summary evaluation

The training form takes on many different sizes and shapes. Ideally a one page document is easy to reproduce and disseminate yet is concise enough to allow the cooperating employer ample time to review it without too much difficulty. It is worth considering to have the form include carbon interleaves so that copies may be disseminated to the appropriate parties, such as the employer, the school, the student, the parent, and state department of education where required. The forms can be interdisciplinary in nature so that one form can be used by all co-op programs. This allows for standardization in the field. Cooperating employers begin to understand that cooperative education is a school function that serves multiple disciplines.

The training agreement is the means by which a link is made between the world of work and school. It demonstrates to all concerned parties that the student-learner is placed at the work site for specific on-the-job instruction. The training agreement helps to dispel the myth that the student-learner is there simply for part-time employment. The training agreement serves as the basis for establishing a sound structured educational program at the work site.

Figure 22

COOPERATIVE VOCATIONAL EDUCATION TRAINING AGREEMENT

Date _____

SCHOOL DISTRICT _____

Employer _____
              Employer's Name   Address

Agrees to employe _____
              Student-Learner's Name   Address

for the purpose of training in _____, Starting Wage: $_____

Student-Learner's date of birth _____ Working Papers _____
                                        Date Issued

Working Conditions:
1. All student-learners must be covered by Workmen's Compensation Insurance.
2. The employer is aware of the educational nature of the program, and agrees to observe all State and Federal laws and regulations relative to the employment of minors.
3. The employer will provide direct and close supervision by a qualified and experienced person, and safety instructions will be provided by the teacher-coordinator and the cooperating employer. **(See New Jersey Child Labor Law Abstract MW-129 and New Jersey State Department of Education T-Letter 268 on prohibited occupations.)**
4. Student-learners will not displace regular workers nor substitute for workers ordinarily needed by the employer.

Other Employer Responsibilities:
1. To take an active part in training and supervising the above named student-learner while providing on-the-job instruction in accordance with the student-learner's training plan.
2. To employ the student-learner for an average of 15 hours a week, for a minimum of 540 hours, until the end of the school year, barring dismissal for cause.
3. To assist in evaluating the student-learner's progress by completing the student evaluation form when required.
4. The student-learner will not be discharged nor status changed without first consulting with the teacher-coordinator.
5. To pay the student-learner the prevailing wage paid similar employees, and to recognize satisfactory service throughout the year with salary increases as awarded to other employees.
6. To allow the student-learner to absent himself/herself from work, without prejudice, when school or vocational student organization activities require his/her presence, with the understanding that notification of the need for such absence will be received from the teacher-coordinator at least one week prior to the absence.
7. To allow the student to be observed on the job periodically by the teacher-coordinator of the Cooperative Education Program.

8. In the event the student-learner's school grades in any major subject fall below passing as a result of time spent on the job, weekly work hours will be reduced according to the advice of the teacher-coordinator until such time as the student-learner is earning passing grades.

9. To notify the teacher-coordinator as soon as possible any time the student-learner fails to appear for work or fails to call in sick at the scheduled time, or fails to stay for the scheduled time.

10. To be available for conference with the teacher-coordinator, the student-learner, or both, as necessary.

_ _

Work Experience

The following will be included in the student-learner's work experience:

1. _____   5. _____
2. _____   6. _____
3. _____   7. _____
4. _____   8. _____

Signed _____
                    Employer

Signed _____
                    Teacher-Coordinator

                                        Phone _____

I have read the above and fully understand my employer's responsibility to me and_____
High School, and my responsibility to my employer and school.

Signed _____   Signed _____
                Student-Learner   Parent/Guardian

Figure 23

ARKANSAS
COOPERATIVE VOCATIONAL EDUCATION
TRAINING PLAN

Name of Service Area	Name of School
City　　　　Date	Name of Training Establishment
Training Supervisor and Position	Student's Name
Birth date　　Social Security No.	Occupational Objective　　O.E. Code
Length of Training Period	Year in Vocational Cooperative Program

1. The school will make provisions for the student to receive related and technical instruction as shown on the attached outline.
2. The employer agrees to offer the student the greatest possible variety of job experiences within the student's individual capabilities to enable him/her to prepare as completely as possible for the occupation for which the training outline prescribes.
3. The amount of compensation shall be determined by the employer in accordance with current wage and hour laws.
4. The coordinator will assist with adjustments of any problems of the trainee while on the job.
5. The trainee is selected without discrimination.
6. Employment shall not be terminated by the trainee without the coordinator's approval.
7. The employment of a regular employee shall not be terminated to create a position for the training of a student.
8. The student agrees to perform diligently the work experiences assigned by the employer according of the same company policies and regulations as apply to regular employees, and his/her employment may be terminated for the same reasons as other employees.
9. Students should average not less than fifteen hours per week on the job during the school term.

THIS TRAINING PLAN IS NOT COMPLETE WITHOUT AN ATTACHED TRAINING OUTLINE

Advisory Committee Member	Employer
State Supervisor	Coordinator
Parent or Guardian	Student

Figure 24

MEMORANDUM OF UNDERSTANDING

State of Maine
Department of Educational
and Cultural Services
Bureau of Vocational Education
Augusta

This vocational education work experience (training) program has been approved by the State Board of Education subject to the terms of this agreement including the following conditions:

1. The program is under the direct supervision of a full-time coordinator.
2. The signatures will indicate approval by all parties involved.
3. The student-learner will be receiving instruction in an approved school and will be employed pursuant to a bona fide Vocational Part-Time Work Experience Education Program in order to further his vocational education.
4. The student-learner will neither displace a regular worker now employed, nor substitute for a worker that would ordinarily be needed by the employer.
5. A schedule of organized and progressive work processes to be performed on the job has been prepared.
6. Safety instruction will be given by the school. While on the job, the student will receive safety instruction from and be under the direct supervision of a qualified representative of the employing organization. Specific machines upon which he will work and other hazardous operations on which he will work are itemized.
7. The student-learner agrees to perform his duties in a loyal and faithful manner and to work for the best interest of all concerned.
8. This program may be terminated at any time by the high school principal or coordinator to assure the best interest of all concerned.
9. This program shall comply with all federal, state, and local laws and regulations.
10. If applicable, the waiver of hazardous occupations restrictions (Section 22, Chapter 30, revised 1954) is granted when this agreement is approved by the Bureau of Labor and Industry.
    NOTE: This exemption for employment of student-learners may be revoked in any individual situation wherein it is found that reasonable precautions have not been observed for the safety of minors employed thereunder (taken from the Maine Department of Labor and Industry Bulletin DLI No. 1, revised 1957, Hazardous Occupations and Operations).
11. The employer agrees to furnish an evaluation of the student-learner's progress, adaptability, and attitude approximately once a month. (Forms will be furnished by the coordinator.)

— —

This program of part-time Vocational Education has been approved by the State Board of Education.

Associate Commissioner, Bureau of Vocational Education

— —

This program, as set forth in the memorandum of understanding, has been reviewed by the Bureau of Labor and Industry for compliance with Maine labor laws. The hazardous occupations restrictions, if any, are hereby waived **during the hours of training as stated herein.**

_____

for the Bureau of Labor and Industry

INFORMATION SECTIONS — All signatures indicating approval must be affixed.

1. SCHOOL CONDUCTING PROGRAM:

Name _____

Address: _____

_____
(Coordinator's Signature)

Type of Program:

DE _____   OO _____   Interrelated _____

T&I _____   HO _____   Other _____

REMARKS: _____

_____

No. of Minutes Related Instruction Wkly: _____

2. STUDENT-LEARNER SECTION

Name _____
(Please Print or Type)

_____
(Student-Learner's Signature)

Grade Level: _____   Date of Birth: _____

Occupational Objective: _____

Social Security No.: _____

No. of Hours in School Daily _____

No. of Hours Employment Daily _____

U.S.O.E. Code No.: _____

_____
(Signature of Parent or Guardian)

- -

3. EMPLOYER'S SECTION:

Name of Establishment: _____ Kind of Business: _____

Address: _____ _____

Beginning Date of Employment: _____

Graduation Date or Anticipated Date of Ending Employment, Whichever is Nearer: _____

Starting Hourly Rate of Pay: _____ Potential Hourly Rate of Pay: _____

As the employer, I am:

subject to the provisions of the Fair Labor Standards Act -------------- Yes_____ No_____

subject to the provisions of the State of Maine minimum wage law ------ Yes_____ No_____

covered under the provisions of the Workmen's Compensation Act ------- Yes_____ No_____

Signature of on-the-job supervisor: _____

Signature of employer: _____

- -

TOPICAL OUTLINE OF on-the-job operations the student will experience:

MACHINE TO BE OPERATED, or hazardous occupation:

_____

_____

_____

_____

_____

_____

_____

_____

_____

_____

Figure 25

COOPERATIVE EDUCATION STUDENT TRAINING AGREEMENT
MIDDLESEX COUNTY COLLEGE
EDISON, NEW JERSEY

1. Students are required to work a full fifteen weeks during the semester. A student-trainee is expected at all times to conform to the rules and regulations of the business in which he/she is working. Special attention is called to the necessity for following regulations concerning dress, conduct, and attendance.

2. Any case of dishonesty or any appearance of dishonesty on the job that causes you to be dismissed will be just cause for your dismissal from the program and loss of all credit therein. Students are cautioned that such an offense is serious and becomes a part of their school and job records.

3. Students who lose their jobs during the school year because of inefficiency, lack of interest, not abiding by company rules and regulations, etc., may be dropped from the program and lose all credit therein.

4. No student may terminate his/her work without the knowledge and consent of his/her coordinator. If the student does, he/she may be dropped from the program.

5. Students who enroll in the program will be expected to work on Saturdays, Sundays, holidays, and school vacations, if needed, and maintain excellent attendance both at school and on the job.

6. Any change in the work schedule or job supervisor must be reported to the coordinator immediately!

   "I understand the above rules and regulations and agree to accept my responsibility in compliance therewith."

                    Student _____

RESPONSIBILITIES

The major purpose of the cooperative education program is to provide valuable vocational education for students in occupational fields of their choice. The training agreement therefore delineates the responsibilities of the cooperating employer, student-learner, school, and employer. The responsibilities of each are discussed below.

The Cooperating Employer

Any or all of the following conditions can be included in the training agreement under the responsibilities of the cooperating employer:

1. To observe all state and federal laws and regulations relative to the employment of the student-learner.
2. To cover the student-learner on the job by Workmen's Compensation Insurance.
3. To provide on-the-job safety instruction that is correlated with the safety instruction given at the school.
4. To guarantee that student-learners will not displace regular workers or substitute for workers ordinarily needed by the employer.
5. To provide on-the-job instruction in accordance with the student-learner's training plan.
6. To keep the student-learner on the job for at least the minimum number of hours specified in the agreement.
7. To pay the student-learner the prevailing wage paid similar employees, and to recognize satisfactory service throughout the year with salary increases as awarded to other employees.
8. To allow the student-learner to absent himself/herself from work, without prejudice, when school or vocational student organization activities require his or her presence, with the understanding that notification of the need for such absence will be reviewed by the teacher-coordinator at least one week prior to the absence.
9. To allow the student to be observed on the job periodically by the teacher-coordinator.

10. To notify the teacher-coordinator as soon as possible any time the student-learner fails to appear for work or fails to call in sick at the scheduled time, or fails to stay for the scheduled time.
11. To provide the student-learner with progressive and challenging work activities.
12. To be available for conference with the teacher-coordinator, the student-learner, or both, as necessary.
13. To assist in evaluating the student-learner's progress by completing the student evaluation form when required.

The Student-Learner

The student-learner agrees as follows:

1. To be honest, punctual, cooperative, courteous, and to make an honest effort to learn and abide by all rules and regulations of the program.
2. To keep regular attendance both at school and on the job.
3. To abstain from work on any school day that he/she fails to attend school. Exceptions are permissible only with the mutual consent of the employer and the teacher-coordinator.
4. To consult with the teacher-coordinator about any difficulties arising at the training station.
5. To conform to the rules and regulations of the training station.
6. To furnish the teacher-coordinator with all necessary information and complete all necessary reports.
7. To refrain from changing his or her place of employment without the prior approval of the teacher-coordinator.
8. To perform classroom responsibilities in an efficient manner.
9. To participate in those co-curricular school activities that are required in connection with the cooperative education program.

The School

The teacher-coordinator, representing the school, will coordinate the training program toward a satisfactory preparation of the student-learner for his or her occupational career objective and agrees as follows:

1. To operate the program in conformity to USOE and state department of education regulations.
2. To grant school credits for successful completion of the program by the student-learner.
3. To comply with all federal and state laws governing the employment of minors especially as it concerns hazardous work.
4. To correlate in-school instruction with the safety instruction provided by the employer on the job.
5. To prepare and organize a progressive work program schedule to be performed by the student-learner on the job.
6. To make periodic visits to the training station to observe the student-learner on the job.
7. To consult with the employer and training supervisor and to render any needed assistance with training problems concerning the student-learner.
8. To correlate the on-the-job learning experience with in-school related instruction, including safety instruction.
9. To assist in the evaluation of the student-learner.

The Parents

The parents of the student-learner, realizing the importance of the training program in the student-learner's attaining his or her career objective, agree as follows:

1. To be responsible for their child in this program.
2. To assist the student-learner in obeying the rules of the cooperative education program.
3. To approve and agree that the student-learner shall participate in said program and training station.
4. To encourage the student-learner to carry out effectively his or her duties and responsibilities.

5. To share the responsibility for the conduct of the student-learner while training in the program.
6. To accept responsibility for the safety and conduct of the student-learner while he or she is traveling to and from school, the training station, and home.
7. To provide ample insurance for the student-learner while traveling to and from school and work.

Each cooperating employer and student-learner knows that the courtesies and responsibilities extended to them are the same as those extended to all others in this category. The training agreement dispells all doubts or misunderstandings that might undermine the cooperative education program. Further, the relationship between the parties to the agreement is given status. Each of the concerned parties receives a copy of the training agreement. For many student-learners, this may be the first document they have ever signed.

A copy of the training agreement should be maintained in the student-learner's personal file folder. The cooperating employer should also maintain a copy of the training agreement in his or her files for future reference. The training agreement and the accompanying training plan should be used by the teacher-coordinator and the cooperating employer in discussing the student-learner's progress on the job during the regular visitation periods by the teacher-coordinator.

TRAINING PLANS

A training plan specifies the nature and extent of occupational training that a student shall receive in a specific trade or occupation. The plan outlines the on-the-job learning experiences and the associated experiences that should be learned and/or reinforced in the classroom. The plans are task-oriented, usually providing estimated time lengths for completion of tasks. The purpose of such plans, how to prepare and use them, and some cautions regarding them are presented in this chapter.

Purpose of Training Plans

A training plan serves as the organizational base for a cooperative education student's learning experience in that it specifies the sequence of the training and learning opportunities the student shall receive. It also provides the instructional plan for the personnel at the training station responsible for supervising the student's occupational training. It assists the teacher-coordinator in planning the related instruction. Although the related instruction may be modified as a result of the coordinator confering with the work station supervisor, to compensate for some area of weaknesses of the student, the plan still identifies the progression of the student's overall learning experience. Finally, training plans provide a means by which employers have some input into decisions regarding the training of possible future employees.

Use of Training Plans

Training plans are an important and useful document to everyone who is associated with the cooperative education program. Among those who find them of particular value are the teacher-coordinator, the training station employer, the school administration, the advisory committee members, the student, and the student's family.

The teacher-coordinator uses the training plan to facilitate planning, supervising, and evaluating the student's progress. Specifically, the teacher-coordinator uses the plan to—

1. Discuss the student's progress with the training supervisors.
2. Identify topics that should be discussed in the related instruction class to preceed or accompany the on-the-job experience.
3. Counsel the student regarding his or her progress in the program.
4. Specify a student's achievement in the learning experience to interested parties, such as the student's family, the guidance personnel, the advisory committee, or the school administration.
5. Evaluate the successfulness of a particular aspect of the cooperative education program.

The training station sponsor uses the training plan to—

1. Identify the parameters of a student's learning experience at the job.
2. Specify what activities the student should be expected to do.
3. Identify how long the student should spend becoming competent at a specific task.
4. Review expectations and attitudes regarding the competence expected of employees in performing a particular skill.

The student and the student's family use the plan as a document to—

1. Clarify the student's career objectives and goals by viewing how much must be learned.
2. Tell approximately how long each skill must be practiced before some degree of competence can be expected.
3. Identify the nature and extent of related instruction necessary for competence in the skill.
4. Compare the progress made with the employer's and coordinator's expectations.

The school administration and advisory committee use training plans—

1. As an indication of the diversity of experiences a cooperative education student receives.
2. To show the nature and extent of training a student receives in preparing for a particular occupation.

Preparation of Training Plans

The preparation of a student's training plan includes several steps. First, the entry level skills and technical knowledges the student should possess are identified and sequenced from simple to difficult. From that list, with consideration to the student's needs, interests, and aptitudes, the employer and coordinator jointly develop a training plan for the student.

Several sources of information are available to help coordinators develop and individualize training plans. Some states have sample listings of the more common occupations that student-learners prepare for in cooperative education programs. Other sources include advisory committee members, people working in the occupations, and information from periodical and occupational study guides. The Dictionary of Occupational Titles (D.O.T.) can also provide much helpful information. In addition, the guidance department and school faculty provide input for the coordinator, which is helpful in individualizing the plan.

The format for the training plan is usually developed by the teacher-coordinator. Irrespective of the format, the following information is often found on a training plan:

1. Job Title—D.O.T. and/or USOE code numbers
2. Student-learner's name
3. Name and place of training station
4. Learning activities, on-the-job and in-school
5. Reference materials
6. Training periods
7. Introductory paragraph describing the occupation.

The teacher-coordinator has the prime responsibility for developing a training plan. The following is a step-by-step procedure of preparing a training plan:

1. Identify, using action verbs of singular tense, the jobs the student will be taught.
2. Sequence those jobs from a simple to complex arrangement in the major areas of responsibility in the occupation.
3. Place the jobs in a column showing the areas of responsibility with the associated tasks located beneath.
4. Identify the related technical information to the jobs the student should know and arrange them in another column beside the activity to which they pertain.
5. Make an estimate of the length of time the student-learner should be expected to devote to each phase of the plan and record it in a column beside the job.
6. Review the student's record regarding interest, abilities, and aptitudes as they relate to the training plan and make necessary adjustments to the plan.

7. Collaborate with the training station sponsor in modifying the plan persuant to the opportunities for training available at the training station.

8. Determine the appropriate number of observations of a job a student should have, and where and if the student should be instructed in how to perform a particular job, including the nature and extent of supervision the student will receive. Note the information in a column beside the job.

9. Secure approval of the plan from the training station employer and the student and have them designate the approval by signing the plan at a designated place on the form.

10. Make several copies of the plan and distribute them to the training station employer and the student, with the original retained as part of the student's permanent record at school.

11. Attach a copy of the laws and regulations that would affect the student learning the occupation to every copy of the training plan and/or training agreement.

Cautions to be Considered

There are certain cautions that should be observed in developing and using training plans. A plan should be individualized, otherwise it will have a poor chance of serving a student's needs and interests. The coordinator must check periodically to determine that the plan is still appropriate. If not, it should be changed. Many coordinators fail to remember a training plan is meant to be a guide and as such should have some degree of flexibility to it. Finally, coordinators should remember that a training plan is only as effective as those who use it.

Figure 26*

ELECTRICIAN

O. E. Code 17. 10 02
D O T Code 821.381
824.281
829.281/.381

SPECIALTY SUMMARY

Assembles, installs, and wires heat, light, power, air conditioning, and refrigeration components.

DUTIES AND RESPONSIBILITIES

1. Performs electrical wiring layout.

   Interprets blueprints, identifies symbols, makes sketches and schematics, describing work for which he receives only verbal orders.

2. Installs rough wiring

   Locates, mounts, installs, and runs electrical wiring, electrical boxes, and conduit.

3. Hooks up wiring

   Splices and connects outlets, switches, lighting fixtures. Splices wires and tests line.

4. Installs special purpose receptacles

   Installs receptacles in floors, walls, appliances, heating units, air conditioning apparatus, outdoor lighting fixtures, and basic security systems.

5. Installs power distribution systems

   Installs and wires service head, mounts meter bases, distribution cabinet. Installs breakers, switches, grounds, and branch circuit panels.

6. Performs preventive maintenance

   Maintains equipment records, cleans controls, uses hand and power tools to keep equipment in safe working conditions.

7. Practices safety

   Follows rules and regulations of the National Electrical Code. Fulfills requirements of state, county, and local electrical codes.

*Natale, Don, Krell, Paul, Snell, Margaret, and Wanat, John A.: *C.I.E. Teacher-Coordinator Training Plans.* New Brunswick, New Jersey, Vocational-Technical Curriculum Laboratory, Rutgers University, 1978. pp. 49-52.

Figure 26b

TRAINING PLAN
for

ELECTRICIAN

SOURCE ___NJ_____

TASKS AND KNOWLEDGES	applicable	observe	perform	master
1. CAREER PROGRESSION				
A. Progression in career ladder				
B. Duties of each career level				
2. ELECTRICAL WIRING LAYOUT				
A. Identify electrical drafting symbols				
1. Convenience outlets				
2. Split wired convenience outlets				
3. Special purpose outlets/appliance symbols				
4. Low voltage signal systems				
5. Riser diagram				
B. Blueprint reading				
1. Room sizes and location				
2. Stairways				
3. Openings such as windows and doors				
C. Specifications				
D. Prepare wiring diagram for residential use				
1. Plain wiring runs				
2. Select wire sizes				
3. Calculate fuse size				
4. Calculate circuit loads				
5. Plan tools required for job completion				
6. Plan equipment required for job completion				
7. Plan materials required for job completion				
8. Perform improvement modification on existing plans				
9. Estimate time-material cost factors				

TASKS and KNOWLEDGES ELECTRICIAN	applicable	observe	perform	master
3. ROUGH WIRE				
A. Locate and mount electrical boxes				
1. Mount outlet boxes				
2. Mount switch boxes				
3. Install junction boxes and fittings				
4. Locate and mount lighting fixtures boxes				
5. Install cabinet and cutout boxes				
B. Bore holes for wire runs				
C. Run electrical wiring				
1. Romex				
2. BX				
3. Conduit				
4. HOOK-UP WIRING				
A. Connect convenience outlets				
B. Connect switches				
1. Single pole - single throw switch				
2. Three-way switch				
3. Four-way switch				
C. Connection of lighting fixtures				
D. Splice wires using:				
1. Solderless connectors and lugs				
2. Soldering copper, flux, and solder				
3. Blowtorch, flux, and solder				
4. Ladle, molten solder, flux				
5. TRIM-OUT				
A. Install special purpose receptacles				
1. Range				
2. Floor				
3. Wall				
4. Appliance				

Figure 26d

TASKS and KNOWLEDGES ELECTRICIAN	applicable	observe	perform	master
B. Electrical System				
1. Perform basic wiring on electrical, gas, and oil fired heating units and controls				
2. Connect air conditioning apparatus				
3. Operate refrigeration control circuits				
4. Develop basic security system plans				
5. Analyze audio system requirements for public address systems				
6. Place outdoor and special effects lighting fixtures and controls				
6. UNDERSTANDING OF POWER DISTRIBUTION SYSTEMS				
A. Service entrance				
B. Distribution box				
C. Service switch				
D. Grounding techniques				
E. Two-wire system				
F. Three-wire system				
7. INSTALL POWER DISTRIBUTION SYSTEM				
A. Install service head on building				
B. Mount meter base on building				
C. Mount distribution cabinet for two-wire system				
D. Mount distribution cabinet for three-wire system				
E. Install service breaker or switch				
F. Install grounds				
G. Install branch circuit power panels				
8. PREVENTATIVE MAINTENANCE				
A. Maintain equipment records				
1. Maintain records of equipment running time				
2. Maintain records on frequency of repair data for electrical units				
B. Clean controls and exposed units of foreign matter				
C. Recommend specific safety procedures				
D. Make mathematical computations for current carrying capacities				
E. Use common hand tools and power tools to keep equipment in good working order.				

Figure 27

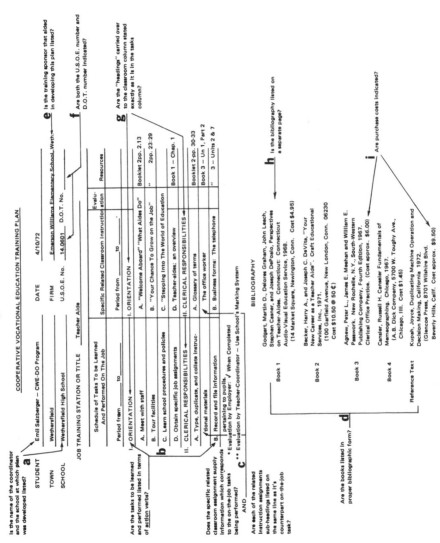

COURTESY — THE CONNECTICUT STATE DEPARTMENT OF EDUCATION, DIVISION OF VOCATIONAL EDUCATION

Figure 28.   Courtesy, Rutgers University Curriculum Laboratory

A CHECKLIST FOR UTILIZING TRAINING AGREEMENTS AND TRAINING PLANS

Yes   No

_____   _____   1. I utilize a written training agreement and plan.

_____   _____   2. I use the training agreement and plan as planning documents for directing and evaluating learning experiences.

_____   _____   3. I update training plans to allow for necessary changes and/or modifications.

_____   _____   4. I utilize the training plan as a basis for training sponsor visits.

_____   _____   5. I prepare the training plan to include the extent of training and the time felt necessary for the various training activities.

_____   _____   6. I develop a training plan in consultation with the cooperating employer and the student-learner.

_____   _____   7. I use the training plan as a basis for discussion with students.

_____   _____   8. I use the training plan to keep track of student's progress.

_____   _____   9. I use the training plan to evaluate prospective training sponsors.

_____   _____   10. I correlate the training plan with the on-the-job instruction and the related classroom instruction.

_____   _____   11. I submit training plans to my advisory committee for their review.

_____   _____   12. I obtain all the appropriate signatures on the training agreement, submit copies to all concerned parties and maintain a copy on file for permanent record.

BIBLIOGRAPHY

Cooperative Vocational Education Handbook for Kentucky.   Frankfort, Bureau of Vocational Education, State Department of Education, 1978.

Cooperative Work Experience Diversified Occupations Training Plans. Hartford, Connecticut State Department of Education, Division of Vocational Education, 1976.

A Guide for Cooperative Vocational Education.   Minneapolis, College of Education, University of Minnesota, September 1969.

Guide for Cooperative Vocational Education.   Denver, The University of Northern Colorado, Department of Vocational Education, State Board for Community Colleges and Occupational Education.

Natale, Don, Krell, Paul, Snell, Margaret, and Wanat, John A.:   *C.I.E.*

Teacher-Coordinator Training Plans. New Brunswick, Vocational-Technical Curriculum Laboratory, Rutgers University, April 1978.

Nelson, Edwin L.: The subject was training agreements. *Current Perspectives in Distributive Education.* The National Association of State Supervisors of Distributive Education, 1974.

Robinson, James B.: *A Standard Training Plan for Distributive Education Cooperative Work Programs.* Trenton, Trenton State College, Division of Business, 1976.

Snell, Margaret Ann: Developing and using training plans. *School Shop,* 23-24, January 1978.

Training Plans — A Guide for the Establishment of Training Plans for Cooperative Vocational Education Programs. Minnesota Association of Distributive Education, 1974.

Training Plans and Work Experience Education. Salem, Oregon State Department of Education, 1974.

Zero In On Cooperative Vocational Education — Training Agreements. Washington, D.C., United States Department of Health, Education and Welfare, January 1974.

Chapter 8

CORRELATING THE RELATED CLASS INSTRUCTION WITH THE WORK EXPERIENCE

An Integral Part of the Cooperative Education Program

COOPERATIVE EDUCATION by definition is a combination of in-school work with on-the-job training. The related class serves as the integral part of the in-school phase of the cooperative education program. The Minneapolis, Minnesota *Guide for Cooperative Vocational Education*, page 46, states—

> Related instruction in Cooperative Vocational Education should facilitate the development of capabilities the student needs to enter, adjust, and advance in a satisfying career. Even though it is expected that a student's career interests and plans may change, the desired vocational capabilities and competencies which he/she will need in future occupations are learned through the medium of a specific job within the context of his/her economic and social environment.

The related class is the setting that—

1. Reinforces the theory behind the skills that are learned on the job.
2. Orients the student-learner to successful employment techniques.
3. Provides student-learners with occupational information on multiple career choices.
4. Eases the student-learner's transition between school and the world of work.
5. Provides the student-learners with a forum to discuss problems and concerns associated with their on-the-job learning situations.

6. Provides students with technical materials relevant to their occupation.
7. Deals with behavioral aspects that are common to all work experiences.
8. Explores activities such as role-playing at job interviews and employer/employee relations.
9. Facilitates individualized learning that will enhance their on-the-job performance.
10. Assists the student-learners in developing leadership skills through participation in a vocational youth organization.
11. Correlates the job instruction with related learning experiences that support the student-learner's understanding and success in the world of work.
12. Develops the student-learner's decision-making process.
13. Prepares the student-learner to be a productive member of society.
14. Reinforces skills, techniques, and principles learned on the job.
15. Evaluates and measures the student-learner's success in school and on the job.

TYPES OF RELATED INSTRUCTION

There are two major types of related instruction that must be presented to the students in order to have a successful cooperative vocational education program. That instruction includes information on specifically related areas pertaining to the job, as well as general information that students need to enter into the world of work. The major types are specific job-related instruction and general related instruction.

The instruction is both group oriented and individualized for the student-learners. Related class instruction, if it is to be most effective, should follow as soon as possible the on-the-job experience of the student-learner.

Job-related instruction that is specific to the student-learner's individual needs on the job is directly related to his or her occupation. It is, for the most part, individualized instruction that utilizes manuals, texts, and other materials that will help the student in performing his or her duties on the job.

Job-related instruction is developed from the training plan that the teacher-coordinator generates with the cooperating employer for the student, prior to the student's beginning work. Students must be instructed in the unique skills associated with their particular job. They must know how to operate equipment that is unique to their job function. They must, therefore, know the safety procedures associated with the equipment that they use, if in fact they use equipment.

Specific related instruction should closely relate to the actual job the student-learner is currently performing. Ideally, it should supplement the on-the-job experience of the day before, the job he or she may still be on, or the job function that will be done within the next day or two. The teacher-coordinator's awareness of the student-learner's daily job schedule is of paramount importance to the success of the specific related instruction phase of the classroom learning experience. Approximately 50 percent of the related classroom instruction is devoted to job-related instruction.

General related instruction is that area of knowledge that all individuals must possess about the world of work if they are to reach any measure of success on the job. It assists the individual to function within his or her occupational environment. General related instruction, for the most part, is taught to the student in a group setting. It is information that all students need to have in order to be successful on the job. There are times, however, when general related instruction becomes specific for an individual student. This happens when the student has an immediate need for information in order to be successful on the job. Furthermore, there are times when students need reinforcement in a given area in order to be successful. The teacher-coordinator's observation of the student-learner on the job will help determine the individualized instruction that is needed by a student-learner.

General related instruction covers topics such as survival skills, human relations, personal grooming, how to apply for and keep a job, how to go for an interview, social manners, personality development, and positive self-concept techniques.

General Related Instruction

Program Orientation
1. Rules and regulations
2. Responsibilities
3. Benefits of the program
4. Training agreement
5. Training plan
6. Working papers
7. Record keeping

Safety
1. Safe work habits
2. Safety facts
3. Unsafe acts
4. Unsafe conditions
5. Safety hints
6. Machine guards and protection
7. Safety devices
8. Fire safety procedures
9. Basic first aid

Knowing Yourself
1. Self inventory
2. Achievement
3. Aptitude.
4. Interest
5. Positive personality trait
6. Desirable characteristics
7. Liabilities
8. Frustration—How to cope
9. Personal appearance
10. Getting along with people

Career Planning
1. Occupational awareness
2. Choosing an occupation
3. Advancing on the job
4. Furthering your education and training

Getting A Job
1. Letter of application
2. Personal data sheet / Resume
3. Preparing for the interview
4. Qualities that employers look for in their employees
5. Finding a job
6. Maintaining good relations with employers and co-workers
7. Handling problems with employers and co-workers
8. Good work habits
9. Following directions
10. Why people fail as employees
11. Successfully meeting work demands
12. Changing jobs

Private Enterprise
1. Business structures
2. Self-employment
3. Problems of operating a business
4. Business profits and your pay
5. The union and the employer

Consumerism
1. Preparing a budget
2. Good buying habits
3. Food and clothing
4. Contracts
5. How and why to borrow money
6. Credit
7. Housing: rental and ownership
8. Insurance for personal protection
9. Checking accounts; savings and investments

Communications
1. Oral skills
2. Writing skills
3. Listening
4. Body language
5. Interaction

  6. Public speaking
  7. Telephone techniques

Job Analysis
  1. Introduction to job analysis
  2. Task detailing sheet
  3. Training plans
  4. Doing and knowing units
  5. Evaluation

Life Skills
  1. Family living
  2. Social Security
  3. Taxes
  4. Human relations
  5. Leadership skills

The above outline should be used as a guide in developing the general related curriculum. It is but one suggestion. It is not all-inclusive. It does, however, cover those essential points that student-learners need to know in order to succeed in the world of work. The ideal way to develop both the specific related instruction and the general related instruction is to discuss the students' in-school curriculum with cooperating employers. Do not overlook the advice that can be obtained from the advisory committee. This group will be willing to share their knowledge and expertise as to what is needed by employees entering the labor market.

A segment of the related class should be devoted to youth organization activities. Youth organization activities are an integral part of vocational teaching and related class instruction. Adequate time should be set aside during the related class to conduct leadership training, business meetings, contest preparation, and general youth organization activities.

It is very difficult for co-op students to gather for youth organization activities after school hours, since these students are employed as part of their cooperative education program. Utilizing related classroom time for this purpose serves not only an educational function but it also provides for social interaction.

Daily Related Classroom Procedures

The key to successfully conducting a related class is a well-organized teacher-coordinator. It is essential for the teacher-coordinator to provide the student-learners with a well-outlined procedural method for conducting the related class. The student-learners should maintain a copy of the procedure outline in their personal file folder for daily reference. A routine procedure is outlined below:

1. Upon entering the class the student-learner secures his/her file folder.
2. Assigned daily forms are completed at the outset of the class, for example: scheduled working hours, wage forms, progress charts, etc.
3. Individual study assignments are begun and/or continued.
4. Completed assignments are checked by the teacher-coordinator before new assignments are issued.

Students have a tendency to learn at different rates and that learning, in the final analysis, is an individual process and achievement. If the related class is to be successful, then the burden must be placed on the student's shoulders. Most of the instruction will become individualized. Guidance and direction by the teacher-coordinator will then become the predominant function of the teacher-coordinator in conducting the related class.

The authors do not mean to imply that teaching the related class is an insurmountable task. It is, however, a task that requires a great deal of preparation and a total understanding of how to provide individualized instruction. It further requires that the teacher-coordinator be thoroughly familiar with a wide range of related instructional materials both in the printed form and in the audiovisual form. It further requires that the teacher-coordinator maximize his or her use of this material to assist the student-learner while they are in a related class.

Figure 29

PERMANENT RECORD CARD   THOMAS A. EDISON VOC. & TECH. HIGH SCHOOL
COOPERATIVE INDUSTRIAL EDUCATION

NAME: LAST NAME   FIRST NAME   MALE   FEMALE   DATE STARTED

ADDRESS   CITY   COUNTY   TRADE

SOCIAL SECURITY NUMBER   DATE OF BIRTH   TELEPHONE NUMBER   STATE APPROVAL NUMBER

EMPLOYER   ADDRESS   CITY   PERSON TO CONTACT

MARKING PERIOD

     1st _____ 2nd _____ 3rd _____ 4th _____

TERMINATED _____

SCHOOL RECORD

19 __ - 19 __   19 __ - 19 __   19 __ - 19 __

MONTH	HOURS WORKED	MONTH	DAYS WORKED	MONTH	AMOUNT EARNED
Sept.		Sept.		Sept.	
Oct.		Oct.		Oct.	
Nov.		Nov.		Nov.	
Dec.		Dec.		Dec.	
Jan.		Jan.		Jan.	
Feb.		Feb.		Feb.	
Mar.		Mar.		Mar.	
Apr.		Apr.		Apr.	
May		May		May	
June		June		June	
TOTAL		TOTAL		TOTAL	

COMMENTS: _____

_____

_____

_____

Specific Job-Related Instruction

The teacher-coordinator has a difficult task. Since no teacher-coordinator is able to understand all aspects of every job, the teacher must rely on instructional material to assist the student with specific and general related instruction. The coordinator's contact with employers can determine areas of occupational ex-

Figure 30

THOMAS A. EDISON VOCATIONAL & TECHNICAL HIGH SCHOOL
COOPERATIVE INDUSTRIAL EDUCATION TRAINING PROGRAM

_____TEACHER-COORDINATOR

PAYROLL SHEET

YEAR_____ STUDENT'S NAME_____

EMPLOYER'S
NAME_____ ADDRESS_____ PHONE_____

STARTING
DATE_____ APPROVAL NO._____ TERMINATED_____

MONTH	WEEK ENDING	DAYS WORKED	PAY RATE	HOURS WORKED	TOTAL WAGES		WEEK ENDING	DAYS WORKED	PAY RATE	HOURS WORKED	TOTAL WAGES
SEPTEMBER						FEBRUARY					
OCTOBER						MARCH					
NOVEMBER						APRIL					
DECEMBER						MAY					
JANUARY						JUNE					

perience that should be reinforced in the related classroom. The teacher-coordinator should constantly seek appropriate materials that will "back up" the skills learned on the job.

Specific instructional information may be acquired from trade manuals, journals, textbooks, pamphlets, and audiovisual materials.

Obtaining related materials is often a cumbersome task. There is an abundance of materials in some areas, while in others there is very little. Where there is an abundance of material, the teacher-coordinator must sift through the material and select only the best. Where there is little or no material, the teacher-coordinator must rely on employers and distributers to provide trade materials and other sources suitable for related instruction. The United States Government Printing Office and most state departments of education have developed comprehensive bibliographies listing text and other materials by occupational education code classification.

The selection of materials is then a prime function of the teacher-coordinator in conducting the related class. A well-equipped related subjects library is essential if the teacher-co-ordinator is to insure a realistic vocational program. Material should be available that will provide the student with knowledge, skills, attitudes, and understanding, which will facilitate the development of the on-the-job competence.

The Arizona Department of Education in their *Guidelines for Diversified Occupations Cooperative Education,* August 1975, page 41, outlines the types of materials that should be contained in the related subjects library. Material may be gathered for teaching the following skills:

1. Manipulation of tools and equipment
2. Gathering, processing, communicating, or applying technical information
3. Construction, assembling, or combining elements
4. Performing a service
5. Other specific occupational skills related to the student's occupational interests area.

Material will be needed to teach the following occupation adjustment capabilities:

1. Learning how to learn a job
2. Interacting with co-workers, supervisors, and employers
3. Participating in worker groups as a member and a leader
4. Developing desirable work habits and attitudes
5. Making rational economic decisions about employment,

spending, saving, and participation in a private enterprise economy

6. Preparing for future jobs
7. Managing work and leisure time
8. Keeping current with developments in the occupation
9. Assessing and analyzing needs, interest, ability, and aspirations

TECHNIQUES OF IMPLEMENTING INSTRUCTIONAL MATERIAL

There is an old saying that variety is the spice of life. If there is any truth to this statement it certainly holds true when we say that a variation in teaching methods will enhance the pro gram and create more interest. Students learn very little when they become bored. Teacher-coordinators, therefore, should make every effort to impart knowledge to students in a variety of tried and true methods of instruction. Listed below are some ideas that have been proven successful over the years. (From *Cooperative Vocational Education*, Maine, January, 1975, pg. 36-37)

Oral and Written Reports
1. Individual
2. Small Groups

Role Playing
1. Filmed and discussed
2. Sensitizing student participants

Student Development of Audiovisual Materials
1. Films
2. Film Strips
3. Slides and Tapes (audio and visual)
4. Bulletin Boards
5. Training Aids

Guest Speakers
1. Panels
2. Individuals

Field Trips
1. Observation
2. Research

Outline Method of Instruction (students fill in topic headings)
1. Previous experience
2. Research

Audiovisuals
1. Show and discuss
2. Hear and discuss
3. Newspaper in the classroom
4. Periodicals

Informal Discussion
1. Job experience
2. Social relations
3. School work

Programmed Instruction
1. General
2. Technical

Debating
Life Simulation Game
Publications—Public Relations
1. Bulletin boards
2. School newspaper
3. Visit service organizations
4. Local and state newspapers
5. Radio and television

Student Organizations
1. Youth organization for students in vocational education
2. Promotes leadership and establishes student identity
3. Brings schools and students together in competitive activities

Student-Developed Aids
1. Employee Guide
2. Student Guide
3. Training Station Evaluation

Being Sensitive to Students' Needs
1. Make student aware of coordinator availability
2. Help student to develop a good self-image
3. Treat student as an individual

Make Sure That Student Self-Image is Good

CLASSROOM FACILITIES

Facility and equipment development represent a planning process, that, when properly developed, produces a curriculum and facility geared to meet the students' interests, needs, employment opportunities, and the needs of the employer. As program planners, teacher-coordinators should keep in mind the following conditions and purposes under which cooperative vocational education programs operate:

1. Bridging the gap between school and the world of work is the primary purpose of the cooperative education program. It is essential for the in-school facilities to have an occupational atmosphere.
2. The facility should be conducive to communicating with employers and the community at large.
3. The program and the facilities for cooperative education program are designed to meet the individual needs of students. Therefore, the facilities must allow for individual counseling and individual instructional materials.

The physical layout of the related classroom should be structured so that it provides the teacher-coordinator with a great deal of flexibility in conducting individualized instruction for student-learners. The classroom should stimulate activity. The ideal arrangement for a related class is flexible seating with spacious areas for multiple arrangements. As with any type of classroom, there should be room to store files, textbooks, workbooks, audiovisual materials, and any other teaching aids that are needed to conduct a related class. Of paramount importance is a related subjects library easily accessible to all the co-op students. It is also equally important that students have storage areas in which they may maintain their individual files and independent study project materials.

Figure 31 is a suggested layout for the related class. This is only one layout with moveable tables and chairs. There are many variations. The classroom should be arranged according to the needs of the students at the time.

Figure 31 Courtesy, Jersey City State College, Center for Occupational Education.

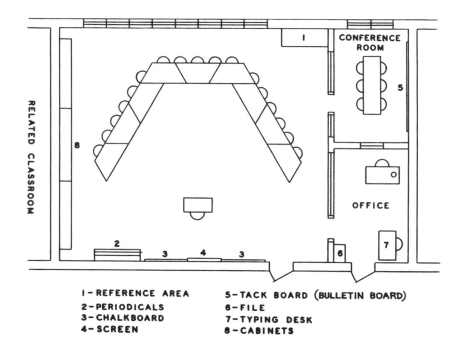

I-REFERENCE AREA   5-TACK BOARD (BULLETIN BOARD)
2-PERIODICALS   6-FILE
3-CHALKBOARD   7-TYPING DESK
4-SCREEN   8-CABINETS

Another important consideration in facility planning is the determination of the location of the classroom to the teacher-coordinator's office. It is essential that the teacher-coordinator's office be located in close proximity to the classroom. The ideal situation is to have the teacher-coordinator's office adjoin the related classroom. There should, however, be separate corridor entrances into the teacher-coordinator's room and into the related classroom so as to avoid traffic problems. The coordinator's classroom and office should be located near a building entrance to reduce the inconveniences that can be created by a great deal of traffic of employers and resource visitors supporting the cooperative vocational education program.

The teacher-coordinator's office should contain the following provisions:

1. Ample space for three or four people to be seated comfortably for individual or group conferences.
2. Provisions for maintaining the privacy of confidential matters with visibility of the classroom.
3. A telephone with connections for outside calls.
4. A desk, typewriter, filing equipment, and clerical assistance.
5. Storage space for audiovisual equipment and teaching materials.

Figure 32

RELATED CLASS CHECKLIST FOR TEACHER-COORDINATORS

Yes   No

_____ _____ 1. I discuss topics in class, such as historic events, scientific facts, current events, etc., that are relevant to the student-learners.

_____ _____ 2. I avoid materials unrelated to the subject area.

_____ _____ 3. I avoid rambling in class and I avoid discussing matters that are not really related to each other.

_____ _____ 4. I allow sufficient time to examine issues that come up in discussion.

_____ 5. I pay attention to students who ask relevant questions.

_____ _____ 6. I run a well-organized related class.

_____ _____ 7. I allow and encourage class discussion.

_____ _____ 8. I make a reasonable effort to "liven things up" by allowing some humor in class.

_____ _____ 9. I exhibit a sincere interest for all student concerns.

_____ _____ 10. I encourage students to come in individually to seek advice.

_____ _____ 11. I assist students in solving job-related problems.

_____ _____ 12. I provide useful related class information.

_____ _____ 13. I correlate on-the-job supervision with related class instruction.

_____ _____ 14. I help students to make decisions concerning their future in the world of work.

_____ _____ 15. I provide information concerning many types of employment opportunities.

_____ _____ 16. I provide the students with a better understanding of working conditions, job benefits, and long-range employment goals.

——— ——— 17. I provide general and specific information about the students' trades and interests.

——— ——— 18. I endeavor to provide the students with a more realistic outlook about the world of work.

——— ——— 19. I use multiple instruction techniques.

——— ——— 20. I endeavor to meet the needs of the individuals and the group as they arise.

——— ——— 21. I integrate the youth organization activities into the related class instruction.

——— ——— 22. I provide sufficient and high quality resource materials to assist the student-learners to succeed on the job.

——— ——— 23. I encompass safety throughout the entire spectrum of the related class instruction.

——— ——— 24. I provide and familiarize students with publications that will keep them informed of new processes and new materials in their particular occupations.

——— ——— 25. I develop an individualized training prescription for each student-learner.

BIBLIOGRAPHY

ACCEPT, Academic Cooperative Career Education Programs Today. Trenton, State of New Jersey, Department of Education, Division of Vocational Education and Career Preparation, December 1977.

Adelman, Everett, Robertson, Dwight, and Webb, Earl: Relating classroom to industry in large-group instruction. *Industrial Arts and Vocational Education,* 14-16, January 1964.

CIE Administrative Handbook. New Brunswick, New Jersey, Vocational Technical Curriculum Laboratory, Rutgers, 1978.

Cooperative Industrial Education, Related Class Manual. Jersey City, Center for Occupational Education, Jersey City State College, 1974.

Coordinators Operating Handbook: A Handbook for Combination Cooperative Vocational Education Program Coordinators. Kansas State Department of Education, Division of Vocational Education.

Cooperative Vocational Education, Administrators and Coordinators Guide for Development, Administration, and Implementation of Cooperative Vocational Education Programs. Maine, State Department of Education and Cultural Services, Bureau of Vocational Education, January 1975.

Diversified Cooperative Training in Florida Schools. Tallahassee, State of Florida, Department of Education, July, 1971.

Dolloph, Frances M.: Time clock grading. *Cooperative Education Quarterly,* 5-19, May 1978.

Fruehling, Rosemary T.: Student self-realization and human relations training in the cooperative work experience curriculum. *Technical Edu-*

cation News, 2-4 October-November 1976.

A Guide for Cooperative Vocational Education. Minneapolis, College of Education, Division of Vocational Technical Education, University of Minnesota, September 1969.

A Guide for Cooperative Vocational Education for Administrators. State of Alabama, Department of Education, Vocational Education and Community Colleges, 1975.

A Guide for Cooperative Vocational Education for Administrators and Coordinators. State of Indiana, Department of Public Instruction, Division of Vocational Education, 1973.

Handbook for Coordinators of Industrial Cooperative Training in Virginia Public Schools. Richmond, Virginia State Department of Education, 1971.

Herr, Edwin L.: Decision making and employability skills and the role of cooperative work experience. *Technical Education News,* 9-11, May-June 1977.

Work Education: Diversified Occupations Cooperative Education Guidelines. Arizona Department of Education, 1975.

Vocational Technical Facility Planning Guide. Trenton, State of New Jersey, Department of Education, Division of Vocational Education, 1976.

Wanat, John A. and Pfeiffer, E. Weston: Preparing students for gainful employment — cooperative vocational technical education. *School Leader,* 20-21, August 1978.

Chapter 9

SAFETY INSTRUCTION AND
COOPERATIVE VOCATIONAL EDUCATION

THE QUESTION might be asked why concern ourselves with teaching safety in a cooperative vocational education program? Are the employers, who provide on-the-job training, not supposed to teach students safe operational procedures? Is it not the employer's responsibility to carry workmen's compensation on the student? Is it not the responsibility of the student-learner to act in a safe manner? The answer to all of these questions is yes. It is the responsibility of the cooperating employer to provide the student-learner with on-the-job safety instruction. It is the responsibility of the employer to carry workmen's compensation on the student learner, and it is the responsibility of the student-learner to act and behave in a safe manner.

COORDINATOR'S RESPONSIBILITY
IN SAFETY EDUCATION

There is, however, another very important consideration that we have not covered in the above three questions. What is the teacher-coordinator's responsibility in teaching safety? It is the teacher-coordinator who prepares the young person for the world of work through the cooperation of the school and the cooperating employer. It is then the responsibility of the teacher-coordinator to provide a sound safety program for the student-learner. It is the responsibility of the teacher-coordinator to make sure that the cooperating employer carries workmen's compensation to protect the student on-the-job, and it is the responsibility of the teacher-coordinator to prepare the student-learner to be a safe worker.

We cannot leave the safety attitude adjustment to the student-learner alone. If the student-learner is going to be a safe productive worker, the time to begin teaching safe work habits should begin early in the student's schooling. A primary responsibility of the teacher-coordinator, then, is to develop within the student a safety attitude. We recognize that cooperative education is not like other in-school vocational programs. It involves a cooperative effort between the employment world and the school world in developing a product. That product is an individual who enters the world of work to earn a living and develop a skill.

From the outset, the coordinator is responsible for finding a safe training station so that the student can develop entry level job skills. The coordinator is responsible for insuring that the activities the student is going to engage in on the job are educationally sound and not injurious to his/her health or well-being. The cooperating employer and the teacher-coordinator share in the responsibility of preparing the student to be a safe productive worker.

Before getting into the area of what we should teach in a safety program, the type of procedures and forms that can be used to assist us in our safety program will be discussed. Since each student is placed in an individualized training station to learn specific skills, it is conceivable that if there are twenty students in class, there will be twenty different job functions.

Students should be given a safety sheet, or a blank piece of paper, where they list at least ten safety rules and regulations that should be adhered to in the performance of their job function at work. Answers may or may not be the same. The students take the ten or more items they have listed on their sheets to their employer to see if the employer agrees with the student's list. The employer should be asked to add or delete items from the list. The students can bring this form back to class where it now becomes the basis for class discussions on safety. These safety lists should be placed in the student's personal folder. Should the occasion arise, the list will act as proof that safety instruction was provided to the student-learner.

Another useful procedure is to have students diagram the

proper safety egress from the employers' premises in case of a fire. Students should be instructed to diagram the location of fire extinguishers and exits. This, too, should be reviewed by the cooperating employer. Once again, the form should be inserted in the student's personal folder for future reference.

Many students are often required to work with power driven equipment in the performance of their learning experience. No student should be allowed to work on any given piece of equipment without first going through a training demonstration on the piece of equipment. Students must not only learn how to use the equipment but how to use the equipment safely. Students should be required to take a test as well as to demonstrate the proper safety operation of equipment before operating the equipment on the job. Two forms that have been useful in the cooperative vocational education programs to demonstrate students' knowledge of proper safety instruction and equipment handling are shown in Figures 33 and 34.

WHY THE CONCERN FOR SAFETY DOCUMENTATION?

Students are placed in the world of work through a cooperative education program as an integral part of their total school program. The cooperating employer and the school share in the training of the cooperative education student. To protect the employer in the case of liability, should an accident occur, the student is covered by workmen's compensation. The federal government, under the OSHA regulations, requires that all employees work in safe environments and wear personal protective clothing.

The school, because of the cooperative arrangement, also shares in the safety responsibility. Just as the employer is responsible for carrying workmen's compensation and adhering to OSHA regulations, the teacher-coordinator is responsible for providing the student with safety instruction. The federal child labor provisions, Bulletin 101, defines a student-learner as one employed under a written agreement that provides " (i) that the work of the student-learner in the occupations declared particularly hazardous shall be incidental to the training; (ii) That such work shall be

Figure 33

SAFETY INSTRUCTION ACKNOWLEDGMENT AND PLEDGE

I have received the SAFETY INSTRUCTIONS regarding the operation of the following power driven machines. I recognize that I may not engage in any activity prohibited by federal or state labor laws. I fully understand the importance of these rules and regulations.

(Name of each machine to be written in by the pupil only after the pupil has received the appropriate safety instruction on its operation.)

Name of Machine	Date	Student's Signature	Coordinator's and Cooperating Employer's Initials

I promise to observe the **Safety Instructions** provided by my teacher-coordinator and co-operating employer. I understand that I may use the machines only after I have been properly instructed in their safe use, and have the approval of the teacher-coordinator.

School _____ Signature _____
                                                                                Pupil

Date _____   _____
                 Cooperating Employer   Teacher-Coordinator

intermittent and for short periods of time, and under the direct and close supervision of a qualified and experienced person; (iii) *That safety instruction shall be given by the school and correlated by the employer with on-the-job training."*

Bulletin 101 of the Fair Labor Standards Act explicitly requires the teacher-coordinator to provide the student-learner with safety instruction when working in hazardous occupations. Not all co-op students work in hazardous occupations. Does this mean that only those co-op students under eighteen years of age who work in hazardous occupations are to receive in-school safety instruction? The answer is obviously No.

Figure 34

SAFETY EQUIPMENT SHEET

Student-Learner's Name: _____

Name and Location of Training Station _____

_____

_____

Date _____

Name of Machine (include model and size): _____

Purpose of Machine: _____

_____

_____

Safety Precautions: _____

_____

_____

Operation Safety: _____

_____

_____

_____

Mechanical Precautions: _____

_____

_____

List of Safe Operating Procedures: _____

_____

_____

_____

_____

Other Safety Hints, e.g. clothing: _____

_____

_____

Figure 35   Courtesy, Rutgers University Curriculum Laboratory.

Accidents can occur in any given occupation. Since students are required to have paid work experience as an integral part of their co-op program, the training station becomes an extension of the school's facilities. Student-learners are considered to be part-time employees. As such, they must be provided with safety instruction, if they are within the Occupational Safety Health Act (OSHA) jurisdiction. If a student is seriously injured on the job as part of the school program, the school might become involved in a class action lawsuit. At this point, it becomes very important for the school to produce documented evidence that the school took all the necessary safety precautions in placing the student on the job. Documented evidence, to substantiate that safety precautions were taken by the school in placing the student on the job, could consist of a written training agreement that indicates the tasks the student is to perform on the job. The training agreement should specifically deliniate those things the student may or may not do on the job. There should also be a provision in the training agreement stipulating that safety instruction will be provided by the teacher-coordinator and the cooperating employer.

There should be on file, preferably in a student folder, evidence that safety instruction was provided to the student-learner.

Figure 36

_____

(Name of School)

I _____ certify that I have received

general safety instruction in terms of the following topics:

			Date
A.	Working papers.		_____
B.	Physical examinations.		_____
C.	Liability insurance.		_____
D.	Getting to the job.		_____
E.	Personal behavior.		_____
F.	Use of personal protective clothing and equipment.		_____
G.	Use of tools and machines.		_____
H.	Material handling.		_____
I.	General company rules and regulations.		_____
Other:	_____		_____
	_____		_____

Student's signature: _____

Date: _____

Coordinator's signature _____

This form should be maintained on file, preferably in a student folder.

The documented safety instruction could consist of a safety test, a checklist, and/or a letter signed by the student indicating that such instruction had indeed taken place. The actual method of instruction will of necessity be left flexible so that the teacher-coordinator can meet the individual needs of the student-learner.

Documented safety evidence in and of itself will not prevent a student-learner from becoming involved in an accident on the job. It will, however, protect the school somewhat should the student become involved in a very serious accident. It will at least demonstrate that the school was not negligent in placing the student in an on-the-job learning experience.

SAFETY INSTRUCTION

The subject of safety is endless. There are thousands of periodical publications and flyers that address safety in every conceivable occupational area. Since the subject of safety is so vast, what should we teach our student-learners about safety? Most of the literature lists at least ten safety rules that should be adhered to in all work experiences:

1. Comply with all safety rules and signs.
2. Follow instructions. Never take chances. If students are unaware of the proper procedure they should ask questions from the teacher-coordinator and/or supervisor.
3. Correct or report all unsafe conditions immediately upon discovery.
4. Use prescribed protective equipment. Wear safety clothing.
5. Report all accidents and get first aid immediately.
6. Never operate, adjust, or repair equipment when unauthorized. Report any unsafe condition immediately.
7. Use the correct tool for the job.
8. When lifting always bend the knees. Never lift with the back. Obtain help for heavy loads.
9. Never "horse" around on the job.
10. Keep the work station orderly and clean.

Subject Outline for Safety Instruction

The following outline should be used as a guide to assist teacher-coordinators in developing a safety program for their students. The National Safety Council has teaching aids on all areas concerning safety. The teacher-coordinator should utilize the catalogue of materials published by the National Safety Council as well as materials provided by insurance companies and private publishers.

SESSION I, SAFETY AND THE CO-OP STUDENT: This session should deal with general safety concerns. It should be the session in which students list those unsafe conditions associated with their particular job and outline a fire evacuation plan from their place of employment; it should be the session in which general safety precautions are discussed.

SESSION II, BE AWARE OF ACCIDENT PROBLEMS: Students should be made aware of the elements of an accident. What are unsafe acts, unsafe conditions, and the financial factors associated

Figure 37 Courtesy, Rutgers University Curriculum Laboratory.

Figure 38

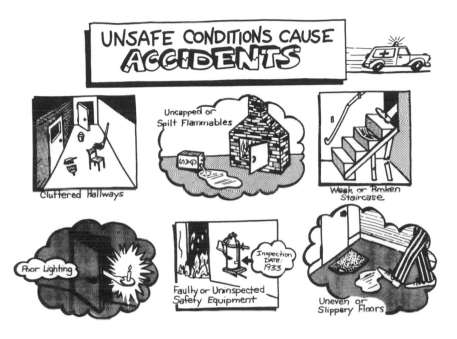

with any accident.

SESSION III, PERSONAL PROTECTIVE EQUIPMENT: This session should concentrate on personal protective equipment for the face, eyes, feet, legs, and hands.   This unit should also contain respiratory protective equipment to comply with OSHA requirements.

SESSION IV, HOUSEKEEPING: This unit should be concerned with maintaining good housekeeping.   A clean work area is often a safe work area.

SESSION V, MACHINE GUARDS: The principals of guarding should be stressed.   Include types of guards; standards and codes; and individualized instruction.

SESSION VI, FIRE PROTECTION: To be studied are how to determine fire hazards, how to use portable fire extinguishers, using the right extinguisher for the right type of fire, and evacuation and emergency procedures.

SESSION VII, FIRST AID SAFETY: This should cover general

medications; first aid supplies; how to control bleeding and shock; mouth-to-mouth resuscitation; what to do in the event of choking, breaks and fractures, open wounds, and chemical burns; and emergency procedures.

SESSION VIII, SAFETY ATTITUDINAL ADJUSTMENTS   This session should concern itself with "horse" playing, taking short cuts, avoiding guards, practical jokes.

SESSION IX, HAND AND PORTABLE POWER TOOLS: Selection and storage, training and safe use of tools.

This is roughly what should be covered in a safety program. It is not all-inclusive nor is it in a sequential order that must be adhered to. Safety instruction is something that should be provided to student-learners throughout the entire year. The ideal time to stress a safety point is when you are demonstrating the proper use of equipment or when a student has a particular question about a safety problem.

METHODS OF TEACHING SAFETY
IN A COOPERATIVE EDUCATION PROGRAM

In addition to regularly scheduled formal classroom units on safety, the ideal time to teach safety is when the teacher-coordinator supervises the student-learner at work. It is at this point the teacher has an opportunity to witness the student-learner in the daily routine activities. If the student is doing something in an unsafe manner, the teacher-coordinator should correct the unsafe act or condition. Reminding people about working in a safe manner is a constant activity. People deviate from established safe practices, and when they do, injuries often occur. In order to prevent possible injuries to student-learners, teacher-coordinators should look for unsafe work methods and correct them as soon as they are observed.

A very productive way to teach safety is to utilize youth organization activities to teach safety. VICA, the Vocational Industrial Clubs of America, has a safety project book contest that is displayed at safety conferences and at the state convention.

Youth organization safety activities can consist of organizing safety committees and activities that will benefit the school and/or the community; working on safety posters during Fire Prevention Week; developing a safety bulletin board for the school with the cooperation of the local fire department; sponsoring a volunteer vehicle safety check; developing and distributing a home fire safety checklist; sponsoring seasonal safety campaigns such as back to school, holiday driving, winter safety, water safety, vacation, and recreational safety. The lists of organization activities in the safety areas can be endless. A little imagination and brainstorming on the part of the teacher-coordinator and the students can result in untold numbers of safety activities.

SELECTING SAFE WORK STATIONS

The teacher-coordinator has the responsibility for selecting safe training stations for the student-learners. Unquestionably, the teacher-coordinator may not be thoroughly schooled in all aspects of safety. There are, however, general concerns that a teacher-coordinator should look for when selecting a training station for the student-learner. The safety conditions that a teacher-coordinator should look for when considering a training station are—

1. Sanitary conditions and facilities
2. General conditions of the floors
   a. Are there grease, oil, and loose materials?
   b. Are there uncovered openings on stairwells?
3. Are there guards on the machines?
4. Is there an adequate exhaust system, especially in industrial locations?
5. Does it appear to be fire safe?

Things to Observe When Viewing the Training Station

Teacher-coordinators should check for—

1. Any lifting the students may be required to do.
2. Whether a student-learner will be supervised on the job or will there be times when a student learner will be left alone?
3. What are the requirements for the students in connection with driving?

4. Is personal protective clothing and equipment provided to the student-learner and is it used by employees?
5. Does the potential employer have a positive safety attitude?

OCCUPATIONAL SAFETY AND HEALTH ACT OF 1970

The Occupational Safety and Health Act of 1970 (OSHA) became an official part of national labor law on April 28, 1971. The mission as declared by Congress is "to assure so far as possible every working man and woman in the Nation safe and healthful working conditions and to preserve our human resources. . ."

Congress was specific on how OSHA was to be implemented:

* by encouraging employers and employees to reduce hazards in the work place, and start or improve existing safety and health programs;
* by establishing employer and employee responsibilities;
* by authorizing OSHA to set mandatory job safety and health standards;
* by providing an effective enforcement program;
* by encouraging the states to assume the fullest responsibility for administering and enforcing their own occupational safety and health programs that are to be at least as effective as the federal program;
* by providing for reporting procedures on job injuries, illnesses, and fatalities.

Coverage by the Act

The Act covers every employer in a business affecting commerce who has one or more employees. The Act does not affect workplaces covered under other federal laws, such as the Coal Mine Health and Safety Act and the Federal Metal and Nonmetallic Safety Act.

Federal, state, and local government employees are covered under separate provisions in the Act for public employment.

Standards

OSHA adopts standards and, among other methods for accomplishing compliance, conducts inspections of workplaces to determine whether the standards are being met. A safety or health standard is a legally enforceable regulation governing conditions, practices, or operations to assure safe and healthful workplaces.

Compliance with national safety and health standards is what a compliance officer looks for when inspecting a workplace. The compliance officer is concerned with what standards apply there and whether the employer and employees are complying with them.

The standards are published in the *Federal Register*. All amendments, corrections, insertions, or deletions involving standards also are printed in the *Federal Register*.

The Role of Employers

The Act requires each employer to provide a workplace free from safety and health hazards and to comply with the standards.

Employer Responsibilities

* Be aware that employers have a general duty responsibility to provide a place of employment free from recognized hazards and to comply with occupational safety and health standards promulgated under the Act.
* Be familiar with mandatory occupational safety and health standards.
* Make sure employees know about OSHA.
* Examine conditions in the workplace to make sure they conform to applicable safety and health standards.
* Remove or guard hazards.
* Make sure employees have and use safe tools and equipment, including required personal protective gear, and that they are properly maintained.
* Use color codes, posters, labels, or signs to warn employees of potential hazards.
* Establish or update operating procedures and communicate them so that employees follow safety and health requirements for their own protection.
* Provide medical examinations when required by OSHA standards.

- Keep required OSHA records of work-related injuries and illnesses (if there are eight or more employees), and post the annual summary during the entire month of February each year.
- Report, to the nearest OSHA area office, each injury or health hazard that results in a fatality or hospitalization of five or more employees.
- Post, in the workplace, the OSHA poster informing employees of their rights and responsibilities.
- Advise OSHA compliance officers of authorized employee representatives to permit their participation in the inspection walkaround. If there are no such representatives, allow a reasonable number of employees to confer with the compliance officer during the walkaround.
- Do not discriminate against employees who properly exercise their rights under the Act.
- Post OSHA citations of violations of standards at the worksite involved.
- Seek advice and consultation as needed by writing, calling, or visiting the nearest OSHA office (OSHA will not inspect work places just because the employer calls for assistance.)
- Be active in the company association's involvement in job safety and health.

The Role of Employees

The Act requires each employee to comply with occupational safety and health standards, as well as all rules, regulations, and orders issued under the Act that apply to his or her own actions and conduct.

EMPLOYEE RESPONSIBILITIES: (This section applies to the cooperative education student-learner on the job.)

- Read the OSHA poster at the jobsite.
- Comply with any applicable OSHA standards.
- Follow all of the employer's safety and health standards and rules.
- Wear or use prescribed protective equipment.
- Report hazardous conditions to the supervisor.

* Report any job-related injuries or illnesses to the employer and seek treatment promptly.
* Cooperate with the OSHA compliance officer conducting an inspection if inquiries are made about conditions at the jobsite.
* Exercise the rights under the Act responsibly.

Penalties

The act provides for mandatory penalties against employers of up to 1,000 dollars for each serious violation and for optional penalties of up to 1,000 dollars for each nonserious violation. Penalties of up to 1,000 dollars per day may be imposed for failure to correct violations within the proposed time period. Also, any employer who willfully or repeatedly violates the Act may be assessed penalties of up to 10,000 dollars for each such violation.

Criminal penalties are also provided for in the Act. Any willful violation resulting in death of an employee, upon conviction, is punishable by a fine of not more than 10,000 dollars or by imprisonment for not more than six months, or by both. Conviction of an employer after a first conviction doubles these maximum penalties.

Voluntary Activity

While providing penalties for violations, the Act also encourages efforts by labor and management, before an OSHA inspection, to reduce injuries and illnesses arising out of employment.

The Department of Labor encourages employers and employees to reduce workplace hazards voluntarily and to develop and improve safety and health programs in all workplaces and industries.

Such cooperative action would initially focus on the identification and elimination of hazards that could cause death, injury, or illness to employees and supervisors. There are many public and private organizations that can provide information and assistance in this effort, if requested.

Records That Must Be Kept

OSHA requires employers of eight or more employees to keep certain records of job-related fatalities, injuries, and illnesses. OSHA requires that only three simple forms be maintained:

1. OSHA 100—A log in which each reportable case is entered on a single line.
2. OSHA 101—A supplementary record with details on each individual case.
3. OSHA 102—An annual summary compiled from the log. This summary must be posted in the workplace by February 1 each year, and kept there one month for employee examination.

If there are no recordable deaths, injuries, or illnesses, there is nothing to fill in.

All employers not exempt (those with eight or more employees) from the recordkeeping requirements must have the forms available when an OSHA compliance officer makes an inspection. The forms do not have to be mailed to any OSHA office.

SOURCES OF SAFETY MATERIALS

A list of organizations that can provide the teacher-coordinator with safety material is almost endless. Free and inexpensive material may be secured from local insurance agents. The National Safety Council provides free and inexpensive material. The Occupational and Safety Health Agencies provide information on OSHA rules and regulations.

The following list will provide the teacher-coordinator with an awareness of the types of services available in the safety and health fields. A more comprehensive list of potential sources can be found in the National Safety Council publication titled "Accident Prevention Manual for Industrial Operations."

Associations Furnishing Materials

• American Industrial Hygiene Association, 210 Haddon Avenue, Westmont, New Jersey 08108
• American Medical Association, Department of Occupational Health

535 North Dearborn Street, Chicago, Illinois 60610

* American National Standards Institute, 1430 Broadway, New York, New York 10018
* American National Red Cross, Safety Services, 17th and D. Streets, N.W., Washington, D.C. 20006
* American Public Health Association, 1740 Broadway, New York, New York 10019
* American Society for Testing and Materials, 1916 Race Street, Philadelphia, Pennsylvania 19103
* American Society of Safety Engineers, 850 Busse Highway, Park Ridge, Illinois 60068
* Human Factors Society, P.O. Box 1369, Santa Monica, California 90406
* Industrial Hygiene Foundation of America, Inc., 5231 Centre Avenue, Pittsburgh, Pennsylvania 15232
* Industrial Medical Association, 55 East Washington Street, Chicago, Illinois 60602
* Industrial Safety Equipment Association, Inc., 60 E. 42nd Street, New York, New York 10017
* The National Fire Protection Association, 60 Batterymarch Street, Boston, Massachusetts 02110
* The National Safety Council, 452 North Michigan Avenue, Chicago, Illinois 60611
* National Society for the Prevention of Blindness, Inc., 79 Madison Avenue, New York, New York 10016
* Underwriters Laboratories, Inc., 207 East Ohio Street, Chicago, Illinois 60611

Publications and Periodicals

FIRE PROTECTION AND CONTROL

* *Fire Engineering:* Reuben H. Donnelley, 466 Lexington Avenue, New York, New York 10017
* *Fire Journal; Fire News; Firemen; Fire Technology:* National Fire Protection Association, 60 Batterymarch Street, Boston, Massachusetts 02110

HAZARDS
* *Occupational Hazards:* Industrial Publishing Corporation, 812 Huron Road, Cleveland, Ohio 44115

HEALTH
* *A.M.A. Archives of Environmental Health:* American Medical Association, 535 North Dearborn Street, Chicago, Illinois 60610
* *American Industrial Hygiene Association Journal:* American Industrail Hygiene Association, 210 Haddon Avenue, Westmont, New Jersey 08108
* *Chemical Abstracts* (Toxicology, Air Pollution and Industrial Hygiene Section): American Chemical Society, 1155 Sixteenth Street, N.W., Washington, D.C. 20036
* *Industrial Hygiene Digest:* Industrial Hygiene Foundation, 5341 Centre Avenue, Pittsburgh, Pennsylvania 15232

SAFETY
* *Journal of the American Society of Safety Engineers:* American Society of Safety Engineers, 850 Busse Highway, Park Ridge, Illinois 60068
* *Safety Standards:* Bureau of Labor Statistics, U.S. Department of Labor, Washington, D.C. 20210
* *National Safety News; Industrial Supervisor; Traffic Safety; Journal of Safety Research; Safe Worker; Safe Driver; Safety Newsletters:* The National Safety Council, 425 N. Michigan Avenue, Chicago, Illinois 60611

OSHA Regional Offices

Region I: Connecticut, Maine, Massachusetts, New Hampshire, Rhode Island, Vermont
              18 Oliver Street
              Boston, Massachusetts 02110

Region II: New York, New Jersey, Puerto Rico, Virgin Islands, Canal Zone
              1515 Broadway (1 Astor Plaza)
              New York, New York 10036

Region III: Delaware, District of Columbia, Maryland, Pennsylvania, Virginia, West Virginia
15220 Gateway Center
3535 Market Street
Philadelphia, Pennsylvania 19104

Region IV: Alabama, Florida, Georgia, Kentucky, Mississippi, North Carolina, South Carolina, Tennessee
1375 Peachtree Street, N.E., Suite 587
Atlanta, Georgia 30309

Region V: Illinois, Indiana, Michigan, Minnesota, Ohio, Wisconsin
230 South Dearborn
32rd Floor—North
Chicago, Illinois 60604

Region VI: Arkansas, Louisiana, New Mexico, Oklahoma, Texas
1512 Commerce Street, 7th Floor
Dallas, Texas 75201

Region VII: Iowa, Kansas, Missouri, Nebraska
823 Walnut Street, Room 300
Kansas City, Missouri 64106

Region VIII: Colorado, Montana, North Dakota, South Dakota, Utah, Wyoming
1961 Stout Street, Room 15010
Denver, Colorado 80202

Region IX: Arizona, California, Hawaii, Nevada, Guam, American Samoa, Trust Territory of the Pacific Islands
450 Golden Gate Avenue, Room 9470
San Francisco, California 94102

Region X: Alaska, Idaho, Oregon, Washington
506 Second Avenue, Room 1808
Seattle, Washington 98104

SUMMARY

Safety instruction is the concern of every teacher-coordinator, irrespective of their discipline.   Teacher-coordinators have the responsibility of insuring that students not only learn a skill but that they learn the skill safely. Every teacher-coordinator should take a self-inventory of safety attitudes and teaching methods. Outlined in Figure 39 is a safety checklist for teacher-coordinators.

Figure 39

SAFETY CHECKLIST FOR TEACHER-COORDINATORS

Yes	No	
_____	_____	1. I am aware of the job safety requirements in my area of supervision.
_____	_____	2. I inspect each and every accident.
_____	_____	3. I make students aware of safety hazards.
_____	_____	4. I acquaint students with personal protective clothing and equipment.
_____	_____	5. I make known to students the purpose of personal protective equipment.
_____	_____	6. I train my students in fire prevention and control.
_____	_____	7. I inform students of the need of good housekeeping.
_____	_____	8. I relate to my students how safety laws are designed to prevent accidents and injuries.
_____	_____	9. I use audiovisual aids to illustrate to my students safety procedures and equipment.
_____	_____	10. I use various teaching methods to demonstrate safety awareness.
_____	_____	11. I test my students to determine how well I am teaching safety.
_____	_____	12. I maintain a personal student folder with documented safety evidence.
_____	_____	13. I make it a practice to give my students a safety tip at least once a week.
_____	_____	14. I provide on-the-job safety instruction.
_____	_____	15. I provide my students with safety reading materials, including newsletters, magazines, and books.
_____	_____	16. I allow no student to undertake a job unless the student has demonstrated how to do the job safely.
_____	_____	17. I allow no student to undertake a job that appears to be unsafe.
_____	_____	18. I have explained general safety regulations to all my students.
_____	_____	19. My employers are aware of their responsibility in teaching students safety on the job.

BIBLIOGRAPHY

American Management Association, Inc.: *Safety for the Supervisor*. New York, Programmed Instruction for Management Education, 1964.

Bird, F.E., Jr. and Germain, G.L.: *Damage Control*. New York, American Management Association, Inc., 1966.

Blake, R.P.: *Industrial Safety*, 3rd ed. Englewood Cliffs, P-H, 1963.

Bureau of National Affairs, Inc.: *ABC's of the Job Safety and Health Act*. Washington, D.C., 1971.

Bureau of National Affairs, Inc.: *The Job Safety and Health Act of 1970*. Washington, D.C., 1971.

Commerce Clearing House, Inc.: *Occupational Safety and Health Act of 1970: Law and Explanation*. Chicago, 1971.

Congress of the United States: Occupational Safety and Health Act of 1970, Public Law 91-596. (91st Congress) Washington, D.C., Superintendent of Documents, U.S. Government Printing Office, December 29, 1970.

Making Safety Work. National Safety Council and Gregg Division/McGraw-Hill, Inc., 1976.

National Safety Council: *Accident Facts*. Chicago, 1976.

National Safety Council: *Accident Prevention Manual for Industrial Operations*, 6th ed. Chicago, 1972.

National Safety Council: *Fundamentals of Industrial Hygiene*. Chicago, undated.

New Jersey State Department of Education: *Safety Manual for Cooperative Industrial Education*. New Brunswick, Division of Vocational Education and Career Preparation, Curriculum Laboratory, Rutgers University, 1977.

Patterson, Lois J.: Effective training and alert supervision can prevent eye injuries. *Cooperative Education Quarterly*, 7, November 1978.

Pope, W.C. and Nicolai, E.R.: *In Case of Accident, Call the Computer*. Washington, D.C., U.S. Department of Interior, 1971.

Smith, William R.: Vocational education accident reporting system. *Cooperative Education Quarterly*, 9, August 1978.

Strong, Merle E. (Ed.): *Accident Prevention Manual for Training Programs*. Chicago, American Technical Society, 1975.

Sugarman, Stephen D.: Accountability through the courts. *School Review*, 82(2):233-259, February 1974.

Tarrants, W.H. (Ed.): *A Selected Bibliography of Reference Materials in Safety Engineering and Related Fields*. Park Ridge, IL, American Society of Safety Engineers, 1967.

Wahl, Ray: *Safety and Health Guide for Vocational Educators — With Emphasis on Cooperative Education and Work-Study Programs*. Harrisburg, Bureau of Vocational Education, Pennsylvania Department of Education, 1977.

Wanat, John A.: What should D.E. students know about safety? *D.E. Today*, 12(1):3-4, Fall 1978.

Chapter 10

LEGAL RESPONSIBILITIES
OF CONDUCTING
COOPERATIVE EDUCATION PROGRAMS

COOPERATIVE VOCATIONAL EDUCATION conducts part of its program in school and the other part of its program in the employment community. The teacher-coordinator should be aware of all those laws that pertain to his/her duties within the school system. This unit will not deal with the legal ramifications of conducting in-school activities. It will center on the legal aspects associated with placing students in the employment community.

Teacher-coordinators at the secondary level placing students under the age of eighteen into employment situations must be thoroughly familiar with the Child Labor Laws and what students can or cannot do in the world of work. In respect to age, teacher-coordinators must be thoroughly familiar with all federal, state, and local laws that pertain to the placement of student-learners in the world of work. Teacher-coordinators are not to act as Labor Department officials in enforcing labor regulations. They are, however, to adhere to all existing regulations so that they do not come into violation of these laws and regulations. The negative effects of not adhering to existing federal and state labor laws can result in giving cooperative education a poor name; it can result in having fines imposed upon cooperating employers who violate existing labor laws. Failure to comply with occupational safety laws, for example, can not only result in a monetary penalty to the cooperating employer but it can endanger the student-learner's health and safety.

The coordinator should not assume that the employer is totally aware of all existing labor laws, especially as it affects the employment of minors in the world of work. The coordinator should have at his/her disposal all pertinent information in this regard. In many cases the coordinator might even be the source of information for an employer who might not be aware of an existing labor law. For this reason, the coordinator should know the source of information on all legal matters and should maintain a complete file of publications and documents that include labor laws and their interpretations.

The following information presents a capsule review of each significant area with which a cooperative vocational teacher-coordinator should be familiar.

FINANCIAL/ACCOUNTING CONSIDERATIONS*
Social Security

Every cooperative industrial education student should have a social security card, and *only one* social security number.

The student should present his or her accurate number to the employer for income tax purposes. This number may later be used for unemployment benefits and disability benefits.

Keep in mind that students might marry at early ages, e.g. eighteen to twenty-four, and possible survivor or auxiliary benefits would accrue to the remaining spouse and children of that marriage in the event of death or disability to the wage earner.

Social Security benefits, therefore, are not solely for the aged. The Social Security Administration states: "If you become disabled before you are 24, you need credit for $1\frac{1}{2}$ years of work in the 3 years before you become disabled." The student-learner should be aware of this fact. In the event of a tragedy, the dependent survivors should contact their nearest Social Security office. An application must be filed before payments can start.

Taxes

All student-learners whose salaries exceed the maximum allowable under I.R.S. regulations within a given year are required

---

*New Jersey State Department of Education: C.I.E. Administrative Handbook. New Brunswick, Division of Vocational Education and Career Preparation, Curriculum Laboratory, Rutgers University, 1977 pgs. 29-45.

to pay federal income taxes. Those student-learners whose salaries fall under this amount are eligible to collect their entire federal withholding contribution as indicated in the W-2 form.

If it is possible for the coordinator to determine that a student-learner's salary will not exceed the I.R.S. maximum salary allowable in a given year, the coordinator should advise the employer to complete a W-4E form for that particular student-learner. A W-4E form permits the employer to give the student-learner an hourly rate without any deduction for federal withholding tax.

Travel Liability

Student-learners are responsible for providing their own transportation to and from the training station. However, if it is necessary for the coordinator to use a private vehicle to transport student-learners, the coordinator should first obtain written assurance, signed by the chief school administrator, that the coordinator is fully covered by school insurance before transporting any student. The coordinator should also seek advice from the insurance company on this subject.

Workmen's Compensation

All student-learners must be covered by Workmen's Compensation Insurance. The coordinator should be extremely careful not to place student-learners in training stations where the employees are not covered by workmen's compensation.

The employer pays the premium for such coverage. Personal injury and liability for injury to other workers must be covered by the policy. Therefore, if a student-learner is injured on the job, the student-learner should receive medical treatment immediately. It is important for the injured party to notify the employer as quickly as possible. The amount of payment is determined by the extent of the injury and the loss of time and wages.

Wages

Cooperative education student-learners should be paid the highest existing statutory minimum wage. The minimum wage is the lowest rate which may normally be paid for employment covered by the Fair Labor Standards Act.

The equal pay provisions of the Fair Labor Standards Act prohibit an employer from discriminating on the basis of sex by paying employees of one sex at rates lower than those paid to employees of the opposite sex in the same establishment, for doing equal work on jobs requiring equal skill, effort, and responsibility and which are performed under similar working conditions. The equal pay provisions apply to all employees subject to the minimum wage provisions of the Act and to every establishment where such workers are employed as well as to executive, administrative, professional, and outside salesworkers.

Special Provisions

Student-learners, apprentices, handicapped workers, and full-time students employed in retail or service establishments, in institutions of higher education, or in agriculture under certain circumstances, may be paid special lower minimum wage rates provided that special certificates are obtained from the division administrator of the nearest office of the Wage and Hour Division, U.S. Department of Labor.

Student-learners may be approved for 75 percent of the applicable minimum wage whereas full-time students employed in retail and service establishments, agriculture, and institutions of higher education may be approved for 85 percent of the applicable minimum wage.

Tips

Many student-learners are employed in training stations where tips are included in the pay. The Fair Labor Standards Act considers a "tipped" employee as one who customarily and regularly received more than twenty dollars a month in tips. The employer may credit up to, and not more than, 50 percent of the minimum wage through tips, provided the student-learner has been notified in advance and has kept all the tips.

STATE CHILD LABOR LAWS

Every state has a child labor law and all but one has a compulsory school attendance law. Whenever a state standard differs from a federal standard, the higher standard must be observed. Only the federal child labor laws are included in this chapter, since state laws vary. The teacher-coordinator should contact his or her state department of labor for state regulations governing the employment of minors and student-learners.

CHILD LABOR REQUIREMENTS IN NONAGRICULTURAL OCCUPATIONS UNDER THE FAIR LABOR STANDARDS ACT

Employment

In Commerce

Employees engaged in interstate commerce are covered. This includes, among others, workers in the telephone, telegraph, radio, television, importing, exporting, and transportation industries; employees in distributing industries, such as wholesaling, who handle goods moving in interstate commerce, as well as workers who order, receive, or keep records of such goods; and clerical and other workers who regularly use the mails, telephone, and telegraph for interstate or foreign communication.

In the Production of Goods for Commerce

Employees who work in places that produce goods for interstate commerce, such as manufacturing establishments, oil fields, mines; or in occupations that are closely related or directly essential to the production of such goods are covered.

In an Enterprise Engaged in Commerce

Employees employed in enterprises having employees handling, selling or working on goods or materials that have been moved in or produced for interstate commerce are covered. Included in this category are employees of hotels, motels, restaurants and other enterprises whose business volume is at least 250,000 dollars a year; and hospitals, establishments for residential care of sick and aged, laundries and dry cleaning establishments, schools, federal, state, and local and interstate governments and agencies regardless of their annual volume of business.

The child labor provisions apply to employment in an establishment of a covered enterprise even though employment in such an establishment is exempt from the monetary provisions of the Act.

The child labor provisions do not apply to domestic service employees employed in or about the household of the employer.

In or About an Establishment Producing Goods for Commerce

Producers, manufacturers, or dealers are prohibited from shipping or delivering for shipment in interstate commerce any goods produced in an establishment in or about which oppressive child labor has been employed within thirty days prior to the removal of the goods. It is not necessary for the employees to be working on the goods that are removed for shipment in order to be covered.

Minimum Age Standards for Nonagricultural Employment

Oppressive child labor is defined as employment of children under the legal minimum ages.

14 — Minimum age for employment in specified occupations outside school hours.

16 — Basic minimum age for employment. At sixteen years of age youths may be employed in any occupation, other than a nonagricultural occupation declared hazardous by the Secretary of Labor.

18 — Minimum age for employment in nonagricultural occupations declared hazardous by the Secretary of Labor.

— No minimum age for employment that is exempt from the child labor provisions of the Act.

No minimum age for employment with respect to any employee whose services during the workweek are performed in a workplace within territory as limited by section 13(f) of the Act.

Exemptions

The child labor provisions do not apply to—

children under sixteen years of age employed by their parents in occupations other than manufacturing or mining, or occupations declared hazardous by the Secretary of Labor.

- children employed as actors or performers in motion pictures, theatrical, radio, or television productions.
- children engaged in the delivery of newspapers to the consumer.
- homeworkers engaged in the making of wreaths composed principally of natural holly, pine, cedar, or other evergreens (including the harvest of the evergreens).

Employment Standards for Fourteen- and Fifteen-Year-Olds

Employment of fourteen- and fifteen-year-old minors is limited to certain occupations under conditions that do not interfere with their schooling, health, or well-being.

Hours-Time Standards

Fourteen- and fifteen-year-old minors may not be employed:

1. During school hours, except as provided for in Work Experience and Career Exploration Programs.
2. Before 7 A.M. or after 7 P.M. except 9 P.M. from June 1 through Labor Day (time depends on local time standards).
3. More than three hours a day on school days.
4. More than eighteen hours a week in school weeks.
5. More than eight hours a day on nonschool days.
6. More than forty hours a week in nonschool weeks.

Permitted Occupations

Fourteen- and fifteen-year-minors may be employed in—

1. Office and clerical work (including operation of office machines).
2. Cashiering, selling, modeling, art work, work in advertising departments, window trimming, and comparative shopping.
3. Price marking and tagging by hand or by machine, assembling orders, packing, and shelving.
4. Bagging and carrying out customers' orders.
5. Errand and delivery work by foot, bicycle, and public transportation.
6. Clean up work, including the use of vacuum cleaners and floor waxers, and maintenance of grounds, but not includ-

ing the use of power-driven mowers or cutters.

7. Kitchen work and other work involved in preparing and serving food and beverages, including the operation of machines and devices used in the performance of such work, such as, but not limited to, dish-washers, toasters, dumb-waiters, popcorn poppers, milk shake blenders, and coffee grinders.

8. Work in connection with cars and trucks if confined to the following:

   Dispensing gasoline and oil.

   Courtesy service on premises of gasoline service station.

   Car cleaning, washing and polishing.

   Other occupations permitted by this section.

   But not including work involving the use of pits, racks, or lifting apparatus or involving the inflation of any tire mounted on a rim equipped with a removable retaining ring.

9. Cleaning vegetables and fruits, and wrapping, sealing, labeling, weighing, pricing, and stocking goods when performed in areas physically separate from areas where meat is prepared for sale and outside freezers or meat coolers.

Excluded Occupations

Fourteen- and fifteen-year-old minors may not be employed in—

1. Any manufacturing occupation.

2. Any mining occupation.

3. Processing occupations such as filleting of fish, dressing poultry, cracking nuts, or laundering as performed by commercial laundries and dry cleaning (except in a retail, food service, or gasoline service establishment in those specific occupations expressly permitted there in accordance with the foregoing list).

4. Occupations requiring the performance of any duties in workrooms or workplaces where goods are manufactured, mined, or otherwise processed (except to the extent expressly permitted in retail, food service, or gasoline service establishments in accordance with the foregoing list).

5. Public messenger service.
6. Operation or tending of hoisting apparatus or of any power-driven machinery (other than office machines and machines in retail, food service, and gasoline service establishments, which are specified in the foregoing list as machines such minors may operate in such establishments).
7. Any occupations found and declared to be hazardous.
8. Occupations in connection with—
    a. Transportation of persons or property by rail, highway, air, on water, pipeline or other means.
    b. Warehousing and storage.
    c. Communications and public utilities.
    d. Construction (including repair).
    Except office or sales work in connection with the above when not performed on transportation media, or at the actual construction site.
9. Any of the following occupations in a retail, food service, or gasoline service establishment:
    a. Work performed in or about boiler or engine rooms.
    b. Work in connection with maintenance or repair of the machines or equipment.
    c. Outside window washing that involves working from window sills, and all work requiring the use of ladders, scaffolds, or their substitutes.
    d. Cooking (except at soda fountains, lunch counters, snack bars, or cafeteria serving counters) and baking.
    e. Occupations that involve operating, setting up, adjusting, cleaning, oiling, or repairing power-driven food slicers grinders, food choppers and cutters, and bakery-type mixers.
    f. Work in freezers and meat coolers and all work in preparation of meats for sale (except wrapping, sealing, labeling, weighing, pricing and stocking when performed in other areas).
    g. Loading and unloading goods to and from trucks, railroad cars, or conveyors.

h. All occupations in warehouses except office and clerical work.

Exceptions

Some of the provisions of Child Labor Regulation No. 3 are varied for fourteen- and fifteen-year-olds in approved school-supervised and school-administered Work Experience and Career Exploration Programs (WECEP). Enrollees in WECEP may be employed—

* during school hours
* for as many as 3 hours on a school day
* for as many as 23 hours in a school week
* in occupations otherwise prohibited for which a variation has been granted by the administrator of the wage and hour division.

The state educational agency must obtain approval from the administrator of the wage and hour division before operating a WECEP program

Hazardous Occupations Orders in Nonagricultural Occupations

The Fair Labor Standards Act provides a minimum age of eighteen years for any nonagricultural occupations which the Secretary of Labor "'shall find and by order declare" to be particularly hazardous for sixteen- and seventeen-year-old persons, or detrimental to their health and well-being. This minimum age applies even when the minor is employed by the parent or person standing in place of the parent.

The seventeen hazardous occupations orders now in effect apply either on an industry basis, specifying the occupations in the industry that are not covered, or on an occupational basis irrespective of the industry in which found:

1. Manufacturing and storing explosives.
2. Motor-vehicle driving and outside helper.
3. Coal mining.
4. Logging and sawmilling.

   5. Power-driven woodworking machines.
   6. Exposure to radioactive substances.
   7. Power-driven hoisting apparatus.
   8. Power-driven metal-forming, punching, and shearing machines.
   9. Mining, other than coal mining.
  10. Slaughtering, or meat-packing, processing or rendering.
  11. Power-driven bakery machines.
  12. Power-driven paper-products machines.
  13. Manufacturing brick, tile, and kindred products.
  14. Power-driven circular saws, band saws, and guillotine shears.
  15. Wrecking, demolition, and shipbreaking operations.
  16. Roofing operations.
  17. Excavation operations.

Exemptions from Hazardous Occupations Orders

Hazardous Occupations Order Numbers 5, 8, 10, 12, 14, 16, and 17 contain exemptions for sixteen- and seventeen-year-old apprentices and student-learners provided they are employed under the following conditions:

APPRENTICES: (1) The apprentice is employed in a craft recognized as an apprenticeable trade; (2) the work of the apprentice in the occupations declared particularly hazardous is incidental to his training; (3) such work is intermittent and for short periods of time and is under the direct and close supervision of a journeyman as a necessary part of such apprentice training; and (4) the apprentice is registered by the Bureau of Apprenticeship and Training of the U.S. Department of Labor as employed in accordance with the standards established by the Bureau, or is registered by a state agency as employed in accordance with the standards of the state apprenticeship agency recognized by the Bureau of Apprenticeship and Training, or is employed under a written apprenticeship agreement and conditions, which are found by the Secretary of Labor to conform substantially with such federal or state standards.

STUDENT-LEARNERS: (1) The student-learner is enrolled in a course of study and training in a cooperative vocational training program under a recognized state or local educational authority or in a course of study in a substantially similar program conducted by a private school and (2) such student-learner is employed under a written agreement, which provides; (i) that the work of the student-learner in the occupations declared particularly hazardous shall be incidental to the training; (ii) that such work shall be intermittent and for short periods of time, and under the direct and close supervision of a qualified and experienced person; (iii) that safety instructions shall be given by the school and correlated by the employer with on-the-job training; and (iv) that a schedule of organized and progressive work processes to be performed on the job shall have been prepared. Each such written agreement shall contain the name of the student-learner and shall be signed by the employer and the school coordinator or principal. Copies of each agreement shall be kept on file by both the school and the employer. This exemption for the employment of student-learners may be revoked in any individual situation where it is found that reasonable precautions have not been observed for the safety of minors employed thereunder. A high school graduate may be employed in an occupation in which training has been completed as provided in this paragraph as a student-learner, even though the youth is not yet eighteen years of age.

Manufacturing or Storage Occupations
Involving Explosives (Order No. 1)

The following occupations in or about plants or establishments manufacturing or storing explosives or articles containing explosives components are prohibited.

(1) All occupations in or about any plant or establishment (other than retail establishments or plants or establishments of the type described in subparagraph (2) of this paragraph) manufacturing or storing explosives or articles containing explosives components except where the occupation is performed in a "non-explosives area" as defined in subparagraph (3) of this section.

(2) The following occupations in or about any plant or establishment manufacturing or storing small arms ammunition not exceeding .60 caliber in size, shotgun shells, or blasting caps when manufactured or stored in conjunction with the manufacture of small-arms ammunition:

(a) All occupations involved in the manufacturing, mixing, transporting, or handling of explosive compounds in the manufacture of small-arms ammunition and all other occupations requiring the performance of any duties in the explosives area in which explosive compounds are manufactured or mixed.

(b)   All occupations involved in the manufacturing, transporting, or handling of primers and all other occupations requiring the performance of any duties in the same building in which primers are manufactured.

(c)   All occupations involved in the priming of cartridges and all other occupations requiring the performance of any duties in the same workroom in which rim-fire cartridges are primed.

(d)   All occupations involved in the plate loading of cartridges and in the operation of automatic loading machines.

(e)   All occupations involved in the loading, inspecting, packing, shipping, and storage of blasting caps.

Definitions

(1)   The term "plant or establishment manufacturing or storing explosives or articles containing explosive components" means the land with all the buildings and other structures thereon used in connection with the manufacturing or processing or storing of explosives or articles containing explosive components.

(2)   The terms "explosives" and "articles containing explosive components" mean and include ammunition, black powder, blasting caps, fireworks, high explosives, primers, smokeless powder, and all goods classified and defined as explosives by the Interstate Commerce Commission in regulations for the transportation of explosives and other dangerous substances by common carriers (49 CFR Parts 71-78) issued pursuant to the Act of June 25, 1948 (62 Stat. 739; 18 U.S.C. 835).

(3)   An area meeting all of the following criteria shall be deemed a "nonexplosive area":

(a)   None of the work performed in the area involves the handling or use of explosives;

(b)   The area is separated from the explosives area by a distance not less than that prescribed in the American Table of Distances for the protection of inhabited buildings;

(c)   The area is separated from the explosives area by a fence or is otherwise located so that it constitutes a definite designated area; and

(d)   Satisfactory controls have been established to prevent employees under 18 years of age within the area from entering any area in or about the plant which does not meet criteria (a) through (c).

Motor Vehicle Occupations (Order No. 2)

(a)   The occupations of motor-vehicle driver and outside helper on any public road, highway, in or about any mine (including open pit mine or quarry), place where logging or sawmill operations are in progress, or in any excavation of the type identified in 29 CFR 570.68(a) are prohibited for minors between 16 and 18 years of age except as provided in paragraph (b).

(b)   Exemptions:

(1)   Incidental and occasional driving.   The finding and declaration in paragraph (a) shall not apply to the operation of automobiles or trucks not exceeding 6,000 pounds gross vehicle weight if such driving is restricted to daylight hours; provided, such operation is only

occasional and incidental to the child's employment; that the child holds a State license valid for the type of driving involved in the job performed and has completed a State approved driver education course; and provided further, that the vehicle is equipped with a seat belt or similar device for the driver and for each helper, and the employer has instructed each child that such belts or other devices must be used. This subparagraph shall not be applicable to any occupation of motor-vehicle driver which involves the towing of vehicles.

(2) School bus driving. The finding and declaration in paragraph (a) shall not apply to driving a school bus during the period of any exemption which has been granted in the discretion of the Secretary of Labor on the basis of an application filed and approved by the Governor of the State in which the vehicle is registered. The Secretary will notify any State which inquires of the information to be furnished in the application. Neither shall the finding and declaration in paragraph (a) apply in a particular State during a period not to exceed 40 days while application for such exemption is being formulated by such State seeking merely to continue in effect unchanged its current program using such drivers, nor while such application is pending action by the Secretary.

(c) Definitions:

(1) The term "motor vehicle" shall mean any automobile, truck, truck-tractor, trailer, semitrailer, motorcycle, or similar vehicle propelled or drawn by mechanical power and designed for use as a means of transportation, but shall not include any vehicle operated exclusively on rails.

(2) The term "driver" shall mean any individual who, in the course of employment, drives a motor vehicle at any time.

(3) The term "outside helper" shall mean any individual, other than a driver, whose work includes riding on a motor vehicle outside the cab for the purpose of assisting in transporting or delivering goods.

(4) The term "gross vehicle weight" includes the truck chassis with lubricants, water and full tank or tanks of fuel, plus the weight of the cab or driver's compartment, body, and special chassis and body equipment, and payload.

Coal Mine Occupations (Order No. 3)

All occupations in or about any coal mine are prohibited except the occupation of slate or other refuse picking at a picking table or picking chute in a tipple or breaker and occupations requiring the performance of duties solely in offices or in repair or maintenance shops located in the surface part of any coal-mining plant.

Definitions

The term "coal" shall mean any rank of coal, including lignite, bituminous, and anthracite coals.

The term "all occupations in or about any coal mine" shall mean all types of work performed in any underground working, open pit, or surface part of any coal-mining plant that contributes to the extraction, grading, cleaning, or other handling of coal.

Logging and Sawmilling Occupations (Order No. 4)

All occupations in logging and all occupations in the operation of any sawmill, lath mill, shingle mill, or cooperage-stock mill are prohibited except the following:

(1) Exceptions applying to logging:

    (a) Work in offices or in repair of maintenance shops.

    (b) Work in the construction, operation, repair or maintenance of living and administrative quarters of logging camps.

    (c) Work in timber cruising, surveying, or logging-engineering parties; work in the repair or maintenance of roads, railroads, or flumes work in forest protection, such as clearing fire trails or roads, piling and burning slash, maintaining firefighting equipment, constructing and maintaining telephone lines, or acting as fire lookout or fire patrolman away from the actual logging operations: Provided, that the provisions of this paragraph shall not apply to the felling or bucking of timber, the collecting or transporting of logs, the operation of powerdriven machinery, the handling or use of explosives, and work on trestles.

    (d) Peeling of fence posts, pulpwood, chemical wood, excelsior wood, cordwood, or similar products, when not done in conjunction with and at the same time and place as other logging occupations declared hazardous by this section.

    (e) Work in the feeding or care of animals.

(2) Exceptions applying to the operation of permanent sawmill or the operation of any lath mill, shingle mill, or cooperage-stock mill; Provided, that these exceptions do not apply to a portable sawmill the lumber yard of which is used only for the temporary storage of green lumber and in connection with which no office or repair or maintenance shop is ordinarily maintained: and Further provided, that these exceptions do not apply to work which entails entering the sawmill building:

    (a) Work in offices or in repair or maintenance shops.

    (b) Straightening, marking, or tallying lumber on the dry chain or the drop sorter.

    (c) Pulling lumber from the dry chain.

    (d) Clean-up in the lumberyard.

    (e) Piling, handling, or shipping of cooperage stock in yards or storage sheds, other than operating or assisting in the operation of power-driven equipment.

    (f) Clerical work in yards or shipping sheds, such as done by ordermen, tallymen, and shipping clerks.

    (g) Clean-up work outside shake and shingle mills, except when the mill is in operation.

    (h) Splitting shakes manually from pre-cut and split blocks with a froe and mallet, except inside the mill building or cover.

    (i) Packing shakes into bundles when done in conjunction with splitting shakes manually with a froe and mallet, except inside the mill building or cover.

(j)   Manual loading of bundles of shingles or shakes into trucks or railroad cars, provided that the employer has on file a statement from a licensed doctor of medicine or osteopathy certifying the minor capable of performing this work without injury to himself.

Definitions

The term "all occupations in logging" shall mean all work performed in connection with the felling of timber; the bucking or converting of timber into logs, poles, piles, ties, bolts, pulpwood, chemical wood, excelsior wood, cordwood, fence posts, or similar products; the collecting, skidding, yarding, loading, transporting, and unloading of such products in connection with logging; the constructing, repairing, and maintaining of roads, railroads, flumes, or camps used in connection with logging; the moving, installing, rigging, and maintenance of machinery or equipment used in logging; and other work performed in connection with logging. The term shall not apply to work performed in timber culture, timber-stand improvement, or in emergency firefighting.

The term "all occupations in the operation of any sawmill, lath mill, shingle mill, or cooperage-stock mill" shall mean all work performed in or about any such mill in connection with storing of logs and bolts; converting logs or bolts into sawn lumber, laths, shingles, or cooperage stock; storing, drying, and shipping lumber, laths, shingles, cooperage stock, or other products of such mills; and other work performed in connection with the operation of any sawmill, lath mill, shingle mill, or cooperage-stock mill. The term shall not include work performed in the planing-mill department or other remanufacturing departments of any sawmill, or in any planing-mill or remanufacturing plant not a part of a sawmill.

Power-Driven Woodworking Machine Occupations (Order No. 5)

The exemptions for apprentices and student-learners apply to this Order.

The following occupations involved in the operation of power-driven woodworking machines are prohibited:

(1)   The occupation of operating power-driven woodworking machines including supervising or controlling the operation of such machines, feeding material into such machines, and helping the operator to feed material into such machines, but not including the placing of material on a moving chain or in a hopper or slide for automatic feeding.

(2)   The occupations of setting up, adjusting, repairing, oiling, or cleaning power-driven woodworking machines.

(3)   The operations of off-bearing from circular saws and from guillotine-action veneer clippers.

Definitions

(1)   The term "power-driven woodworking machines" shall mean all fixed or portable machines or tools driven by power and used or designed for cutting, shaping, forming, surfacing, nailing, stapling, wire stitching, fastening, or otherwise assembling, pressing, or printing wood or veneer.

(2)   The term "off-bearing" shall mean the removal of material or refuse di-

rectly from a saw table or from the point of operation. Operations not considered as off-bearing within the intent of this section include: (a) The removal of material or refuse from a circular saw or guillotine-action veneer clipper where the material or refuse has been conveyed away from the saw table or point of operation by a gravity chute or by some mechanical means such as a moving belt or expulsion roller, and (b) the following operations when they do not involve the removal of material or refuse directly from a saw table or from a point of operation: the carrying, moving or transporting of materials from one machine to another or from one part of a plant to another; the piling, stacking, or arranging of materials for feeding into a machine by another person; and the sorting, tying, bundling, or loading of materials.

Occupations Involving Exposure to Radioactive Substances And to Ionizing Radiations (Order No. 6)

Any work is prohibited in any workroom in which (a) radium is stored or used in the manufacture of self-luminous compound; (b) self-luminous compound is made, processed, or packaged; (c) self-luminous compound is stored, used, or worked upon; (d) incandescent mantles are made from fabric and solutions containing thorium salts, or are processed or packaged; (e) other radioactive substances are present in the air in average concentrations exceeding 10 percent of the maximum permissible concentrations in the air recommended for occupational exposure by the National Committee on Radiation Protection, as set forth in the 40-hour week column of Table One of the National Bureau of Standards Handbook No. 69 entitled "Maximum Permissible Body Burdens and Maximum Permissible Concentrations of Radionuclides in Air and in Water for Occupational Exposure," issued June 5, 1959.

Any other work which involves exposure to ionizing radiations in excess of 0.5 rem per year.

Definitions

As used in this section: the term "self-luminous compound" shall mean any mixture of phosphorescent material and radium, mesothorium, or other radioactive element; the term "workroom" shall include the entire area bounded by walls of solid material and extending from floor to ceiling; the term "ionizing radiations" shall mean alpha and beta particles, electrons, protons, neutrons, gamma, and x-ray and all other radiations which produce ionizations directly or indirectly, but does not include electromagnetic radiations other than gamma and x-ray.

Power-Driven Hoisting Apparatus Occupations (Order No. 7)

The following occupations involved in the operation of power-driven hoisting apparatus are prohibited:

(1) Work of operating an elevator, crane, derrick, hoist, or high-lift truck, except operating an unattended automatic operation passenger elevator or an electric or air-operated hoist not exceeding 1 ton capacity.

(2) Work which involves riding on a manlift or on a freight elevator, except a freight elevator operated by an assigned operator.

(3) Work on assisting in the operation of a crane, derrick, or hoist performed by crane hookers, crane chasers, hookers-on, riggers, rigger helpers, and like occupations.

Definitions

The term "elevator" shall mean any power-driven hoisting or lowering mechanism equipped with a car or platform which moves in guides in a substantially vertical direction. The term shall include both passenger and freight elevators (including portable elevators or tiering machines) but shall not include dumbwaiters.

The term "crane" shall mean a power-driven machine for lifting and lowering a load and moving it horizontally, in which the hoisting mechanism is an integral part of the machine. The term shall include all types of cranes, such as cantilever gantry, crawler, gantry, hammerhead, ingot-pouring, jib, locomotive, motor truck, overhead traveling, pillar jib, pintle, portal, semigantry, semiportal, storage bridge, tower, walking jib, and wall cranes.

The term "derrick" shall mean a power-driven apparatus consisting of a mast or equivalent members held at the top by guys or braces, with or without a boom, for use with a hoisting mechanism and operating ropes. The term shall include all types of derricks, such as A-frame, breast, Chicago boom, gin-pole, guy, and stiff-leg derricks.

The term "hoist" shall mean a power-driven apparatus for raising or lowering a load by the application of a pulling force that does not include a car or platform running in guides. The term shall include all types of hoists, such as base-mounted electric, clevis suspension, hook suspension, monorail, overhead electric, simple drum, and trolley suspension hoists.

The term "high-lift truck" shall mean a power-driven industrial type of truck used for lateral transportation that is equipped with a power-operated lifting device usually in the form of a fork or platform capable of tiering loaded pallets or skids one above the other. Instead of a fork, or platform, the lifting device may consist of a ram, scoop, shovel, crane, revolving fork, or other attachments for handling specific loads. The term shall mean and include high-lift trucks known under such names as forklifts, fork trucks, forklift trucks, tiering trucks, or stacking trucks, but shall not mean low-lift trucks or low-lift platform trucks, that are designed for the transportation of, but not the tiering of, material.

The term "manlift" shall mean a device intended for the conveyance of persons which consists of platforms or brackets mounted on, or attached to, an endless belt, cable, chain or similar method of suspension; such belt, cable, or chain operating in a substantially vertical direction and being supported by and driven through pulleys, sheaves or sprockets at the top or bottom.

Exception

This section shall not prohibit the operation of an automatic elevator and an automatic signal operation elevator provided that the exposed portion of the car interior (exclusive of vents and other necessary small openings), the car door, and the hoistway doors are constructed of solid surfaces without any opening through which a part of the body may extend; all hoistway openings at floor level have doors which are interlocked with the car door so as to prevent the car from starting until all such doors are closed and locked; the elevator (other than hydraulic elevators) is equipped with a device which will stop and hold the car in case of overspeed or if the cable slackens or breaks; and the elevator is equipped with upper and lower travel limit devices which will normally bring the car to rest at either terminal and a final limit switch which will prevent the movement in either direction and will open in case of excessive over travel by the car.

Definitions as used in this exception: For the purpose of this exception the term "automatic elevator" shall mean a passenger elevator, a freight elevator, or a combination passenger-freight elevator, the operation of which is controlled by pushbuttons in such a manner that the starting, going to the landing selected, leveling and holding, and the opening and closing of the car and hoistway doors are entirely automatic.

For the purpose of this exception, the term "automatic signal operation elevator" shall mean an elevator which is started in response to the operation of a switch (such as a lever or pushbutton) in the car which when operated by the operator actuates a starting device that automatically closes the car and hoistway doors — from this point on, the movement of the car to the landing selected, leveling and holding when it gets there, and the opening of the car and hoistway doors are entirely automatic.

Power-Driven Metal Forming, Punching, and Shearing Machine Occupations (Order No. 8)

The exemptions for apprentices and student-learners apply to this Order.

The occupations of operator of or helper on the following power-driven metal forming, punching, and shearing machines are prohibited:

(1) All rolling machines, such as beading, straightening, corrugating, flanging, or bending rolls; and hot or cold rolling mills.

(2) All pressing or punching machines, such as punch presses, except those provided with full automatic feed and ejection and with a fixed barrier guard to prevent the hands or fingers of the operator from entering the area between the dies; power presses; and plate punches.

(3) All bending machines, such as apron brakes and press brakes.

(4) All hammering machines, such as drop hammers and power hammers.

(5) All shearing machines, such as guillotine or squaring shears; alligator shears; and rotary shears.

The occupations of setting up, adjusting, repairing, oiling, or cleaning these machines including those with automatic feed and injection.

Definitions

The term "operator" shall mean a person who operates a machine covered by this Order by performing such functions as starting or stopping the machine, placing materials into or removing them from the machine, or any other functions directly involved in operation of the machine.

The term "helper" shall mean a person who assists in the operation of a machine covered by this Order by helping place materials into or remove them from the machine.

The term "forming, punching and shearing machines" shall mean power-driven metal-working machines, other than machine tools, which change the shape of or cut metal by means of tools, such as dies, rolls, or knives which are mounted on rams, plungers, or other moving parts. Types of forming, punching, and shearing machines enumerated in this section are the machines to which the designation is by custom applied.

Note: This order does not apply to a very large group of metal-working machines known as machine tools. Machine tools are defined as "power-driven complete metal-working machines having one or more tool-or-work-holding devices, and used for progressively removing metal in the form of chips." Since the Order does not apply to machine tools, the 18-year age minimum does not apply. Such machine tools are classified below so that they can be readily identified.

Milling function Machines
Horizontal Milling Machines
Vertical Milling Machines
Universal Milling Machines
Planer-type Milling Machines
Gear Hobbing Machines
Profilers
Routers
Turning function Machines
Engine Lathes
Turret Lathes
Hollow Spindle Lathes
Automatic Lathes
Automatic Screw Machines
Planing function Machines
Planers
Shapers
Slotters
Broaches
Keycasters
Hack Saws
Grinding function Machines
Grinders
Abrasive Wheels
Abrasive Belts
Abrasive Disks
Abrasive Points
Polishing Wheels
Buffing Wheels
Stroppers
Lapping Machines
Boring function Machines
Vertical Boring Mills
Horizontal Boring Mills
Jig Borers
Pedestal Drills
Radial Drills
Gang Drills
Upright Drills
Drill Press, etc.
Centering Machines
Reamers
Honers

Occupations in Connection with Mining, Other Than Coal (Order No. 9)

All occupations in connection with mining, other than coal, are prohibited except the following:

(1) Work in offices, in the warehouse or supply house, in the change house, in the laboratory, and in repair or maintenance shops not located underground.

(2) Work in the operation and maintenance of living quarters.

(3) Work outside the mine in surveying, in the repair and maintenance of roads, and in general clean-up about the mine property such as clearing brush and digging drainage ditches.

(4) Work of track crews in the building and maintaining of sections of railroad track located in those areas of open-cut metal mines where mining and haulage activities are not being conducted at the time and place that such building and maintenance work is being done.

(5) Work in or about surface placer mining operations other than placer dredging operations and hydraulic placer mining operations.

(6) The following work in metal mills other than in mercury-recovery mills or mills using the cyanide process:

    (a) Work involving the operation of jigs, sludge tables, flotation cells, or drier-filters.

    (b) Work of hand sorting at picking table or picking belt.

    (c) General cleanup work.

Provided, however, that nothing in this section shall be construed as permitting employment of minors in any occupation prohibited by any other hazardous occupations order issued by the Secretary of Labor.

Definitions

As used in this section: The term "all occupations in connection with mining, other than coal" shall mean all work performed underground in mines and quarries; on the surface at underground mines and underground quarries; in or about open-cut mines, open quarries, clay pits, and sand and gravel operations; at or about placer mining operations; at or about dredging operations for clay, sand or gravel; at or about bore-hole mining operations; in or about all metal mills, washer plants, or grinding mills reducing the bulk of the extracted minerals; and at or about any other crushing, grinding, screening, sizing, washing or cleaning operations performed upon the extracted minerals except where such operations are performed as a part of a manufacturing process. The term shall not include work performed in subsequent manufacturing or processing operations, such as work performed in smelters, electro-metallurgical plants, refineries, reduction plants, cement mills, plants where quarried stone is cut, sanded and further processed, or plants manufacturing clay, glass, or ceramic products. Neither shall the term include work performed in connection with coal mining, in petroleum production, in natural-gas production, nor in dredging operations which are not a part of mining operations, such as dredging for construction or navigation purposes.

Occupations Involving Slaughtering, Meat-Packing or Processing, or Rendering (Order No. 10)

The exemptions for apprentices and student-learners apply to this Order.

The following occupations in or about slaughtering and meat-packing establishments, rendering plants, or wholesale, retail or service establishments are prohibited:

(1) All occupations on the killing floor, in curing cellars, and in hide cellars, except the work of messengers, runners, hand-truckers, and similar occupations which require entering such workrooms or workplaces infrequently and for short periods of time.

(2) All occupations involved in the recovery of lard and oils, except packaging and shipping of such products and the operations of lard-roll machines.

(3) All occupations involved in tankage or rendering of dead animals, animal offal, animal fats, scrap meats, blood, and bones into stock feeds, tallow, inedible greases, fertilizer ingredients, and similar products.

(4) All occupations involved in the operation or feeding of the following power-driven meat-processing machines, including the occupation of setting-up, adjusting, repairing, oiling, or cleaning such machines: meat patty forming machines, meat and bone cutting saws, knives (except bacon-slicing machines*), head splitters, and guillotine cutters; snout pullers and jaw pullers; skinning machines; horizontal rotary washing machines; casing-cleaning machines such as crushing, stripping, and finishing machines; grinding, mixing, chopping, and hashing machines; and presses (except belly-rolling machines).

(5) All boning occupations.

(6) All occupations that involve the pushing or dropping of any suspended carcass, half carcass, or quarter carcass.

(7) All occupations involving hand-lifting or hand-carrying any carcass or half carcass of beef, pork, or horse, or any quarter carcass of beef or horse.

Definitions

The term "slaughtering and meat-packing establishments" shall mean places in or about which cattle, calves, hogs, sheep, lambs, goats, or horses are killed, butchered, or processed. The term shall also include establishments which manufacture or process meat products or sausage casings from such animals.

The term "rendering plants" shall mean establishments engaged in the conversion of dead animals, animal offal, animal fats, scrap meats, blood, and bones into stock feeds, tallow, inedible greases, fertilizer ingredients, and similar products.

---

*Note: The term "bacon-slicing machine" as used in this Order refers to those machines which are designed solely for the purpose of slicing bacon and are equipped with enclosure or barrier guards that prevent the operator from coming in contact with the blade or blades, and with devices for automatic feeding, slicing, shingling, stacking, and conveying the sliced bacon away from the point of operation.

The term "killing floor" shall include that workroom or workplace where cattle, calves, hogs, sheep, lambs, goats, or horses are immobilized, shackled, or killed, and the carcasses are dressed prior to chilling.

The term "curing cellar" shall include that workroom or workplace which is primarily devoted to the preservation and flavoring of meat by curing materials. It does not include that workroom or workplace where meats are smoked.

The term "hide cellar" shall include that workroom or workplace where hides are graded, trimmed, salted, and otherwise cured.

The term "boning occupations" shall mean the removal of bones from meat cuts. It shall not include work that invovles cutting, scraping, or trimming meat from cuts containing bones.

Exemptions

This order shall not apply to the killing and processing of poultry, rabbits, or small game in areas physically separated from the "killing floor."

Power-Driven Bakery Machine Occupations (Order No. 11)

The following occupations involved in the operation of power-driven bakery machines are prohibited:

(1)   The occupations of operating, assisting to operate, or setting up, adjusting, repairing, oiling, or cleaning any horizontal or vertical dough mixer; batter mixer; bread dividing, rounding, or molding machine; dough brake; dough sheeter; combination bread slicing and wrapping machine; or cake cutting band saw.

(2)   The occupation of setting up or adjusting a cooky or cracker machine.

Note: This Order does not apply to the following list of bakery machines which may be operated by 16 and 17-year-old minors:

Ingredient Preparation and Mixing:
flour-sifting machine operator
flour-blending machine operator
sack-cleaning machine operator
Product Forming and Shaping:
roll-dividing machine operator
roll-making machine operator
batter-sealing machine operator
depositing machine operator
cooky or cracker machine operator
wafer machine operator
pretzel-stick machine operator
pie-dough sealing machine operator
pie-dough rolling machine operator
pie-crimping machine operator

Finishing and Icing:
depositing machine operator
enrobing machine operator
spray machine operator
icing mixing machine operator

Slicing and Wrapping:
roll slicing and wrapping machine operator
cake wrapping machine operator
carton packing and sealing machine operator

Pan Washing:
spray-type pan washing machine operator
tumbler-type pan washing machine operator

Power-Driven Paper-Products Machine Occupations (Order No. 12)

The exemptions for apprentices and student-learners apply to this Order.

The occupations of operating or assisting to operate any of the following power-driven paper-products machines are prohibited:

(1) Arm-type wirestitcher or stapler, circular or band saw, corner cutter or mitering machine, corrugating and single- or double-facing machine, envelope die-cutting press, guillotine paper cutter or shear, horizontal bar scorer, laminating or combining machine, sheeting machine, scrap-paper baler, or vertical slotter.

(2) Platen die-cutting press, platen printing press, or punch press which involves hand feeding of the machine.

The occupations of setting up, adjusting, repairing, oiling, or cleaning these machines including those which do not involve hand feeding are prohibited.

Definitions

The term "operating or assisting to operate" shall mean all work which involves starting or stopping a machine covered by this Order, placing materials into or removing them from the machine, or any other work directly involved in operating the machine.

The term "paper-products machine" shall mean power-driven machines used in the remanufacture or conversion of paper or pulp into a finished product. The term is understood to apply to such machines whether they are used in establishments that manufacture converted paper pulp products, or in any other type of manufacturing or non-manufacturing establishment.

Note: There are many machines not covered by this Order. The most important of these machines are the following:

Bag Machine, Bag-Making Machine
Bottoming Machine (Bags)
Box-making Machine (Collapsible Boxes)
Bundling Machine
Calender Roll and Plating Machines
Cigarette Carton Opener and Tax Stamping Machine
Clasp Machine
Counting, Stacking and Ejecting Machine
Corner Stayer
Covering, Lining or Wrapping Machines (Set-up Boxes)
Creping Machine
Dornbusch Machines (Wall Paper)

Ending Machine (Set-up Boxes)
Envelope Machine
Folding Machine
Gluing, Scaling, or Gumming Machine
Interfolding Machine
Jogging Machine
Lacer Machine
Parchmentizing, Waxing, or Coating Machines
Partition Assembling Machine
Paper Cup Machine
Quadruple Stayer
Rewinder
Rotary Printing Press
Ruling Machine
Slitting Machine
Straw Winder
Stripping Machine
Taping Machine
Tube Cutting Machine
Tube Winder
Tube Machine (Paper Bags)
Window Patch Machine
Wire or Tag Stringing Machine

Occupations Involved in the Manufacture of Brick, Tile and Kindred Products (Order No. 13)

The following occupations involved in the manufacture of clay construction products and of silica refractory products are prohibited:

(1) All work in or about establishments in which clay construction products are manufactured, except (a) work in storage and shipping; (b) work in offices, laboratories, and storerooms; and (c) work in the drying departments of plants manufacturing sewer pipe.

(2) All work in or about establishments in which silica brick or other silica refractories are manufactured, except work in offices.

(3) Nothing in this section shall be construed as permitting employment of minors in any occupation prohibited by any other hazardous occupations order issued by the Secretary of Labor.

Definitions

The term "clay construction products" shall mean the following clay products: Brick, hollow structural tile, sewer pipe and kindred products, refractories, and other clay products such as architectural terra cotta, glazed structural tile, roofing tile, stove lining, chimney pipes and tops, wall coping, and drain tile. The term shall not include the following non-structural-bearing clay products: Ceramic floor and wall tile, mosaic tile, glazed and enameled tile, faience, and similar tile, nor shall the term include nonclay construction products such as sand-lime brick, glass brick, or nonclay refractories.

The term "silica brick or other silica refractories" shall mean refractory products produced from raw materials containing free silica as their main constituent.

Occupations Involved in the Operation of Power-Driven Circular Saws, Band Saws and Guillotine Shears (Order No. 14)

The exemptions for apprentices and student-learners apply to this Order.

The occupations of operator of or helper on the following power-driven fixed or portable machines are prohibited except for machines equipped with full automatic feed and ejection:

(1) Circular saws.
(2) Band saws.
(3) Guillotine shears.

The occupations of setting up, adjusting, repairing, oiling, or cleaning circular saws, band saws, and guillotine shears are prohibited.

Definitions

The term "operator" shall mean a person who operates a machine covered by this Order by performing such functions as starting or stopping the machine, placing materials into or removing them from the machine, or any other functions directly involved in operation of the machine.

The term "helper" shall mean a person who assists in the operation of a machine covered by this Order by helping place materials into or remove them from the machine.

The term "machines equipped with full automatic feed and ejection" shall mean machines covered by this Order which are equipped with devices for full automatic feeding and ejection and with a fixed barrier guard to prevent completely the operator or helper from placing any part of his body in the point-of-operation area.

The term "circular saw" shall mean a machine equipped with a thin steel disc having a continuous series of notches or teeth on the periphery, mounted on shafting, and used for sawing materials.

The term "band saw" shall mean a machine equipped with an endless steel band having a continuous series of notches or teeth, running over wheels or pulleys, and used for sawing materials.

The term "guillotine shear" shall mean a machine equipped with a movable blade operated vertically and used to shear materials. The term shall not include other types of shearing machines, using a different form of shearing action, such as alligator shears or circular shears.

Occupations Involved in Wrecking, Demolition, And Shipbreaking Operations (Order No. 15)

All occupations in wrecking, demolition, and shipbreaking operations are prohibited.

Definitions

The term "wrecking, demolition, and shipbreaking operations" shall mean all work, including cleanup and salvage work, performed at the site of the total or partial razing, demolishing, or dismantling of a building, bridge, steeple, tower, chimney, other structure, ship or other vessel.

Occupations in Roofing Operations (Order No. 16)

The exemptions for apprentices and student-learners apply to this Order.
All occupations in roofing operations are prohibited.

Definitions

The term "roofing operations" shall mean all work performed in connection with the application of weatherproofing materials and substances (such as tar or pitch, asphalt prepared paper, tile, slate, metal, translucent materials, and shingles of asbestos, asphalt or wood) to roofs of buildings or other structures. The term shall also include all work performed in connection with: (1) The installation of roofs, including related metal work such as flashing and (2) alterations, additions, maintenance, and repair, including painting and coating, of existing roofs. The term shall not include gutter and downspout work; the construction of the sheathing or base of roofs; or the installation of television antennas, air conditioners, exhaust and ventilating equipment, or similar appliances attached to roofs.

Occupations in Excavation Operations (Order No. 17)

The exemptions for apprentices and student-learners apply to this Order.
The following occupations in excavation operations are prohibited:

(1) Excavating, working in, or backfilling (refilling) trenches, except (a) manually excavating or manually backfilling trenches that do not exceed four feet in depth at any point, or (b) working in trenches that do not exceed four feet in depth at any point.

(2) Excavating for buildings or other structures or working in such excavations, except (a) manually excavating to a depth not exceeding four feet below any ground surface adjoining the excavation, or (b) working in an excavation not exceeding such depth, or (c) working in an excavation where the side walls are shored or sloped to the angle of repose.

(3) Working within tunnels prior to the completion of all driving and shoring operations.

(4) Working within shafts prior to the completion of all sinking and shoring operations.

Penalties for Violation

For each violation of the child labor provisions or any regulation issued thereunder, employers may be subject to a civil money penalty of up to 1,000 dollars.

The Act was amended, effective May 1, 1974, authorizing the Secretary of Labor to assess a civil money penalty not to exceed 1,000 dollars for each violation of the child labor provisions of the Act or any regulation issued thereunder. When a child labor civil money penalty is assessed against an employer, the employer has the right, within fifteen days after receipt of the notice of such penalty, to file an exception to the determination that the violation or violations of the child labor provisions occurred.   When such an exception is filed with the administrator of the Wage and Hour Division, the matter is referred to the chief administrative law judge, and a formal hearing is scheduled.   At such a hearing the employer, or an attorney retained by the employer, may present such witnesses, introduce such evidence, and establish such facts as the employer believes will support the exception.   The determination of the amount of any civil money penalty becomes final if no exception is taken to the administrative assessment thereof, or if an exception is filed, pursuant to the decision and order of the administrative law judge.

The Act also provides, in the case of willful violation, for a fine up to 10,000 dollars; or, for a second offense committed after the conviction of such person for a similar offense, for a fine of not more   than 10,000 dollars, or imprisonment for not more than 6 months, or both.   The Secretary of Labor may also ask a federal district court to restrain future violations of the child labor provisions of the Act by injunction.

Age Certificates

Employers may protect themselves from unintentional violation of the child labor provisions by keeping on file an employment or age certificate for each minor employed to show that the minor is the minimum age for the job.   Certificates issued under most state laws are acceptable for purposes of the Act.

Assistance

Inquiries about the Fair Labor Standards Act will be answered by mail, telephone, or personal interview at any office of the Wage and Hour Division of the U.S. Department of Labor.   Offices are listed in the telephone directory under U.S. Department of Labor in the U.S. Government listing.   These offices also supply publications free of charge.

Figure 40

A CHECKLIST FOR THE TEACHER-COORDINATOR IN COMPLYING WITH
LEGAL RESPONSIBILITIES

Yes   No

———   ———   1. I place student learners at job sites that comply with occupational safety laws.

———   ———   2. I adhere to all existing federal, state and local laws in placing student-learners on the job.

———   ———   3. I keep abreast of all legal matters concerning the employment of minors.

———   ———   4. I maintain a complete file of publications and documents that include labor laws and their interpretations.

———   ———   5. I require all student-learners to take out additional around-the-clock insurance.

———   ———   7. I endeavor to have all student-learners paid the highest existing statutory minimum wage.

———   ———   8. I ensure that all student-learners under eighteen years of age have valid employment or age certificates prior to beginning their on-the-job learning experience.

———   ———   9. I ensure that student-learners are employed under a written training agreement.

———   ———   10. I ensure that copies of the written training agreement are kept on file by both the school and the employer.

———   ———   11. I am thoroughly familiar with the Child Labor Provisions of the Fair Labor Standards Act.

———   ———   12. I enforce the Child Labor Provisions of the Fair Labor Standards Act.

———   ———   13. I ensure that student-learners do not work beyond hours prescribed by law.

———   ———   14. I do not place student-learners in positions that are detrimental to their health and well-being.

———   ———   15. I do not place student-learners in prohibited occupations.

BIBLIOGRAPHY

Alabama Guide for Cooperative Vocational Education. Montgomery, State of Alabama, Department of Education, Division of Vocational Education, 1970.

Child Labor Requirements in Nonagricultural Occupations Under the Fair Labor Standards Act. Child Labor Bulletin No. 101. Washington, D.C.,

United States Department of Labor Employment Standards Administration, Wage and Hour Division, U.S. Government Printing Office, 1977.

C.I.E. Administrative Handbook. New Brunswick, State of New Jersey, Department of Education, Division of Vocational Education and Career Preparation, Curriculum Laboratory, Rutgers University, April 1978.

Employment of Full-time Students at Subminimum Wages — Fair Labor Standards. Part 519, U.S. Department of Labor, Washington, D.C., W H Publication 1223 (Rev.) 2/13/75.

Guide For Cooperative Vocational Education. Denver, University of Northern Colorado, Department of Vocational Education, State Board of Community Colleges and Occupational Education, 1972.

Handbook for Coordinator of Industrial Cooperative Training in Virginia's Public Schools. Richmond, Trade and Industrial Education Service, Division of Vocational Education, State Department of Education, January 1971.

Handbook on Work-Experience Education. Sacramento, California State Department of Education, 1965.

Selected Procedures for Working Paper Issuance In New Jersey School Districts. Trenton, New Jersey Department of Education, Division of Vocational Education and Career Preparation, 1972.

Workmen's Compensation Law, Revised Statutes 1937. Trenton, State of New Jersey, Department of Labor and Industry, March 2, 1972.

Wyoming Management System for Cooperative Education, 2nd Ed. Cheyenne, Wyoming State Department of Education, 1974.

Chapter 11

VOCATIONAL STUDENT
ORGANIZATIONS ARE COCURRICULAR

THE ACTIVITIES of the vocational student organizations are an integral part of the students' field of study. Combined with related classroom instruction and cooperative education, the organizations complement, supplement, strengthen, and enrich the total instructional program.

The involvement of students, teachers, and citizens in the activities of vocational student organizations fosters a greater knowledge and respect for vocational competencies and leadership development. Community service projects comprise a major portion of local chapter activities. These projects utilize occupational and leadership skills of members. Regional, state, and national meetings and contests involve members in skill competitions, projects, and leadership training.

The seventh report from the National Advisory Council on Vocational Education, entitled "Vocational Student Organizations," explains why the student group is so important to the Cooperative program.

> "there is an increasing disparity between what society needs and what our educational institutions are producing . . . Industry, still by far the principal source of opportunities, is changing very, very rapidly. These changing needs (of industry) are not being met by institutions that are changing much more slowly . . . It is much easier to identify the relevance gap than it is to prescribe a comprehensive solution. But one part of the solution is perfectly clear: There must be direct daily involvement of business and industry in practically all phases of the educational enterprise.
>
> One splendid, yet neglected, mechanism for industry involvement is already in place: our national vocational student organizations . . .

But much more important, thousands of business, industry, labor, and community representatives participate in the daily activities of these organizations. The value of the time they contribute is inestimable, but infinitely more valuable are the solid links between industry and our young people that are being built. These vocational youth organizations . . . are quietly doing more to close the relevance gap than any other movement on the educational scene . . . .

POLICY OF THE UNITED STATES OFFICE OF EDUCATION ON VOCATIONAL STUDENT ORGANIZATIONS

The United States Office of Education maintains a close relationship with the eight vocational student organizations and welcomes their cooperation and support in strengthening our programs of vocational and technical education. Recognizing that the past performance and demonstrated potential of these eight organizations are compatible with the overall purposes and objects of education today, the United States Office of Education strongly endorses their objectives and seeks to involve their thinking in the development of our policies and plans.

In view of this, their policy is as follows:

1. The United States Office of Education recognizes the concept of total student development as being necessary for all vocational-technical education students to enter the labor market and to assume successful roles in society.
2. The United States Office of Education recognizes the educational programs and philosophies embraced by the following vocational education student organizations as being an integral part of our vocational education system of training.
   * American Industrial Arts Student Association (AIASA)
   * Distributive Education Clubs of America (DECA)
   * Future Business Leaders of America—Phi Beta Lambda (FBLA-PBL)
   * Future Farmers of America (FFA)
   * Future Homemakers of America—Home Economics Related Occupations (FHA-HERO)
   * Health Occupations Students of America (HOSA)
   * Office Education Association (OEA)
   * Vocational Industrial Clubs of America (VICA)

3. The United States Office of Education will provide technical and supportive services to assist vocational student organizations and state agencies in their efforts to improve the quality and relevance of instruction, develop student leadership, enhance citizenship responsibilities, overcome sex and race discrimination and sex stereotyping, and serve students with special needs.
4. Federal and state grant funds for vocational education may be used by the states to give leadership and support to vocational student organizations and activities directly related to established vocational education instructional programs at all levels under provisions of approved state plans for vocational education.

The responsibility for instructional programs and related activities rests with the states and localities. It is the belief of the U.S. Office of Education that increased efforts on the part of state education agencies to recognize and encourage the growth and development of these vocational student organizations are highly important and deserve the support of all leaders in American education.

Membership in one of the eight vocational student organizations should be encouraged for all cooperative education students. Teacher-coordinators provide the incentive and encouragement to join and become active members. The activities of the student organizations provide opportunities to further develop competencies normally learned in the classroom and on the job.

The following is a summary of the eight major national vocational student organizations and their specific goals and activities.

AIASA

The American Industrial Arts Student Association, known as AIASA (Eye-Ay-Zsa), is a national organization for elementary, junior high, and senior high school students who are presently enrolled in, or who have completed, industrial arts courses.

AIASA is the only national student organization devoted exclusively to the needs of industrial arts students. Purposes of AIASA are—

1. To provide opportunities for the development of leadership in social, civic, scholastic, and community activities;
2. To encourage scholastic motivation by providing opportunities to integrate and use the knowledge and skills of other educational disciplines in practical ways;
3. To increase the knowledge and broaden the understanding of all students living in our industrial-technological society;
4. To assist in the making of informed and meaningful occupational choices;
5. To provide opportunities to promote industrial arts in school, community, state, and nation;
6. To inspire students to respect the dignity of labor, and to appreciate craftsmanship.

AIASA chapter activities are an integral part of the school industrial arts program and provide added dimensions to school/community activities. AIASA activities improve the industrial arts instructional program by offering the instructor additional means of creating interesting and productive situations to benefit the student. AIASA increases the opportunity for individual student growth, development, and maturation according to his or her own interests and abilities.

The address of the national organization is American Industrial Arts Student Association, 1201 16th Street, N.W., Washington, D.C. 20036.

DECA

Distributive Education Clubs of America serve youths preparing for careers in marketing and distribution.

DECA is recognized by educational and business groups as being an integral part of the total distributive education curriculum. It encourages free enterprise and economic awareness through individual instruction, competitive activities, exposure to successful business leaders, and practical experience in the business world. It encourages civic responsibility through participation in conferences, chapter activities, and community projects.

In addition, DECA sponsors state and national competitive events designed to stimulate and motivate classroom interest, career encouragement, and vocational competence. DECA's philosophy is to encourage competition. It offers awards and recognition to members for outstanding accomplishment.

The organization also maintains a scholarship loan award program to assist and encourage its members to pursue post secondary education programs.

The address of the national organization is Distributive Education Clubs of America, Inc., 200 Park Avenue, Falls Church, Virginia 22046.

FBLA/PBL

Future Business Leaders of America is for high school students enrolled in business and office programs. It operates as an integral part of the school business program under the guidance of business teachers, state supervisors, school administrators, and the business community.

Phi Beta Lambda is the national organization for all young adults in post secondary institutions who are enrolled in business and office programs.

Besides high school students the membership is also open to persons in community colleges, junior colleges, regular colleges and universities, vocational-technical schools, and private business schools.

All FBLA and PBL chapters are under the guidance of qualified business teachers who have the recognition of the local, state, and national headquarters.

The activities of the organization provide students with the opportunity to better prepare for business careers. Members learn how to engage in individual and group business enterprises; how to work with representatives of other youth organizations; and how to compete honorably with their colleagues on the local, state, and national levels.

The address of the national organization is Future Business Leaders of America—Phi Beta Lambda, Inc., P.O. Box 174 17—Dulles, Washington, D.C. 20041.

FFA

Future Farmers of America is open to high school students preparing for careers in agricultural production, agribusiness, ornamental horticulture, food processing, and natural resources occupations.

Chapters of the FFA are established in schools that offer instruction in agricultural and natural resources occupations as provided for under various vocational education acts and are specifically designed as part of those types of instructional programs.

FFA strives to develop leadership, cooperation, and citizenship in its students. Through participation in FFA activities, students learn how to speak in public, conduct and take part in meetings, handle financial matters, and assume civic responsibilities.

Founded nationally in 1928, FFA received a federal charter from Congress in 1950. FFA has over 8,000 chapters in fifty states, Puerto Rico, and the Virgin Islands and a membership of more than 500,000 young people.

The address of the national organization is Future Farmers of America, National FFA Center, P.O. Box 15160, Alexandria, Virginia 22309.

FHA/HERO

Secondary students interested in home economics and related occupations can become members of Future Homemakers of America—Home Economics Related Occupations.

FHA/HERO strives to help individuals improve personal, family, and community living and gives emphasis to career education.

It has two types of chapters: FHA chapters are for students in homemaking, consumer, and family-life education. HERO chapters are for students in home economics related occupation courses.

Established in 1945 as an integral part of the home economics education curriculum, FHA/HERO provides opportunities for developing individual and group initiative in planning and carrying out activities related to the multiple roles of homemaker and wage-earner.

State and national conferences are held annually to plan work and give recognition to chapters and individuals who have proven to be outstanding leaders in furthering the purposes of FHA/HERO.

The address of the National organization is Future Homemakers of America, 2010 Massachusetts Avenue, N.W., Washington, D.C. 20036.

HOSA

Health Occupations Students of America serve students interested in careers in the health field. Membership includes students enrolled in health occupations education programs and students enrolled in prevocational health occupations related programs.

Founded in 1976, HOSA provides students with recognition, prestige, the tools to develop leadership abilities, and practical experience in how the democratic process works.

Competitive events are planned continually to develop various skills needed in the work world, such as public speaking and job interviews. Awards are given annually to winners of these competitions both as individuals and chapters.

The primary purposes of HOSA are to help members be the leaders of today and to lead the world of tomorrow. This is accomplished in the following ways:

1. Broadening members physical, mental, social, citizenship, and leadership abilities.
2. Through their involvement with HOSA, members learn to respect the responsibilities of work and develop personal and occupational skills which guide them for future planning of careers affiliated with the health field.

The address of the national organization is Health Occupations Education, Kenora Enterprises 2 East 7th Street, Suite 102, Wilmington, Delaware 19801.

OEA

The Office Education Association, founded in 1966, is the vocational student organization for high school, postsecondary, and collegiate students enrolled in vocational business and office programs. OEA's purpose is to develop vocational competency in business and office occupations.

Secondary members participate in local, state, and national activities directed toward promoting skill competency, leadership traits, and social awareness at the high school level.

OEA provides co-curricular instruction in business and related areas of clerical, secretarial, data processing, and accounting studies. The secondary division encourages participation in the academic areas as well as community, civic, and professional endeavors.

For those students who enroll in postsecondary programs, OEA offers a program designed to further their vocational training for careers they have chosen. Members include students enrolled in legal and medical secretarial, computer programmer, word processing, reprographics clerk, accounting, and many other courses. Like the secondary division, many postsecondary students participate in cooperative employment positions during their education process.

The newest division of OEA is the collegiate division, designed for students enrolled in a baccalaureate or postbaccalaureate program in an accredited college or university and whose career goal is teaching vocational business and office education.

Collegiate members assist in administering tests at state and national conferences, serve on secondary or postsecondary advisory committees, and participate in other activities preparing them to work with similar students upon graduation.

The address of the national organization is Office Education Association, 1120 Morse Road, Columbus, Ohio 43229.

VICA

The Vocational Industrial Clubs of America serve students in trade, industrial, health, and technical education programs through the development of their leadership, citizenship, and skill abilities.

VICA emphasizes respect for "the dignity of work," high standards in trade ethics, workmanship, scholarship, and safety. In each chapter meeting the members recite the VICA pledge which begins: "Upon my honor, I pledge myself by diligent study and ardent practice to become a worker whose services will be recognized as honorable by my employer and fellow workers."

Competitive activities in skill and personal achievement are important aspects of the VICA program. Members can also participate in an individual achievement program to receive recognition for both skill and personal accomplishment. There are also national, state, and regional conferences on leadership.

VICA was established through the efforts of the National Association of State Supervisors of Trade and Industrial Education. The American Vocational Association, U.S. Office of Education, AFL-CIO, and the Chamber of Commerce of the United States also participated in the founding of VICA.

The address of the national organization is Vocational Industrial Clubs of America, P.O. Box 3600, Leesburg, Virginia 20075.

IMPORTANCE

Importance to the Student

Students belonging to vocational student organizations have common objectives and interests in that each is studying for a specific career objective. Vocational student organization activities have a tremendous psychological effect upon the attitudes of students, many of whom have no other opportunity to participate in planned activities of the school or to develop leadership competencies and citizenship responsibilities.

Vocational student organization members learn to serve as leaders and followers, and are offered state and national recognition that they would not have otherwise.

Importance to the School

Activities of the vocational student organizations are always school-centered, thus contributing to the school's purpose of preparing well-adjusted, employable citizens. Chapter activities serve the teacher-coordinator as a teaching tool by creating interest in all phases of vocational education and serve as an avenue of expression for individual talent.

The chapter is the vehicle for student achievement and progress. It attracts students who are interested in vocational programs leading to a career or further study upon graduation from high school.

Importance to the Community

Members of the vocational student organizations have made numerous contributions to aid the economic development of their communities.

Many businesses favor employing members of the vocational student organizations because of industry's interest in education and their related school study of the particular career area. Leaders in business and government have praised the programs of the vocational student organizations for their civic-related activities.

Importance to the State and Nation

The activities of the vocational student organizations constantly emphasize America's system of competition, free enterprise, and democracy. Self-help among members is the rule rather than the exception, with advisors giving constant encouragement to continuous education.

These organizations offer practical opportunities for young people to participate in, and prepare for, a leadership role in our highly industrialized nation.

Vocational student organization members understand the *importance* of competition, recognize sound values, work cooperatively with others, learn responsibilities of leadership, and gain recognition for their accomplishments.

The Vocational Industrial Clubs of America in their publication "Directions—A Guide for VICA Club Advisors" September, 1973, listed (on pages 28-29) ninety-four ideas for student organization activities, which are typical for all student organizations:

1. Safety poster contest
2. Clean up, paint up project
3. Adopt a needy family
4. "Get Out the Vote"
5. Faculty recognition tea, reception, assembly

6. Ushering at school events
7. Raise funds for a community drive
8. Visit a local industry
9. Visit a labor union hall
10. Guest speakers—on just about any subject
11. Parliamentary procedure study
12. Public speaking workshop
13. Debate or round-table discussion
14. Inter-club visits or socials
15. Occupational display or occupational library section
16. Career program or career open house
17. State legislature visit
18. Parents' banquet
19. Employer-employee banquet
20. Picnic
21. Dance
22. Hayride
23. Skating party
24. Talent Show
25. Alumni Day
26. Present honorary life membership
27. Follow-up survey of former members
28. Radio show on local station
29. Parade float
30. Carnival or fair
31. Rummage sale
32. Bake sale
33. Dinner meeting in local restaurant
34. Parties—Thanksgiving, Christmas, Valentine's Day, or any other day
35. Welcome new teachers, new students
36. Operate concession stand
37. Help PTA or other organizations put on programs
38. Decorate trash receptacle in school colors
39. Put up school's signs (and a VICA sign!)
40. Anti-dropout campaign
41. Program on highway safety, home safety

42. Collect toys for needy children
43. Christmas caroling
44. Visit nursing homes, hospitals, orphanages
45. Develop a community park
46. Sponsor a consumer education program
47. VICA newsletter or VICA column in school paper
48. Send flowers and greetings to teachers who are sick
49. Assist churches with special projects
50. Display VICA billboard poster
51. Citizenship week
52. Used clothing drive for the needy
53. Babysitting service so parents may attend school functions
54. Plant flowers, trees, shrubs
55. Repair and paint community homes
56. Leadership workshops on public speaking, parliamentary procedures, job interview
57. New member initiation
58. Officer installation
59. International Understanding Week
60. National VICA Week
61. Earth Day
62. Recycling drive or a recycling center
63. Speak Up for America Day
64. Color Day (everyone wear official colors or red, white, gold, or blue)
65. Raise money with a mani-cur-athon, a hair-a-thon
66. Sandlot football
67. VICA Sweetheart Contest
68. Mr. and Miss VICA Contest
69. Offer cosmetology or nursing services to nursing homes or hospitals
70. Go sightseeing in your State Capital
71. "Sacrifice Day"—use money saved from snacks, etc. for a special project
72. VICA display in shops, banks, etc.
73. Scholarship fund
74. Design and distribute VICA bumper stickers

75. Repair services for nursing homes, hospitals, or orphanages
76. Ecology survey
77. Drug seminar
78. Volunteer service at hospitals, nursing homes, youth service institutions
79. Volunteer to help local Boys' or Girls' clubs with activities
80. "Adopt" foster children or foster grandparents
81. Man booth at county or state fair
82. Job opportunities program
83. Pen-pal exchange with a "sister" VICA club
84. Grooming and hygiene workshop
85. Fashion show
86. Promote police community relations
87. Music festival
88. Essay contest
89. Oustanding citizen award
90. Vocational Education Week
91. Promote careers in teaching
92. National VICA Youth Center fund drive
93. Speakers' bureau participants talk to school and civic groups
94. "Rent-a-Kid" (a day's worth of odd jobs—money used for a special project)

Figure 41 is a sample letter introducing the VICA program to parents and students. Similar letters may be sent by any student organization, signed by superintendent, principal, or other school official, to potential vocational student organization members and their parents. Chapters throughout the country have found that such a letter can successfully boost membership; an additional benefit is that parental support can greatly enhance participation in your programs and activities.

Figure 41*

TO: Vocational/Technical Students and Parents

SUBJECT: Membership and Participation in Vocational Industrial Clubs of America (VICA)

The Vocational Industrial Clubs of America (VICA) is a national vocational student organization serving over 300,000 students who are preparing for careers in trade, industrial and technical occupations. The programs of VICA are strongly supported by business, labor, and industry as well as by the United States Office of Education and the New Jersey Department of Education.

VICA, as an integral part of the vocational education curriculum, provides numerous activities through which students develop their leadership and skill abilities for future success in the world of work.

Parliamentary procedure, public speaking, job interview, and demonstration programs and contests provide an unequaled opportunity for self-improvement and enhancement of self-concept. Trade skill contests motivate students to excellence and recognize them for achievement in their chosen occupational field.

Community, school, service, and social activities provide an avenue for students to learn planning, cooperation, and responsibility. The Vocational Initiative and Club Achievement program, administered by an Advisory Council of business/industry representatives, allows the individual student to work at his or her own pace to further develop leadership and trade knowledge and rewards each participant for his or her accomplishments.

Each shop class will have its own VICA section and will elect officers and plan a program of work which relates to vocational training. Students may also participate in school-wide activities.

Membership in VICA is $3.00 per year for state and national dues. Each member will receive:

- Four issues of the National VICA magazine
- Membership Card
- Opportunity to participate in all functions and activities and achieve recognition on the local, state, and national levels.

I am sure that you will be most pleased with the results of the VICA leadership/citizenship skills experience and the challenge and rewards its offers. I strongly urge participation in the programs of the Vocational Industrial Clubs of America.

Sincerely,

_____

          (Superintendent)

_____

*New Jersey VICA Manual, Meredith C. Hentschel, State VICA Advisor.

Figure 42

VOCATIONAL STUDENT ORGANIZATION CHECKLIST FOR TEACHER-COORDINATORS

Yes   No

_____ _____ 1. I assist and guide students in all aspects of the vocational student organization.

_____ _____ 2. I encourage use of the democratic process in all youth group functions.

_____ _____ 3. I am thoroughly familiar with the organization's goals, purposes, structure, constitution, and by-laws.

_____ _____ 4. I integrate the student organization program into my related class.

_____ _____ 5. I encourage self-initiative on the part of all members of the organization.

_____ _____ 6. I am committed to the vocational student group and its purposes.

_____ _____ 7. I endeavor to relate chapter experiences to life experiences.

_____ _____ 8. I act as a resource person.

_____ _____ 9. I provide leadership development experiences.

_____ _____ 10. I keep members informed about local, state, and national events.

_____ _____ 11. I encourage formation of alumni and advisory groups.

_____ _____ 12. I accept responsibility for supervising students participating in organizational activities in or out of school.

_____ _____ 13. I encourage members to hold state and national office.

_____ _____ 14. I endeavor to develop leadership abilities in all my students.

_____ _____ 15. I instill enthusiasm for vocational student organizations in the students.

_____ _____ 16. I assist the student in setting up adequate records and accounts.

_____ _____ 17. I help new members take part and get into the spirit of the various vocational student organization activities.

_____ _____ 18. I instruct newly elected officers in their duties.

_____ _____ 19. I keep school authorities and the public posted on vocational student organization activities and developments.

_____ _____ 20. I counsel individual members and committees on problems.

BIBLIOGRAPHY

America's turned on youth. *American Vocational Journal*, *46(6)*:22-59, September, 1971.
Carlson, Richard E.: *Memorandum, Vocational Student Organizations.*

Washington, D.C., Department of Health, Education and Welfare, Office of Education, March 20, 1978.

Directions — A Guide for VICA Club Advisors. Publication #73C2. Falls Church, Va., Vocational Industrial Clubs of America, September, 1973.

A Guide for Cooperative Vocational Education for Administrators and Coordinators. State of Indiana, Department of Public Instruction, Division of Vocational Education, 1973.

List Student Groups in Vocational Areas, Interact, Vol. 4, #2. Trenton, New Jersey State Department of Education, October, 1977.

National Advisory Council on Vocational Education, 7th Report. Washington, D.C., Vocational Student Organizations, November 15, 1972.

Work Education Diversified Occupations Cooperative Education Guidelines. Arizona Department of Education, August, 1975.

Youth With A Purpose. Youth Organizations Associated with Vocational Education. Unpublished paper, New Jersey Department of Education, 1976.

Chapter 12

PUBLIC RELATIONS PRACTICES
IN COOPERATIVE EDUCATION

COOPERATIVE EDUCATION is not like other vocational education programs and definitely not like academic programs. It is a program that requires a great deal of public relations. The school community, parents, business and industrial community, and the public at large should be kept abreast of the program's goals, what students are trying to achieve, and how they are meeting success. Cooperative vocational education is a program that can be misunderstood. It can easily become known as the program that simply finds kids a job; that only "runs a half day"; where the students are released from school to do "heaven only knows what"; where students are placed for disciplinary reasons. A good public relations program can correct these misconceptions.

Good public relations evolves around the teacher-coordinator. It involves effective communications with the public describing the program's concepts, objectives, ideals, and successes. Public relations is a constant activity. The teacher-coordinator must not assume for a moment that all is well with the understanding of the program if they merely place an occasional article in the newspaper or have a general discussion with teachers about the program. Because cooperative education is an alternative to the traditional classroom, because it involves the business/industrial community, and because parents are concerned with their sons' and daughters' learning pursuits, public relations becomes the means by which the general public is kept abreast of the program.

Public relations can become a difficult chore if one tries to do it all at once. If that is the approach one chooses to pursue, the public relations campaign will probably fail. Public relations requires systematic planning, step-by-step on a monthly basis. It is wise for a teacher-coordinator to sit down either before school begins or shortly thereafter and map out the public relations program for the year. Public relations should be spread across the entire school year to maintain a positive image. Before you begin mapping out your yearly activities, you should first identify the persons and/or agencies you wish to reach through your campaign.

PERSONS AND AGENCIES

Boards of Education

It is essential that the Board of Education have a working knowledge of the co-op program. Cooperative education can be reviewed by an unknowing board as a costly program in relation to the total number of students it serves. A public relations program for the board of education should include a slide/tape presentation followed by statistical data on the success of the program. The statistics should include the total number of students served on a yearly basis, the total dollars earned, the hours worked, and the types of training establishments in which student-learners received on-the-job experiences. The coordinator should field questions from board members. Invite them, whenever possible, to attend functions such as youth organization activities, employer/employee banquets, and on-site visitations to training stations.

School Administrators

The boss must know what the employee is doing. This is an old axiom taken from the business world. It is important that the school administration know what is taking place in the cooperative education program. A well-informed administration will be most supportive. If the administration does not know what is taking place in the co-op program, it could be the first program cut in time of a budget crunch. The coordinator should submit quarterly statistical reports on the program's activities to the administration. The coordinator should always submit a summary report on any professional conference or in-service activity attended. The coordinator should also provide the administration with a report that outlines the monthly visitations made to students on the job.

Most importantly, the teacher-coordinator should invite administrators to spend a day or two with them supervising students on the job in various job training stations. The coordinator should schedule a normal supervisory day. Administrators should be requested to participate in the entire supervisory experience even if the time element exceeds the normal school day.

Community Organizations

A major target group for public relations is the Chamber of Commerce, Lions Club, and PTA. Members often serve as judges for youth organization activities and donors of equipment to co-op programs. Community organizations will invite coordinators to be guest speakers at their meetings. Quite often, they will provide the speaker with favorable publicity before and after the event. Most importantly, it provides the coordinator with an audience who can promote the program.

Merchants and Other Business/Industry Persons in the Community

The business/industry community is a major target population for a massive public relations campaign. Merchants and business-industry people are more than delighted to come into the school system to make presentations. They are eager to discuss the benefits to be derived from their company operations. They will prepare talks on job interviews, safety, consumerism, and a host of other areas.

Local Employment Agencies

The employment bureau is a major source of job training stations. If they are aware of your program, they could make referrals for you and they could be attuned to your particular needs. When job opportunities come up they could forward information that would benefit your program. They need to know that there is a way for the school and their agency to work harmoniously toward a common end. A good public relations program with the local employment bureau will pay off in great dividends.

Labor Organizations

It has been proven through multiple examples and studies that when teacher-coordinators make contact with labor unions there are very few, if any, problems in having a cooperative education program initiated in a "union shop." On the contrary, where teacher-coordinators do not make contact with the labor organizations, they have much difficulty in trying to promote a cooperative vocational education program in unionized companies.

Labor organizations have to be made aware of the cooperative education concept, namely, that student-learners are not employees but student-learners; that the job is a training station and not merely a part-time work station; that students are going to receive a diversity of on-the-job training activities that would not normally be afforded to the regular employee. Once the concepts of cooperative education are understood by organized labor leaders, there is very little difficulty in initiating a cooperative education program. It is also wise to involve organized labor in the co-op advisory committee. They can be of tremendous assistance in providing the program with employment outlook projections, assistance in overcoming labor disputes, and easy acceptability to employment training stations.

Legislators

An enlightened legislator, one who understands a cooperative vocational education program, will be a tremendous asset to any school program. Legislators are often involved in writing bills that affect Child Labor Laws and employers. Legislators who are aware of coordinators' needs for program improvement, financial support, and vocational objectives will initiate legislation that can benefit co-op programs. Legislators should be invited to see programs, they should be invited to participate in award ceremonies, and they should be invited, as presenters, to in-service teacher-organization conferences.

Guidance Counselors

One of two things will happen if guidance counselors do not understand the cooperative vocational education program: no students will be forwarded to your program and/or only undesirable problem students will be forwarded to your program. Guidance counselors should be thoroughly provided with information about your program. They should also be given in-service training in cooperative education.

Teachers

The majority of teachers in a school system teach five or six subjects per day. They do not understand the role of the teacher-coordinator, who may only teach one or two related classes and then be released from the school's premises to do on-the-job supervision. It is important that they understand the coordinator's involvement in cooperative vocational education. It is important that other teachers in the school system respect the co-op program and the students it serves. There has to be a very close working relationship among all teachers in the school system. Teachers can provide feedback to the teacher-coordinator on a student's progress in an academic area that can be strengthened in a related class. If teachers do not understand the program, they will discourage students from entering the program.

Parents and Guardians

If parents are not aware of what the cooperative education program is all about, they will not allow students to participate in it. Parents are traditionally geared to have students go to class from 9:00 A.M. to 3:00 P.M. They are not accustomed to having their children released at the noon hour to go to a job training station for a learning experience. Parents have to be assured that learning will take place, that the program is educationally sound, and that it meets the needs of their youngsters.

Students

If students are not aware of the program, there is no program. Obviously, students will not elect a cooperative vocational education program if they are not aware of the program. They must be made aware that they have to commit themselves to the program, that it involves more than simply earning a dollar, and that there is an educational component.

Newspapers, Radio, and Television Personnel

It will serve the cooperative vocational education program well if the teacher-coordinator makes friends or acquaintances with personnel in the newspaper, radio, and television media. A great many action-oriented activities take place in a cooperative vocational education program; if the teacher-coordinator has access to individuals within the communications media who can assist in getting their material in print, or on the air, it will benefit the program tremendously. Students can be invited to be participants in radio talk shows and television programs. Articles on students at their job-training stations are good newspaper reading material. The media can be invited to view youth organization contests, open house days at the school, vocational and education career days, and any educational activity that has community appeal.

PUBLIC RELATIONS ACTIVITIES

The list of public relations activities is endless. Listed below are thirty public relation activities that teacher-coordinators have successfully used in the past.

1. Preparation and dissemination of timely brochures on cooperative education programs to meet target populations of potential employers, parents, students, and the community at large.
2. Speaking invitations.
3. Radio and television spot announcements.
4. Editorials, feature stories in newspapers and magazines.
5. Advanced notices about upcoming events.
6. Employer-Employee banquets.
7. Proclamations for Cooperative Education Week by public officials such as the mayor and/or governor.

8. Slide/tape presentations on the program.
9. Follow-up news releases of special events.
10. Charitable activities such as Christmas toys for orphans and needy youngsters, visits to old-age homes, turkey dinners for the elderly and the poor.
11. Effective utilization of advisory committees.
12. Distribution of course enrollment statistics.
13. Participating in student organization activities.
14. Involving the community as judges in student organization activities.
15. Exhibits at educational conventions.
16. Participation in career days at the school.
17. Community surveys.
18. Periodic status reports on the program.
19. Billboards taken out by cooperating employers that exemplify the values of co-op.
20. Advertisements taken out in newspapers by cooperating employers.
21. Recognition of an outstanding student as "Cooperative Student of the Year."
22. Recognition of an employer as "Cooperative Employer of the Year."
23. Holding co-op exhibits at shopping malls.
24. High school bulletin boards in heavy traffic school corridors.
25. Buttons stating "Co-op Works."
26. Certificates of recognition for outstanding achievement in the area of cooperative education.
27. Decals and/or certificates to be displayed in cooperating employers windows or on walls saying "We Participate in the Cooperative Education Program."
28. Conducting conferences and/or in-service workshops for administrators, guidance counselors, parents, and cooperating employers.
29. Disseminating favors such as printed mugs, glasses, pens, calendars, etc., that place the Cooperative Education logo and the name of the school on the items.
30. Automobile decal with the co-op logo on it.

TARGET DATES

Once you have identified your audience and the types of public relation activities you wish to engage in, you should then take a calendar and mark off potential dates to fulfill the public relation activities. Remember that the teacher-coordinator is not expected to do everything by him– or herself. Use the management technique of delegating. Students are more than willing to assist when given proper instructions and the freedom to carry out the assignment. They can be a tremendous asset to your public relations campaign.

If your school system has a public relations director, meet with that person frequently and work out arrangements for that individual to assist you in your public relations campaign. Utilize your advisory committee members effectively in the public relations campaign. There should be a standing public relations committee to promote the cooperative education program.

Calendar for Public Relations Activities

Summer Months

1. Canvas job training stations, secure new ones, maintain contact with old ones.
2. Prepare news releases for both school and community newspapers.
3. Begin selecting training stations and sending students for placement.
4. Schedule presentation time for faculty orientation to the co-op program.
5. Begin visitation of parents.
6. Check the physical equipment, arrangement of rooms, availability of textbooks and supplies.
7. Work on related class materials, review audiovisual materials.
8. Get acquainted with owners and managers of business and industrial firms.
9. Review current minimum wage and hour laws.
10. Review and update career information materials with counselors and librarians.
11. Arrange to speak to as many civic organizations as possible.

September

1. Plan orientation program for new students and teachers.
2. Conduct an employer training sponsor meeting.
3. Contact newspaper editor and reporters, radio and television program managers. Send releases on expansion of programs and projects and arrange for at least five or six articles on individual students while they are on the job.
4. Initiate plans for conducting a vocational student organization for the year. Publicize the organization through the local community newspaper as well as the school newspaper.
5. Prepare a list of advisory committee members and request your superintendent to mail invitations from his/her office.

October

1. Plan a schedule for advisory committee meetings.
2. Have students prepare a bulletin board or window display regarding the objectives of the co-op program.
3. Visit and observe students at their training stations.
4. Invite board members and school administrators to attend related classes, as well as visits to on-the-job training stations.
5. Contact your audiovisual coordinator and arrange to make a slide or film presentation on your co-op program.
6. Prepare news releases regarding employer follow-up surveys.
7. Have your youth organization participate in Education Week activities.
8. Sponsor your first youth organization fund-raising project.

November

1. Plan and conduct a radio or television program explaining the purposes of the organization as well as the values of the program.
2. Invite state and federal legislators to visit and observe the program.
3. Invite community resource speakers to the related class and submit news releases regarding the speakers to your community and school newspapers.

4. Plan an outdoor billboard display somewhere within the community.
5. Schedule and develop an agenda for your second training sponsor program and emphasize techniques for evaluation.
6. Arrange to speak at another civic organization meeting.
7. Arrange for a free spot announcement on a local radio program regarding a youth organization activity.
8. Change bulletin boards and displays.

December

1. Attend the American Vocational Association (AVA) national meeting and prepare news releases covering your attendance and participation.
2. Plan and conduct a student assembly program.
3. Have youth organizations participate in a civic activity such as visits to a retirement home, orphanage, pediatrics ward, etc.
4. Submit quarterly reports to administrators, advisers, and SEA personnel.
5. Visit training stations regularly.
6. Schedule monthly club meetings and plan activities for state leadership conference.
7. Write a professional article about cooperative vocational education to trade papers and professional journals such as the *AVA Journal, DE Today, Cooperative Education Quarterly.*

January

1. Prepare brochures and submit them to business and community representatives.
2. Submit the next article in your series on individual students on the job to your local newspaper. Remember to include photos of the student on the job.
3. Prepare additional newspaper articles on the progress of your vocational students.
4. Arrange for students to speak to local civic groups.
5. Arrange for students to conduct career awareness sessions at the elementary schools.

6. Conduct a five-year follow-up study.
7. Prepare for Vocational Education Week in February.
8. Prepare for Cooperative Work Experience Education Day in February.

February

1. Contact cable or public television stations for a program on the values of co-op. Include students, teacher-coordinators, cooperating employers, and state department personnel in the program activities.
2. Encourage youth organization members to individually prepare themselves for any competitive events at the state leadership conference.
3. Conduct an advisory committee meeting.
4. Begin employer-employee banquet plans.

March

1. Continue to visit training stations regularly.
2. Conduct an alumni meeting.
3. Attend professional association meetings and in-service training sessions. Submit report on your activities to your administration.
4. Prepare bumper sticker stating "Cooperative Education Works."
5. Prepare releases regarding participation in student organizations as well as advisory committee meetings and the alumni follow-up study.
6. Collect occupational information and give this information to your school guidance counselors.

April

1. Arrange for school newspaper coverage of an employer of the month.
2. Change bulletin boards and school marquees.
3. Arrange for free radio spot announcements on your upcoming employer-employee appreciation banquet.
4. Plan a co-op and youth organization exhibit at one of the local shopping malls.

  5. Conduct a student-parent night for those who wish to enter the cooperative education program next school year.

May

  1. Visit training stations to thank employers personally for participating in the cooperative education program. Prepare an in-school display of trophies and/or certificates for any state or national competitive event winners.

  2. Select an outstanding cooperative education student to receive an award at graduation.

  3. Conduct an employer-employee appreciation breakfast, lunch, or dinner. Invite council members, parents, newspaper reporters, members of the board of education, and administrative staff to the banquet. Invitations may be on a rotating basis so as to minimize costs.

  4. Present every employer with a certificate of appreciation.

  5. Present every advisory committee member with a certificate of participation.

  6. Prepare your annual report.

June

  1. Prepare letters of appreciation to training sponsors, advisory committee members, parents, news media personnel, and other individuals who have contributed to your cooperative education program.

  2. Prepare and submit all state-required forms prior to the deadline.

  3. Submit releases regarding permanent job placements.

  4. Show a slide/tape presentation to in-school assembly groups and community organizations on the activities of your co-op students for the year.

GETTING YOUR MESSAGE HEARD

There is no mystery behind getting your program into the news media. It simply requires a great deal of planning and some initiative on the part of the teacher-coordinator and the students. A few simple rules will assist the teacher-coordinator immensely in carrying out an effective public relations campaign.

News Releases

Newspapers are in the business to sell local interest items. Multiple newspaper copies are bought by individuals who see their names in the newspaper. Every teacher-coordinator should keep this fact in mind. "Names make the news," therefore, take every opportunity to list as many local newsworthy names as you can when developing a news release.

Before writing any news release, the teacher-coordinator should compile a list of all of the newspaper media in the vicinity. This should include local, area, county, and tri-county newspapers. The coordinator should list the names, addresses, and telephone numbers of individuals to contact at the newspaper. Heading the list should be the educational editor for each newspaper.

Coordinators should also canvas the school, advisory committee members, and cooperating employers to see if they have relatives and/or friends associated with the news media. Do not be hesitant in following through with these potential contacts. A wise coordinator gets to know the news media on a personal first name basis. Remember, the teacher-coordinator has to take the initiative to bring the information to the newspaper. Very little effective public relations will occur if the coordinator sits back and waits for the newspaper to come to the school.

Tips on Writing an Effective News Release

Every good news release should have a lead that captures the attention of the reader and makes them want to know more. The article should answer the five basic questions of who, what, when, where and why. The first paragraph should be the most important paragraph providing the major lead and giving the story in a nutshell. Each succeeding paragraph should be of declining importance, the last paragraph being the least important paragraph; if cut it would make very little difference to the article. When writing a news release adhere to the following principles:

1. Write short sentences.
2. Write short paragraphs.

3. Type the news release on 8½ by 11 plain paper on one side of the sheet.
4. Leave margins of at least an inch and a half on each side of the paper.
5. Type the name of the individual who can be contacted at the school, namely, the teacher-coordinator, along with the address and telephone number.
6. Type double spaced.
7. Use names, dates, times, and places accurately.
8. Whenever possible, include photographs.
9. Deliver your release well in advance of the deadline.
10. Submit an article at least once a month.

Photographs

Photographs enhance any news release and definitely should be used when submitting articles for publication. When submitting photographs always adhere to the following simple rules:

1. Submit 8 by 10 black and white glossies.
2. Attach captions that tell the complete story.
3. Identify the people in the picture.
4. Never use paper clips on a picture.
5. Never write on the back of a picture.
6. Type out the caption and paste it to the photograph.
7. Avoid Polaroids® or small prints.
8. Forward only clear pictures that tell the story you want told.
9. If you desire to have your photographs returned, state so and provide a self-addressed stamped envelope.
10. If you cannot provide your own photographs, request a photographer from the news media.

Radio and Television

The same principles should apply to the radio and television media as apply to the newspaper and publications media. Compile a list of all of the radio and television stations. Identify individuals who are associated with the media who could be of assistance to you in getting your messages on the air. List names, addresses, and telephone numbers and keep an up-to-date file on your contacts. Remember that both the radio and television networks are looking for public spot announcements that can easily fit into a program and that will be of community interest.

Radio spot announcements should be usually ten, thirty, or sixty seconds. They should be typewritten, double spaced on plain white paper, and submitted to the radio station at least ten days in advance of the time that they are to be aired. These radio spot announcements are normally provided free of charge if they deal with a community activity.

Spot announcements can be used effectively to announce a car wash that is going to gain money for a state competitive event contest, to announce an open house at the school, to encourage cooperating employers to participate in the co-op program. In addition to the free spot announcements, radio also provides opportunities for interview shows between an individual or two, as well as panel or group discussions. A great deal of thought should be given to what can be done on the radio show. It is up to the teacher-coordinator to take the initiative to contact the radio to offer suggestions for a show.

In the area of television promotion, the public broadcasting authority often is looking for interesting activities to air, such as youth organization contests, career days, skits and talk shows put on by cooperative education teacher-coordinators and students. Cable television is another major source that can be utilized by the teacher coordinator.

Audiovisual Material

Almost every school district has access to audiovisual equipment to prepare slides, films, and videotapes. Most schools have a media specialist and even offer classes in the subject; the students can assist the teacher coordinator in preparing homemade but professionally done sound slide tape presentations and videotapes. The making of a film usually requires a little bit more professional assistance, but this too can be secured from local colleges and universities who have programs in the communications media and who would be willing to assist in preparing a film on cooperative education.

Of the three visual methods presented above, slides are perhaps the easiest and most effective visual presentation. Slides are relatively inexpensive to produce. All that is required is a 35 millimeter camera. You can take many still shots of co-op students with cooperating employers on the job, of youth organization activities, of parent nights, etc. A slide/tape presentation is a tremendous way of wrapping up the year by showing the community the activities in which the cooperative education students participated throughout the year.

Printed Materials

The most inexpensive public relations media is the printed material that can be provided through brochures, flyers and bulletins. Although relatively inexpensive to produce, a great deal of thought and planning should go into everything that comes out in the form of printed public relations. The teacher-coordinator can request the assistance of the graphic arts class and the print shop to prepare attractive brochures, flyers, and bulletins. Within any given school system there usually is a pool of individuals who have typing skills, from students to clerical help, that can possibly be utilized in developing a professional looking brochure. If you solicit in-school assistance, it should be a cooperative effort. Teaching must be the primary purpose. An attractive public relations brochure will emanate from a well-coordinated in-school public relations activity.

Additional Public Relations

ANNUAL REPORTS: Many teacher-coordinators are required to submit to their state department an annual report on the number of students who participated in the program, the total dollars earned, and locations of employment. This type of information should not only be used to supply information to administrators and state department staff, it can also be used as a public relations tool to inform the school community, the parents, and the employment community of the cooperative education program.

SPEAKERS BUREAU: The teacher-coordinator and the cooperative education students should prepare talks on multiple aspects of vocational education, cooperative education, and youth organization activities. These topics can be presented to service organizations such as the PTA, Chamber of Commerce, and Lions Club. Participating students can be rotated to accommodate their on-the-job learning schedule. Additions to the speakers bureau can be advisory committee members and cooperating employers who may wish to make presentations on behalf of the school.

PREPARATION OF DISPLAYS: Teacher-coordinators should take advantage of preparing exhibits and displays for fairs and statewide conventions. With the increasing number of shopping malls that have come into existence, the enclosed malls are constantly looking for community and civic activities that can take place in their main walking corridors. This is an ideal place for an exhibit on cooperative education. It can be manned by cooperative education students who explain the purposes and goals of their co-op program and their youth organization.

Another avenue for display is to prepare a float that can be used in local community parades. This float can be used at baseball and football games as well as scout jamborees.

OUTDOOR ADVERTISEMENT: Attractive billboards displayed within the community are an excellent source of public relations. The cost factor for putting up a billboard could be expensive; however, the teacher-coordinator should check with the alumni to see if they have anyone who is in the business or can request that cooperating employers help defray the cost of putting up an advertisement. Often overlooked, but an ideal source for billboard displays, are banks and hotels that have marquees outside of their establishment, including the school system that has a marquee to announce school activities. Bus or taxi display cards are other possibilities.

Employer-Employee Banquet

One of the most demanding, and probably the most rewarding, public relations activity of the cooperative education program is the employer-employee banquet. It is an activity that requires a great deal of planning and it is an activity that should involve all the student-learners in the program.

As the name suggests, the employer-employee banquet is one at which the student-learners demonstrate their appreciation to the cooperating employers for their participation in the program. These appreciation functions are usually held toward the end of the school year. The appreciation banquet need not be an elaborate dinner function, although many are semiformal dinner engagements. The function can be a breakfast, lunch, brunch, outdoor picnic, or dinner. It can be held at a fancy restaurant or it can be held within the school complex. What is important is the fact that the student-learners, in cooperation with the school administration and the cooperative education advisory committee, acknowledge the cooperating employer as an essential member of the cooperative education team.

The purposes of the employer-employee banquet are—

1. To express appreciation to cooperating employers for their participation in the program.
2. To recognize the linkages between the school and the community through the cooperative vocational education program.
3. To provide the student-learners with a major learning function, since they must plan, coordinate, and implement the entire banquet function.
4. To present to cooperating employers and advisory committee members certificates of appreciation for their involvement in the success of the program.
5. To publicize the program and maintain a positive image within the business/industry community.

The planning for the employer-employee banquet should begin shortly after the school year begins. A great deal of preparation and student involvement must occur if the banquet function is to be a success. Committees must be appointed and there must be close coordination between the committee chairpeople and the teacher-coordinator.

Items to be considered in planning the function include—

1. The location (restaurant, school, picnic grounds)
2. The source of funds to cover the costs of the entire function

Figure 43

In recognition and appreciation for service as a Cooperating Training Agency
for students enrolled in the Diversified Cooperative Training Program.

(donations, school board appropriation, fund raisers, student assessment)

3. The invitational list (all cooperating employers, state officials, school administrators, school board members, selected faculty, and advisory committee members)

4. The guest speaker (who, topic, length of time)

5. The recognition of employers (certificates, favors, introductions). See Figure 43.

6. The publicity (printed invitations, printed program booklet, news releases, photographer-newspaper coverage)

7. The establishment of a detailed task chart and a calendar of assignments to be completed (committees, restaurant, invitations, menu).

Figure 44

PUBLIC RELATIONS CHECKLIST FOR TEACHER-COORDINATORS

Yes   No

_____ _____   1. I keep the public informed of the program's concepts, objectives, ideals, and successes.

_____ _____   2. I systematically plan the public relations program, step-by-step, on a monthly basis.

_____ _____   3. I keep the board of education informed of the goals, objectives, and outcomes of the cooperative education program.

_____ _____   4. I submit quarterly statistical reports on the program's activities to the administration.

_____ _____   5. I utilize members of community organizations, as well as business and industry, to prepare talks to students on a host of pertinent topics.

_____ _____   6. I familiarize labor organizations with the cooperative education concept.

_____ _____   7. I maintain contact with the communications media.

_____ _____   8. I invite the communications media to view youth organization contests, open house days at the school, and all educational activity that has community appeal.

_____ _____   9. I prepare slide-tape presentations on the program.

_____ _____   10. I effectively utilize my advisory committee members in the public relations campaign.

_____ _____   11. I prepare and disseminate timely brochures on cooperative education programs.

_____ _____   12. I prepare a yearly calendar of public relations activities.

_____ _____   13. I prepare spot announcements on cooperative education for radio and television coverage.

_____ _____   14. I utilize the employer-employee banquet to express appreciation to cooperating employers for their participation in the program.

_____ _____   15. I assist the student-learners in preparing the employer-employee banquet by coordinating their activities.

BIBLIOGRAPHY

Bagin, Don and Lefever, Dave: *How to Gain Public Support for Your School's Budget and Bond Issue.* Glassboro, NJ, Glassboro State College Press, 1971.

———: Grazian, Frank, and Harrison, Charles H.: *School Communications: Ideas that Work.* Woodstown, NJ, Communicaid Incorporated, 1972.

Bortner, Doyle M.: *Public Relations for Public Schools.* Morristown, NJ, General Learning Press, 1972.

Ferguson, Ralph (Ed.): *School/Community Relations Innovative Program Techniques Handbook.* Phoenix, Arizona Department of Education and the Arizona School Public Relations Association 1978.

Ferrucci, Francis A.: On the track. *Cooperative Education Quarterly,* 6, May 1978.

Hoffner, Jack: *News Writing For Education and Cooperative Programs.* Cherry Hill, NJ, Cherry Hill High School East, 1975.

Marx, Gary: *Radio: Your Publics are Listening.* Washington, D.C., National School Board Association, 1976.

National Association of Broadcasters: *If You Want Air Time.* Washington, D.C., 1970.

New Jersey Advisory Council on Vocational Education: *Practical Public Relations Program.* Trenton, New Jersey, 1970.

Newsom, Doug and Scott, Alan: *This is PR: The Realities of Public Relations.* Belmont, CA, Wadsworth, 1976.

Pemberton, Evelyn Deloris: Selling vocational education during vocational education week. *Cooperative Education Quarterly,* 15, November 1978.

Public Relations Guide. Cincinnati, Proctor and Gamble Educational Services, 1975.

A Resource for New Jersey Cooperative Office Education Coordinator. New Jersey State Department of Education, Division of Vocational Education and Career Preparation, June 1973.

Tilden, Scott W.: *Communicating Via Radio: 101 How-to-Ideas.* Mr. Scott W. Tilden, 560 North Madison Road, Guilford, CT, 06437, 1975.

Van Gulik, Richard and Pfeiffer, E. Weston: Commercializing co-op. *Cooperative Education Quarterly,* 8-9, May 1978.

Walker, John E. and Perez, Richard L.: *Public Relations: A Team Effort.* Midland, MI, Pendell Pub, 1976.

Chapter 13

MANAGERIAL TECHNIQUES
FOR TEACHER-COORDINATORS

TIME MANAGEMENT

IN THE CHAPTER ON THE ROLE of the teacher-coordinator, it was stated that a teacher-coordinator's job description often has many similarities to several careers. It is not uncommon for a teacher-coordinator to function in five distinct roles in one day. A typical example illustrating the many roles of the teacher-coordinator can be found in the daily work schedule (Fig. 45). The typical daily routine of a teacher-coordinator is varied and very time-consuming. A teacher-coordinator has to be able to do, and handle, several different activities on a routine daily basis in order to accomplish the duties and objectives of his or her program.

Bill G. Gooch in an article appearing in the *Cooperative Edu-*

Figure 45

Role	Time	Activity
Teacher	9:00 A.M.	Teach related class. Begin unit on job interview.
Guidance Counselor	11:00 A.M.	Conduct student counseling session on post-secondary schools on an individualized basis.
Coordinator	1:00 P.M.	On-the-job supervision. Review the training plan for the student-learner with his/her cooperating employer.
Administrator	3:00 P.M.	Advisory committee meeting. Establish scholarship fund and report on the five-year follow-up study of cooperative education graduates.
Public Relations	7:30 P.M.	Chamber of Commerce meeting. Making a presentation to the members on the advantages of providing training opportunities for cooperative education students.

cation Quarterly (Volume I, Number 3, November 1978), entitled "The Key to Success" states the following: "Shock is likely to be the initial reaction of the person who studies the responsibilities of the teacher-coordinator. After the shock subsides, disbelief normally sets in. This shock and disbelief will likely result if Cotrell's 385 performance activities associated with the duties and responsibilities of a coordinator are studied or if one of the numerous state Cooperative Education manuals are investigated." In order to accomplish all that needs to be done, a teacher-coordinator should know how to manage his or her time effectively.

In order to effectively manage one's time, one has to be organized. There are simple techniques that a teacher-coordinator can use in order to get the most use of his or her time. Step number one, according to all the literature on the study of time management, is to have a "things I have to do today" list. This "things I have to do today" list can be something that can be purchased at a stationery store or it can be a plain piece of paper on which you list and prioritize your daily activities. Column space should be set aside for the coordinator to check off completed items. The first thing a coordinator should do at the beginning of the work day, or at the conclusion of work for the next day, is to prepare a "things I have to do today" list. Once the list is made out, a coordinator should review the list to determine which of the items have greatest priority and prioritize them accordingly.

Because of the heavy work load and the things that have to be done, it is conceivable that you will never get to item number two— to prepare the financial report for next week's Teacher-Coordinator Association meeting (Fig. 46). What you should be able to do is determine which is more important, item number two or item number eight. Both requre some extensive writing, thinking, and preparation. To let items two and eight go by the wayside completely would be a fallacy because, if you keep procrastinating, neither one of these two activities is going to be accomplished in time. Prioritize to determine which is more important and begin to piecemeal it, even if you only have fifteen minutes left in your regular school day. Fifteen minutes today, another half hour or twenty minutes squeezed in tomorrow, and the financial report

Figure 46

THINGS I HAVE TO DO TODAY

Date: October 20, 1978

Completed

———— 1. Call the Labor Department on their latest regulations concerning student-learner's minimum wages.

———— 2. Prepare the financial report for next week's Teacher-Coordinators Association Meeting.

———— 3. Call Joe White of XYZ Safety Company to see if he will speak to the related class sometime next month on OSHA standards.

———— 4. See Mary White of E-Z Insurance Company and review the training plan for student-learner Joe Blake.

———— 5. Order flowers for Arlene's birthday tomorrow.

———— 6. Make sure everything is set for the Advisory Committee meeting this afternoon — agenda, coffee and danish, name tags and plates, conference room, etc.

———— 7. Pick up slide projector for this evening's Chamber of Commerce presentation on "The Values of Participating in a Cooperative Vocational Education program."

———— 8. Finish class assignment on certification standards for Thursday evening class.

and class assignment will be accomplished.

Many items that are not completed on Monday's "things I have to do today" list should be transferred to Tuesday's "things I have to do today" list.   And again, one must prioritize.

Steps to Save Time

The steps involved in organizing your time are (1) list all the things you have to do; (2) determine how much time each activity requires to accomplish the job; (3) prioritize activities in their order of importance; (4) determine if you can get others to perform some of the tasks; (5) group activities that can be done at a given time, such as making telephone calls during a certain period of the day when you know that you will be able to reach the parties you are attempting to contact; (6) prepare a realistic timetable to complete given assignments, including time for long-range planning and thinking; (7) review your emergency situations to better plan and forecast your work load so you do not run into situations that require immediate attention.

Finally, place your plan of action into motion, review long-range and short-range goals, and determine those things that need to be done at the precise time that you need to do them.

Short and Long Range Planning

It will save the teacher-coordinator a great deal of time in the long run if he or she spends several hours, or even a day, sitting down and developing long-range goals and short-range goals for the school year. Teacher-coordinators know that there are times of the year when they have to perform certain functions. For example, the teacher-coordinator knows that sometime during the fall he or she will hold an advisory committee meeting. Plans can be made and a tentative date set aside for an advisory committee meeting. From past experience the coordinator will know during which months organization activities will take place, when vocational education week will be held, etc. The coordinator should take his or her calendar book and begin to pencil in target dates to complete activities. For example, coordinators know that they have to complete an end-of-the-year report to their board of education and possibly to the department of education, that includes the total number of students enrolled in the program, the total hours they worked, their total earnings, the types of occupations they held, and the job placement rate after graduation. The teacher-coordinator should have some kind of mechanism to gather this information beginning day one of the school year.

A review of the chapter on public relations, specifically the calendar for public relations activities, will give the teacher-coordinator an idea of the type of planning that can be done on a monthly basis for long-term planning. The activities that are listed for the month can be broken down further for the daily "things I have to do today" list. The coordinator should develop a specific time frame to allow ample time to accomplish the set objectives. Frequently, the teacher-coordinator must initiate action in September to implement an activity in November. If a coordinator doesn't outline those activities that he or she wants to do for the entire year, it will be almost impossible for the coordinator to accomplish all the activities they would like to see done.

Some Proven Time-Saving Ideas[1]

A review of the literature has indicated the following tips on how to maximize an individual's time:

1. Develop specific goals for the year, long- and short-range.
2. Make a "things I have to do today" list at a regular time each day.
3. Prioritize the "things I have to do today" list.
4. Endeavor to beat or meet your designated deadline.
5. Schedule as many activities in your day as is practical.
6. Do not allow interruptions to keep you from completing your priority—return to your priority item immediately after interruptions.
7. Do not overact to crises situations, stick to the priorities you have set.
8. Establish a quiet time at home or at work in which you can concentrate on assigned tasks.
9. Let everyone know that you do not wish to be disturbed during your quiet hour.
10. Avoid a cluttered desk—when things are in order it is easier and more efficient to get work done.

Telephone Time-Saving Tips

1. Arrange to make as many telephone calls as you can at any one given time.
2. Jot down on a sheet of paper, prior to making your telephone calls, the telephone numbers and notations on what you want to cover before you make the call.
3. Keep all calls to a short time frame.
4. Make all telephone calls businesslike and to the point.
5. Make sure that you use the telephone to your advantage,

---

[1]Adapted from an unpublished conference handout "Time Saving Ideas" by J.V McGuigan, 1978.

making outgoing calls to individuals at times when you know you will catch them in their office.

6. Know the different time zones and make these time zones work for you.
7. If you cannot reach your party on the phone, do not waste time—leave a message.
8. If your party is not available to take your call, speak to someone else who may be able to help you.
9. Provide your secretary with training so that she can take messages and answer questions whenever possible.

Time-Saving Tips for Conducting Meetings

1. Start and end all meetings on time.
2. Stick to predetermined time schedules.
3. Begin meetings even if one or two people are missing or late.
4. Arrange to hold formal meetings just before quitting time or just before lunch.
5. Schedule meetings and appointments back-to-back—this forces you to keep deadlines.

Tips on Handling Mail

1. Do not concentrate on junk mail—either save it and read it when you have a few hours to kill or file in the wastebasket.
2. Do not read incoming mail unless you have time to act on it.
3. As you read your mail make notations on the letter outlining a response.
4. Only handle mail once, do something with it; for example delegate it to someone to take further action, dictate a letter or a memo as a response, circulate it to others for their information, or file it in the wastebasket.

REMEMBERING NAMES

The teacher-coordinator comes in contact with many individuals on any given day, for example, there are students, parents, cooperating employers, advisory committee members, fellow teacher-coordinators, state department officials, labor department officials, fellow teachers in the school system, and general acquaintances.

A common complaint of the teacher-coordinator is "I know so many people by sight, but I cannot recall their names and it is embarrassing to say, " 'Hi, there,' 'Hello,' 'How are You?' 'How is it going?' " These are all phrases of individuals who do not remember another person's name. A teacher-coordinator is like a salesperson. They meet many individuals and they must know their names if they are going to be successful in selling their product, namely, student-learners.

There are some simple techniques that a teacher-coordinator can use in assisting him or her to remember peoples' names. The first technique is to get the person's name the first time that you meet them. How many times have you been introduced to someone by a third party and you nod your head and shake their hand but you quite frankly never get to hear the name? The reason is quite common. People who introduce others frequently mumble the other person's name; frequently the individual who is being introduced does not listen to the name of the other person; or no concerted effort is made to retain the name in their memory.

A simple technique that can be used by the coordinator to remember a person's name is to repeat the name immediately after hearing it. For example, when someone says "I would like to introduce you to Mr. Bill Smith," repeat "How do you do Mr. Smith? It is nice to know you Mr. Smith." By repeating the person's name you are fixing it in your memory.

Another clue to remembering someone's name is to try to make an association with that name. If you were introduced to a Mr. William Shefsky, in addition to the techniques given above, an association you can make with Mr. Shefsky would be a mental picture of Bill with a chef's hat on skiing down a slope. Of course, you don't have to tell the other person the type of association you made, but you should try to fix into your mind some kind of an association that would help you to recall that name at a later date. The sillier and the more absurd the association the better the chances of your retaining the name.

If you can recall even part of the name, like chef, and forget about the association you made about him skiing down the slope, the mere fact that you remembered the first half of the name will automatically help you to recall the second part. People have the tendency to remember things if they can get a portion of the name they are trying to recall. Continue to repeat the name throughout the conversation as often as you can. This repetition will enable you to fix the name in your memory.

Another technique is to take a genuine interest in the people you are introduced to. Make specific mental images of their looks and personalities, and inquire about their jobs and their families. Try to learn at least one or two names a day. At your leisure, in the evening or later during the day after you have met someone, write down their name. By using multiple senses (writing the name using your manual dexterity; seeing their name in print; spelling out the name; pronouncing the name; and then associating the name) you will have that much more of an opportunity to recall the name.

The techniques outlined above are only techniques that will work if they are put into practice on a daily basis. Coordinators cannot possibly forget a name if they have never taken the time to hear or know the name. Therefore, listening is a very important factor in the remembering process.

Teacher-coordinators must be attentive to the introduction of individuals. If a teacher-coordinator cannot recall the name of the student, parent, cooperating employer, or an advisory committee member, this places the teacher-coordinator in a very poor light. The following summary will provide a teacher-coordinator with pointers on remembering names:

1. The teacher-coordinator will make a considerable effort to learn people's names.
2. The coordinator will make sure to hear the name clearly.
3. The coordinator should repeat the name frequently in the conversation so as to implant it in the mind.
4. The coordinator should request that a person repeat their name or even spell their name, if they were unable to get the name the first time.
5. Look for some associations to help you recall the name.

6. On a daily basis, write down the name (s) of people you meet.

7. Attempt to learn at least one new name a day.

COMMUNICATIONS

A major barrier to effective communications is the inability of individuals to listen. A teacher-coordinator cannot afford to have this kind of barrier in his or her communication process. Much of what a coordinator does depends on the ability to listen to other individuals. For example: a teacher-coordinator should listen attentively to what an advisory committee member has to say about future employment trends in the labor market. If coordinators do not listen to what is being communicated to them, they might find themselves having students who are unemployable because the occupational choices their students wish to enter no longer exist in the job market. Equally important is the communications that are transmitted by cooperating employers to teacher-coordinators during regular visitations to the training sites. Teacher-coordinators must listen attentively to what the employer has to say about the student-learner's progress or lack of progress on the job. The coordinator visits the training station to ascertain from the cooperating employer how well the student is performing. If the coordinator's communication is totally one-sided, the coordinator does all the talking and does not allow for the listening process to occur, the coordinator will not be in a position to assist that student back in the related class.

Some Basic Rules to Improve Listening

BE ATTENTIVE. The teacher-coordinator should constantly strive to keep in mind what the speaker is saying. Human nature being what it is, it is easy to become distracted by outside elements; however, the coordinator should not allow him- or herself to be swayed by the distraction. They should refocus their attention back to the speaker.

LISTEN TO THE MESSAGE NOT THE DELIVERY. Quite frequently, teacher-coordinators are caught in the trap of concentrating on a poor delivery of a speaker instead of the message of the speaker.

It is the message that counts, not the eloquence or the mannerism of the speaker.

AVOID CONCENTRATING ON EMOTIONALLY CHARGED WORDS. Studies have shown that certain words have a tendency to arouse the emotions of the listener. Words such as sexist, chauvinist, elitist, crook, pig, and many others are emotionally upsetting words for a great number of individuals. The teacher-coordinator should learn to control his or her emotions and not pay attention to the individually "charged" words that would distract them from listening to the message of the speaker.

STRIVE FOR ACCURACY. It is of the utmost importance that the listener and the speaker have the same understanding of what is being said. Quite frequently meanings and interpretations of what was said can differ from what the speaker intended. A typical example might be how the students perceive the instructions of the teacher-coordinator. A good practice is to have the listener repeat back to you what was said. This will eliminate a great deal of confusion and misconception for the future.

GO AFTER IDEAS. Do not try to memorize facts. With the exception of a few gifted people, it is impossible for the average individual to memorize all the facts that a speaker presents. In listening to a speech the listener should concentrate on the central ideas and should not endeavor to memorize all the facts. If the listener, in this case the teacher-coordinator, listens attentively to the ideas and grasps the central idea that is being conveyed, the supporting facts to substantiate the idea will fall into place in the listener's mind.

SCREEN AND WEIGH WHAT IS BEING SAID. A very important aspect of listening is analyzing what is being heard. The coordinator should focus on those points, and only those points, that have a bearing on what is being said. An important question that a listener has to answer each and every time is "How valid is the evidence and how complete is it?"

Non-Verbal Communication

Communication can and does take place without ever speaking a word. Teacher-coordinators communicate to employers by their body movement.   Frequently, a lot more is said by the body than is conveyed by the tongue.   For example, a teacher-coordinator who constantly keeps fidgeting in the chair and looking at his or her watch while interviewing a potential cooperating employer is not engaging in effective communication.   The spoken words say "I am interested in having the student work here and I think that the training station will be a true link between the school and the world of work."   The body language is saying "I really want to get out of here and I am not too interested in whether I land this training station or not."

Figure 47

MANAGERIAL TECHNIQUES,
A CHECKLIST FOR TEACHER-COORDINATORS

Yes   No

——— ——— 1. I establish achievable long- and short-range goals for the school year.

——— ——— 2. I maintain a calendar with penciled-in target dates for completing activities.

——— ——— 3. I maintain a "Things I have to do today" list.

——— ——— 4. I prioritize my daily activities in their order of importance.

——— ——— 5. I maintain a routine quiet hour in order to concentrate on assigned tasks.

——— ——— 6. I delegate tasks where applicable.

——— ——— 7. I maximize my telephone usage time by grouping calls, keeping calls to a short time frame, and making notations of what I want to cover prior to making the call.

——— ——— 8. I start and end all meetings on time.

——— ——— 9. I don't waste my time concentrating on junk mail.

——— ——— 10. I only handle a piece of mail once.

——— ——— 11. I am attentive to people's names.

——— ——— 12. I make an effort to remember at least one new name a day.

——— ——— 13. I make an effort to listen to what others are saying.

——— ——— 14. I practice good communications.

——— ——— 15. I am conscious of my body language.

The above situation is but one example in an unending array of examples that point out how actions and body movements convey messages. Teacher-coordinators must be very serious in the communication process. The entire body must be in harmony with the words spoken. If teacher-coordinators express by word and gestures sincere interest in student-learners, cooperating employers, advisory committee members, parents, and all those they serve, they will be welcomed by the majority of people. Failure to engage in effective communications can possibly mean the demise of the program at the school.

BIBLIOGRAPHY

Brothers, Joyce and Egan, Edward P.F.: *Ten Days to a Successful Memory.* New York, Darryl Publ., 1967.

The Bureau of Business Practice, Inc.: *Solving Time Problems, Dynamic Supervision Number 489.* Waterford, C, 1978.

The Bureau of Business Practice, Inc.: *The Standard Manual for Supervisors.* Waterford, C, 1969.

De Simone, George A.: M.B.O.—Is there a place for it in cooperative education? *Cooperative Education Quarterly,* 10-11, February 1979.

Finley, Thomas Kaye: *Mental Dynamic-Power Thinking for Personnel Success.* Englewood Cliffs, P-H, 1969.

Furst, Dr. Bruno. *Stop Forgetting.* Garden City, NY, Garden City Books, 1948.

Gooch, Bill G.: The key to success. *Cooperative Education Quarterly, 1 (3):* 1978.

McGuigan, Jack V.: *Time Saving Ideas,* Unpublished Paper, 1978.

———: One Hundred Time Saving Ideas. *Cooperative Education Quarterly, 2 (12):* 1979.

Wanat, J.A., Merrigan, John J. Jr., and Guy, Edward T.: *Supervisory Development for Security Officers.* Springfield, Thomas, 1980.

Wood, Merle W.: The time line: An effective tool for planning and management. *Business Education World,* 24-25, September-October, 1978.

Chapter 14

TECHNIQUES FOR CONDUCTING
TRAINING SPONSOR PROGRAMS

BECAUSE COOPERATIVE EDUCATION is a combination of an in-school and a community-based effort to train young people for the world of work, cooperating sponsors must be thoroughly familiar with the objectives, goals, and outcomes of cooperative education in order to provide a realistic learning experience for their student-learners. The teacher-coordinator should assume the responsibility for sharing information about the program with the cooperating sponsors. It is impractical to assume that an employer is well-informed about a program just because the person has agreed to train a teenager and work cooperatively with the school.

There are several ways available to teacher-coordinators to provide information about their program to cooperating sponsors. Two of them are discussed in this chapter.

A TRAINING SPONSOR CONFERENCE

A technique that has been used successfully by some teacher co-ordinators is to invite training station employers to a conference or meeting co-sponsored by the cooperative education advisory committee. Besides the obvious advantages to the coordinator and the school, the cooperating sponsors receive several advantages from such a meeting:

* an opportunity to meet with other sponsors
* become acquainted with the school administration and advisory committee

250

- share their interest in the program and discuss common problems and concerns
- demonstrate their willingness to cooperate with the school
- share information and teaching techniques with other sponsors

The invitational letter to the meeting should be sent to the training station sponsors by the advisory committee chairperson after it has been reviewed and approved by the school administration. The coordinator usually assumes responsibility for preparing the letter. On some occasions the letter is sent over the signatures of both the advisory committee chairperson and the superintendent of schools. The letter should state the purpose of the meeting and the benefits to the sponsor of attending the meeting. In addition, some invitational letters list the entire advisory committee's names on the bottom.

While the meeting should be short, it should be well-planned and provide comprehensive details about certain parts of the program that would be of concern to the training sponsors. Training experts in the field of business and industry along with educators in the school should conduct short sessions on various aspects of the program that would assist the cooperating employer to provide a realistic program for student-learners. Some time also should be left for the training sponsors to ask questions, state concerns, or share information.

While a variety of topics is possible for the conference or meeting, the following topics should be included:

- an overview of the cooperative education program
- techniques of providing on-the-job supervision
- evaluation techniques for student performance
- motivational techniques to use with students

In addition to the topics listed above, the program should include a welcome by the chief school administrator, remarks from the advisory committee, and a comment on contributions that business and industry can make toward the cooperative education students' career objectives. The benefits that employers can derive from participating in a cooperative education program should be stressed. Adequate coverage by the communication media also will help to emphasize the importance the school places on cooperating sponsors' help.

TRAINING STATION SPONSOR MANUAL

Whether or not an in-service conference or meeting is held, an employer's handbook should be provided to every cooperating employer. The manual should be specific to the program with which the sponsor is cooperating in order to familiarize them with the guidelines of the program and the various procedures used in it.

Following is a list of items that would be found in most manuals:

- a description of the program
- an overview of the operation of the program
- some advantages to the training station employer
- the relationships between the employer and the school
- the coordinator's responsibilities to the employer and to the students in the program
- rules and regulations for cooperative education students
- the involvement of the students' parents in the program
- background information regarding federal and state laws connected with the program
- safety procedures and operational procedures
- the names of members of the advisory committee and the advisory committee chairperson's name and telephone number
- the names of the school administration and the board of education
- the name and home and school telephone number of the teacher-coordinator of the program
- sample forms

Cooperating employers are busy people and they may have limited time to attend evening programs. The coordinator should schedule an appointment that is mutually convenient, and review in some detail the handbook or manual for the training sponsor. To simply hand an employer a copy of it could result in the manual being put aside for review at a more convenient time, which might never be found.

The manual should be prepared by the teacher-coordinator. While it is helpful to review manuals used by other coordinators, each manual should be individualized for the particular cooperative education program in which it will be used. Following are some guidelines to use in developing a manual.

Description of the Program

The program description should be brief. It should contain some information about cooperative education in general and the particular program in detail. The reader should understand what constitutes their specific type of program and what makes it different from other cooperative education programs. The description should be limited to half a page, if possible.

Overview of the Operation of the Program

The cooperating sponsor may have an understanding of the program operation on the part of the employer but little knowledge about how the student is scheduled at school, how the student will be supervised by the coordinator, and how the school and the training station employer are expected to work together to provide the student with a meaningful learning experience. In a brief paragraph or two, the coordinator should describe how the program operates in school. Included in the description should be how the grade is determined, how the related course is structured, and the requirements for students to be eligible to enroll in the program.

Some Advantages to the Training Station Employer

The advantages to a training station employer of participating in a cooperative education program are discussed elsewhere in this text. The advantages should be reviewed and stated briefly in the manual. How the information is presented will vary from one manual to another; however, limited space should be devoted to listing them.

The Relationships Between the Employer and the School

In a paragraph or two, the relationships between the employer and the school should be discussed. The various relationships could be subdivided into those of the school administration, the coordinator, the student, and the advisory committee.

The Coordinator's Responsibilities to the Employer And to the Students in the Program

Cooperating training station sponsors are interested in knowing what the coordinator's responsibilities are to the employer and to the student-learners in the program. A list of the various responsibilities should be included in the manual. The responsibilities should be listed in the sequence that the coordinator would follow in developing, initiating, and maintaining a cooperative education program.

Rules and Regulations for Cooperative Education Students

Most programs have a list of rules and regulations prepared for the students. That list can provide the structure for this section. Along with the list, the coordinator might wish to explain the rationale behind any item that might be confusing to the training station sponsor.

The Involvement of the Students' Parents in the Program

The information regarding the nature and extent of the parents' involvement in the program should be explained in a few sentences. Most employers will be satisfied to know that some attempt is made to involve the parents.

Background Information Regarding Federal and State Laws

This part should consist of two sections. One should list the federal and state laws that are pertinent to cooperative education programs. The other part should discuss the procedures used in the program as a means of following the laws.

Safety Procedures and Operational Procedures

This section will vary from one program to another. It is a very important section and should be described in a thorough and complete manner. Any instruction given to students should be identified. Procedures used by the coordinator should be described, and ways in which the employer and coordinator can work together should be discussed.

Information About the Advisory Committee

The names of the advisory committee members and the advisory committee chairperson should be listed in the manual. In addition, the business telephone number of the committee chairperson should be listed.

School Administration Information

The names and telephone numbers of the school administration should be listed. In addition, the members of the board of education should be included.

Information About the Teacher-Coordinator

It may be important for the training sponsor to contact the teacher-coordinator. Therefore, the name and both home and office telephone numbers of the coordinator should be listed in a prominent place in the manual. Some coordinators list the times they can be reached most conveniently on the telephone. Other coordinators list their entire schedule.

Sample Forms

Training station sponsors are interested in the forms they have to complete. Copies of forms should be included with some brief explanation regarding when and how they are used.

RESPONSIBILITIES OF TRAINING SPONSOR IN TRAINING COE STUDENTS[1]

Just as the coordinator has definite responsibilities in teaching his/her students, so does the on-the-job training sponsor have definite responsibilities in teaching his/her student-trainees.

---

[1]*Cooperative Office Education Related Class Manual,* State of New Jersey, Department of Education, Division of Vocational Education, Trenton, New Jersey June 1971 pgs. 311-312.

What Teaching Responsibilities Does the Sponsor And/or Supervisor Have?

1. Understand the goal of the training program
2. Know units being studied in the classroom
3. Know enough about student-trainee to be able to teach him/ her effectively
4. Work in partnership with coordinator
5. Give accurate information about the student-trainee to the coordinator
6. Take time to be a teacher
7. Provide "learning by doing" experiences
8. Give support to the youth club program
9. Teach specific job skills
10. Teach "values" in human relations
11. Teach technical information
12. Teach business ethics and responsibility
13. Teach policies, systems, methods of training agency
14. Help student develop judgment and a mature outlook

How Can the Coordinator Help the Sponsor Carry Out His/Her Teaching Responsibilities?

1. Develop a plan to follow in training the sponsor
2. Make a training timetable for training the sponsor
3. Set an appropriate place for training sessions with the sponsor
4. Get sponsor into adult classes on how to train and how to supervise
5. Develop a "clinic" for sponsors
6. Keep the sponsor's training needs in mind during all co-ordination activities
7. Invite the sponsor to club activities early in the year
8. Show appropriate film on orientation if available
9. Develop and make available to sponsors reports and records to be used in the program
10. Review unit content throughout the year
11. Develop project in relation to job and class discussions
12. Give personal data on the student-trainee with discretion

13. Interpret school policies
    a. Calendar (vacations, schedules, events)
    b. Regulations
14. Suggest experiences student is ready for in the training agency
    a. Give student an opportunity to learn by doing
    b. Find ways for student to develop in the job assignments
15. Suggest evidences of progress to look for in student's performance
16. Analyze the job in terms of the student's needs for training
    a. Skills
    b. Technical information
    c. Systems, regulations, policies of the company
    d. Physical requirements
17. Suggest additional training directed towards promotional opportunities

TENTATIVE SPONSOR TRAINING CALENDAR[2]

These activities can be carried out by personal interviews or at the sponsors' meetings.

August—September
1. Stress advantages of participating
2. Explain how the co-op program works
    a. Types of students
    b. Hours a week
    c. Rate of pay
    d. Relationships to coordinator and student
    e. Time and red tape involved
    f. Credits
    g. Curriculum overview
    h. School rules
3. Discuss labor laws involved
4. Interpret school policies

---

[2]*Cooperative Office Education Related Class Manual,* State of New Jersey, Department of Education, Division of Vocational Education, Trenton, New Jersey, June 1971, pgs. 313-314.

5. Introduce techniques of supervision
   a. Induction
   b. Morale
6. Go over content of orientation unit
   a. Classwork application
   b. Progress on the job
7. Review production report and its purpose

October—November—December
1. Discuss follow-up as a technique of supervision
2. Go over contents of unit(s) being studied
   a. Classwork application
   b. Progress on the job
3. Review use and purpose of progress report
4. Invite to club get-acquainted session
5. Encourage evaluation by supervisor
   a. Self-evaluation
   b. Student evaluation
6. Go over content of unit(s) being studied through Christmas
   a. Classwork application
   b. Progress on the job
7. Study ways student may develop on the job
8. Discuss ways of seeing how student performs
9. Use sponsor as guest trainer for part-time employment trainees
10. Interpret school policies regarding time off for co-op employment trainees

January—February—March
1. Arrange downtown showing of co-op film
2. Enlighten sponsor on club contests
3. Review progress during semester
4. Re-train on progress report
5. Start how-to-train class for sponsors
6. Encourage attendance at employer-employee function
7. Get participation in area club convention
8. Invite sponsor to cooperate in classroom activity

9. Give public recognition to sponsor at employer-employee banquet
10. Re-train on practices needing adjustment
11. Follow through on "how-to-train"
12. Point way towards permanent employment for co-op student trainee

April—May

1. Get overall evaluations
   a. Of student (Fig. 48)
   b. Of training given sponsor
   c. Of cooperative relationships
2. Clear way for summer employment of co-op trainees
3. Continue to build good relations between sponsor and co-ordinator

Figure 48

UNION COUNTY VOCATIONAL CENTER

COOPERATIVE EDUCATION PROGRAM

EMPLOYER'S EVALUATION OF COOPERATIVE STUDENT

Name --- Major ------------------ Work Period --------------------

Employer -- Location ------------------------------

INSTRUCTIONS: The immediate supervisor should evaluate the student objectively, comparing him with other students of comparable academic level with other personnel assigned the same or similarly classified jobs, or with individual standards. *Remarks are particularly helpful.*

ATTITUDE—APPLICATION TO WORK
- ☐ Outstanding in enthusiasm
- ☐ Very interested and industrious
- ☐ Average in diligence and interest
- ☐ Somewhat indifferent
- ☐ Definitely not interested

ABILITY TO LEARN
- ☐ Learned work exceptionally well
- ☐ Learned work readily
- ☐ Average in understanding work
- ☐ Rather slow in learning
- ☐ Very slow to learn

DEPENDABILITY
- ☐ Completely dependable
- ☐ Above average in dependability
- ☐ Usually dependable
- ☐ Sometimes neglectful or careless
- ☐ Unreliable

INITIATIVE
- ☐ Proceeds well on his own
- ☐ Goes ahead independently at times
- ☐ Does all assigned work
- ☐ Hesitates
- ☐ Must be pushed frequently

QUALITY OF WORK
- ☐ Excellent
- ☐ Very good
- ☐ Average
- ☐ Below average
- ☐ Very poor

RELATIONS WITH OTHERS
- ☐ Exceptionally well accepted
- ☐ Works well with others
- ☐ Gets along satisfactorily
- ☐ Has difficulty working with other
- ☐ Works very poorly with others

MATURITY—POISE
- ☐ Quite poised and confident
- ☐ Has good self-assurance
- ☐ Average maturity and poise
- ☐ Seldom asserts himself
- ☐ Timid   ☐ Brash

QUANTITY OF WORK
- ☐ Unusually high output
- ☐ More than average
- ☐ Normal amount
- ☐ Below average
- ☐ Low out-put, slow

JUDGMENT
- ☐ Exceptionally mature in judgment
- ☐ Above average in making decision
- ☐ Usually makes the right decision
- ☐ Often uses poor judgment
- ☐ Consistently uses bad judgment

ATTENDANCE: ☐ Regular   ☐ Irregular | PUNCTUALITY: ☐ Regular   ☐ Irregular

OVER-ALL PERFORMANCE: Outstanding ‖ Very Good ‖ + Average − ‖ Marginal ‖ Unsatisfactory

The student's outstanding personal qualities are —

The personal qualities which the student should strive most to improve are —

For additional remarks, please use reverse side.

This report has been discussed with. the student: Yes ☐   No ☐

(Signed) -- (Date) ----------------------
         (Immediate Supervisor)

Figure 49

A CHECKLIST FOR CONDUCTING TRAINING SPONSOR PROGRAMS

Yes   No

_____ _____   1. I prepare and disseminate training sponsor guidelines to each co-operating sponsor.

_____ _____   2. I thoroughly familiarize training sponsors with the objectives and procedures of the cooperative education program.

_____ _____   3. I plan and conduct an orientation meeting.

_____ _____   4. I contact each training sponsor individually and prepare a training agreement prior to the student's commencement on the job.

_____ _____   5. I contact each training sponsor individually and prepare a training plan for each student-learner at the job site.

_____ _____   6. I prepare and disseminate a training sponsor manual for each cooperating sponsor.

_____ _____   7. I encourage training station sponsors to discuss problems and concerns that student-learners may be having on the job.

_____ _____   8. I suggest alternate ways of dealing with student-learner problems on the job.

_____ _____   9. I suggest teaching techniques that cooperating employes can use to instruct student-learners on the job.

_____ _____   10. I provide in-service training sessions for cooperating employers.

_____ _____   11. I correlate classroom instruction with job experiences through information gained from training sponsor visits.

_____ _____   12. I make periodic visits to student-learner training stations to determine student's progress on the job.

_____ _____   13. I make an effort to have the training sponsor feel that he or she is an integral part of the school program.

_____ _____   14. I work through my administration and advisory committee in establishing and conducting training sponsor conferences.

_____ _____   15. I work closely with the training sponsor chairperson in developing relevant and timely topics on the agenda.

BIBLIOGRAPHY

An Articulated Guide For Cooperative Occupational Education. Springfield, State of Illinois, Board of Vocational Education and Rehabilitation, Division of Vocational and Technical Education, Bulletin #34-872.

Ehrlich, Dan J.: Employer assessment of a cooperative education program. *Journal of Cooperative Education,* 74-87, March 1978.

Evans, Rupert N.: Employer and employee groups. *Foundations of Vocational Education,* 1971.

Gold, M.J.: Work and school as partners in education. *International Review of Education,* 449-453, 1962.

Hayes, Richard A.: Employer experience with the work performance of cooperative education employees. *Journal of Cooperative Education,* 93-103, March 1978.

Johnson, Peter: Co-op programs extend skill training. *School Shop,* 62-64, April 1977.

Notgrass, Troy: *Handbook for Industrial Cooperative Training Sponsors.* Austin, Tx, Instructional Materials Services, Division of Extension, The University of Texas at Austin, 1973.

A Resource for New Jersey Cooperative Office Education Coordinator. Trenton, New Jersey State Department of Education, Division of Vocational Education and Career Preparation, 1973.

Scally, Leslie J.: *Selling Co-op to Training Station Sponsors.* New Brunswick, New Jersey State Department of Education, Division of Vocational Education and Career Preparation, Rutgers University Curriculum Laboratory, 1979.

Chapter 15

COMPREHENSIVE PROGRAM EVALUATION TECHNIQUES

IN ONE WAY or another, whether by formal or informal process, covert or overt manner, consciously or subconsciously, almost everything a person thinks and does is evaluated by others. As a result of that evaluation, other people determine how one should act and what one should think.

Evaluation serves several purposes in a cooperative education program. It enables people to review responsibilities, identify trends, and define weaknesses. It pinpoints parts of the program that are in need of upgrading, modification, or deletion. It provides a basis for comparing similar programs and checks on the presence and quality of relationships. In addition, it provides a rationale for action being contemplated.

A cooperative education program needs periodic evaluation regardless of how successfully it seems to be fulfilling its role and purpose. The need for, and process of, evaluating a cooperative education program are discussed in this chapter.

NEED FOR EVALUATION OF A COOPERATIVE EDUCATION PROGRAM

Depending on the extensiveness of the investigation, formal evaluation of a cooperative education program provides the structure for retrieval and analysis of data associated with every aspect and phase of the program. It examines such things as the structure and format of a program, the delineation of responsibility, and the effectiveness with which that responsibility is performed. Among the various components that are discussed are the program objectives; the effectiveness of the school administration relative to the program; the process of student selection; the nature and extent of related class instruction; the work experience students receive; the various forms used in the program; ways to check student performance and the support organization of the program; ways to check the effectiveness of the teacher-coordinator and the use of public relations; and finally, how well the program meets the needs of its students.

Evaluation procedures can be conducted for various purposes which in turn influence the extensiveness of the procedure and how frequently it is scheduled. Sometimes the evaluation is concerned with process and other times with the product of the program. Evaluation can have an economic orientation and be conducted as a cost-benefit analysis. It also can be conducted to determine the value perception of various groups of people associated with the program.

The frequency of evaluation varies from one program to another. Some are examined sporadically, others on a systematic on-going basis, some yearly and some every five years. The evaluation suggested in this chapter is too comprehensive for most coordinators to conduct on a yearly basis. As most coordinators complete a yearly report about their program, which provides an informal assessment of sorts, the comprehensive examination discussed in this chapter should be conducted every few years. The frequency should be determined by the apparent effectiveness of the program and the number of years the program has been established.

Just as there are various purposes for evaluating a cooperative education program and various frequencies with which it is done, the people conducting the evaluation can also vary. Members of the investigative task force can include any number and any combination of people from the following: school administration, school faculty, advisory committee, training station employers, other cooperative education coordinators, and students who are in the program or who have completed it. Occasionally, private consultants and college professors are part of the evaluation team. Regardless of the various groups that are represented, the investigating team should be limited to ten to fifteen people. A larger group tends to be too cumbersome and a smaller group might be overwhelmed by all the items to be checked.

EVALUATION OF THE OBJECTIVES OF A COOPERATIVE PROGRAM

While the objectives of one cooperative education program may vary from one to another, all programs have some similar objectives. Following are some objectives which relate to activities of the program coordinator, purposes of the program, and the outcomes desired for the students in the program.

Is the cooperative education program structured to—

1. Assist the students in the program to identify their occupational interests, aptitudes, and activities? It is assumed that such a process involves more than just talking to each student. Such things as career information readings and interest and aptitude tests should be a regular part of this investigatory procedure.

2. Provide an awareness and appreciation of the social and economic values of this society and encourage the students to cultivate the generally acceptable habits of society? Many programs encourage the students to have a budget and start a savings program. In addition, some programs attempt to reinforce the desirable work, study and personal habits of co-op education students.

Does the cooperative education teacher-coordinator—

1. Arrange for each student to receive instruction pertaining to general information about the world of work and specific technical information related to the occupation in which the student is receiving training?

2. Insure that all students in the program are encouraged to develop skills for interpersonal interaction with their peers and people they encounter at work, at school, or during their leisure pursuits?

3. Provide meaningful learning experiences for all the stu-

dents in the program according to their interest, aptitude, and ability?

Are students in the program encouraged to—

1. Practice generally accepted work, study, and personal habits, such as health habits and habits associated with acceptable values and performance?
2. Share responsibility for their educational preparation in terms of identifying problems and concerns, specifying remedial action, and planning for their future?

EVALUATION OF THE ADMINISTRATION OF A COOPERATIVE EDUCATION PROGRAM

Evaluation of the administration of a cooperative education program includes more than checking to determine that the leadership is sympathetic to the basic goals of the program and effective in carrying out its responsibilities relating to the program. Some people think that—if the school administration and the program coordinator work closely together regarding the various operations of the program and if that program follows the policies and practices prescribed by their state department of education—there is no need to evaluate it. Certainly, their program may fill a legitimate educational need and it may function without apparent problems. However, until a formal evaluation is conducted, these conclusions can only be presumed.

Administration of a cooperative education program involves responsibilities relating to the overall program, the teacher-coordinator and the student-learners in the program. The following overview identifies the various aspects of the program that fall under the purview of administrative authority and decision making.

The school administration should make provisions for the cooperative education program:

1. Are there facilities for related instruction and practice in the school facility where students can study or have hands-on activities? In addition, is there an office area for the coordinator, a telephone with an outside line, and office equipment such as a typewriter?

2. Is there part-time secretarial assistance to help the coordinator with correspondence and record-keeping activities?

The administration should provide for students in the cooperative education program:

1. Is a procedure established for students that enables them to receive guidance regarding how to obtain working papers? In addition, is there a related monitoring system on all issued working papers?
2. Is a policy implemented by which the school grants credit to students in cooperative education programs toward high school graduation requirements?
3. Are provisions identified in scheduling practices that allow cooperative education students to spend half of their school time in a training situation at a work site? Do scheduling policies exist for such occasion as when a student is unable to continue working at a training station? Are student policies flexible to enable student-learners ample time to fulfill the work experience requirements of the cooperative education program?

The school administration must make provisions for the cooperative education teacher-coordinator:

1. Is the coordinator, in cooperation with the school administration, responsible for all aspects of the cooperative education program?
2. Does the coordinator have a stipulated number of students as identified by state department of education recommendations?
3. Do the coordinator's duties include conference and consultation in the community as well as training station supervision?

In addition to the other administrative considerations, the budget for the program should be reviewed. Items to be scrutinized are the type of contract provided for the coordinator and what allocations are made for the coordinator's travel, professional meetings, and conferences. The budget also would be checked to determine what funds were provided for instructional materials, support materials, and equipment.

EVALUATION OF THE PROCESS OF STUDENT SELECTION

The process of selecting students can vary from one cooperative education program to another. Such considerations as the number of students interested in the program, the involvement of the advisory committee, and the number of years the program is established affect which candidates will be accepted into the program.

Most evaluative procedures would include questions to determine the nature and extent of the student selection process. Following are questions that could be used to examine the criteria that frequently are used to select students for a cooperative education program. The criteria are listed sequentially as they would occur in the process of selecting students for a cooperative education program. Some of the activities occur concurrently to each other. The process occurs in the spring so that the new students can enter the program in the fall without scheduling complications.

1. Does the advisory committee specify general characteristics, aptitudes, and abilities that the candidates should have for successful employment in various trades?
2. Does the coordinator personally interview students who are interested in entering the cooperative education program and discuss the program with other students who are recommended by guidance counselors as possible candidates?
3. Do students complete an application form for the cooperative education program that contains questions on interest, career goals, and work experience?
4. Does the guidance department provide the coordinator with background information on students' school records and results of interest and ability tests?
5. Does the coordinator check each student's personal data to see that the candidate meets the entrance requirements and that the type of training desired by the student can be provided in the program?

6. Does the coordinator provide written material about the program for the students and are students' parents provided an overview of the program that specifies the responsibilities of students in the program?
7. Does the coordinator evaluate each candidate regarding ability level, aptitude and interest, personal health, attendance, and behavior in the school and community before selecting the students for the following academic year?

EVALUATION OF THE SCHEDULING PRACTICES

Scheduling practices can create many problems in a cooperative education program or they can contribute to making a program successful. Scheduling must be flexible in order to survey students and to allow for the many demands of the coordinator's job.

Evaluation of the scheduling process entails investigating whether or not scheduling practices are sufficiently flexible to schedule students initially and reschedule them at various times throughout the academic year. Flexible scheduling in a cooperative education program requires being able to handle the following situations:

* Temporary lay-off from a training station
* Failing a subject
* Change in work station
* New arrivals
* Students requiring extra credits
* Student violation of the discipline code
* Students wishing to participate in extracurricular sports
* Students wishing to reenter a full-time school program

The teacher-coordinator's duties present several scheduling difficulties to the administration, although once the schedule is made, it rarely has to be changed. A coordinator's schedule has to be considered separately from the rest of the faculty because the responsibilities are different. Then, too, the responsibilities of coordinators vary from one program to another.

Some coordinators are responsible for teaching one or more

related instruction classes, others spend much of their time working individually with various students, teachers, and support personnel in the school. Regardless of their duties, ample time must be left in a schedule for a coordinator to fulfill the responsibilities of the job description; otherwise, the cooperative education program will suffer. A major factor in determining the teacher-coordinator's schedule is to allow ample time to supervise the students on the job.

EVALUATION OF RELATED CLASS INSTRUCTION

Because related instruction is one of the most important components of a cooperative education program, the examination must be thorough in nature and comprehensive in its scope. Among the items that might be evaluated are the comprehensiveness and effectiveness of the instructional content and associated resource; the effectiveness of the teaching methods; and the provisions made for the individual differences of students.

Some of the more common items in an evaluation of related class instruction are discussed in this section. They are grouped relative to considerations about instruction provided to the students, the supplemental support available for students, and the program policies associated with related instruction.

When evaluating the nature and extent of the related instruction available to students, the following questions should be asked:

1. Are student's instructional assignments correlated with the work activities? The employers should recommend to the teacher-coordinator those areas in which the student-learner needs additional study or preparation in advance of some work experience.

2. Is safety instruction given at periodic intervals and are records kept of the test results? An 85 percent grade on a safety test is not acceptable. Students should be required to retake the test until they demonstrate 100 percent understanding of the proper safety procedures associated with their on-the-job experience.

3. Are instructional aids available for students to use and

are students encouraged to use them? While a great variety of audiovisual material may be available, students sometimes have to be encouraged to use them.

4. Do students maintain notebooks containing the related class information? Some students need to be encouraged to keep notes and reference material in an organized fashion. Most students would benefit from having to maintain a notebook.

5. Are students required to maintain and keep current the required records associated with the program, such as wage, hours, and work progress?

Evaluation of the policies and practices of the program regarding related instruction should include some of the following questions:

1. Do students receive a variety of topics in related class in addition to the learning experiences indicated on the training plan, such as safety and health instruction, sources of job information, new and evolving technology problems relating to the world of work, and how to use their income effectively?

2. Is reference material available in suitable quantity and variety and is it geared to the interest, ability, and needs of the students? Included in the type of reference materials should be self-study materials, tests, library resources, and audiovisual materials.

3. Are a variety of school services available to help students who need review or remedial instruction or support services? Students might need assistance in math, reading, English, or science. In addition, they might need the service of the guidance department, the health department, or the Child Study Team.

EVALUATION OF THE WORK EXPERIENCE

There are several criteria to selecting a training station. Not only must the business be respected in the community, but it must have a functioning safety program, adequate equipment and facili-

ties, and a sufficient volume of production to provide a meaningful educational experience for the cooperative education student-
learner.   In addition, the management must agree to follow the
program guidelines relative to Child Labor Laws and state department of education regulations.

Besides the criteria for selecting a training station, evaluation
of the work experience might also include the way other rules and
regulations pertaining to the student-learner are observed.   An
investigator would check to see that a qualified person was responsible for the student's training and that the student-learner
worked the specified number of hours per day and week within
the proper time framework.

EVALUATION OF COOPERATIVE EDUCATION FORMS

A teacher-coordinator uses a variety of forms when working
with a training station.   Two forms involving the student-learners,
and essential to a meaningful work experience for them, are the
training agreement and the training plan.   Both should be reviewed in an evaluation process.

A training agreement is required by most states.   Quite often,
the agreement is on a form specified by the state.   Every student
should have an agreement for the current job and all the involved
parties should have copies of it.   The original should be kept on
file at the school.   A training agreement should be reviewed
periodically and updated as necessary.

A training plan is the other type of form that guides students
in their experience.   An evaluation process would check to see
whether or not the plan provided for detailed training based on
the individual student's career interest, abilities, and aptitudes.
The plan also would provide for rotation and upgrading of skill
experiences during the training period.

In addition to the above two types of forms, an evaluation of
the cooperative education record-keeping system would check on
the required local and state records.   Requirements for such
records might vary from state to state.   However, there are some
records that must be kept regarding the hours students work and
the pay they receive.   Other records are kept according to the

school policy.

One type of record that most schools keep is a follow-up record on graduates. Some state departments of education require that information. Sometimes the guidance personnel maintain such records and at other times the cooperative education teacher-coordinator keeps them.

Follow-up study is important because it indicates labor market trends, information on unemployment, job advancement, and the mobility of the labor force. Evaluation of a cooperative education program would include checking on an alumni follow-up study, how frequently it was done, and what mechanics were used.

Other forms that are checked during an evaluative procedure are the student records. Again, this information might be maintained in the guidance department, though it usually is kept in the teacher-coordinator's files. Among the contents of such files should be the application form to the program, the training agreement and plan, safety tests, copies of working papers and proof of age, supervision reports, and grades achieved.

The coordinator should have available for review some type of record regarding what instructional material was provided for each student and the results achieved. In addition, inventory reports and supervision schedules would be checked. Finally, the coordinator should have copies of all reports submitted to various agencies and people.

EVALUATION OF STUDENT PERFORMANCE

A student's performance is determined on the basis of the achievement made at the training station and the related class work. The evaluation process would entail checking each one of those records for frequency of rotation and comprehensiveness of the data. Some coordinators also consider discipline reports and attendance records. Other determinants that would be examined are how the coordinator arrived at a grade for a student. An evaluator would check to see that a student's program was specified in writing and that several sources were used to determine a grade.

EVALUATION OF SUPPORT ORGANIZATIONS

Cooperative education programs have two types of support organizations. One is the student organization associated with the field of study. The other is the advisory committee for the program.

Some of the criteria that would be used to evaluate how well a student organization functions are whether or not it is affiliated, as applicable, with the state and national organizations. Also, the nature and extent of the cooperative education students' understanding would be checked. An investigator also would find out if the officers were identified, if periodic meetings were held, and whether or not minutes of those meetings were kept on record. Finally, the type and frequency of activities of the club would be checked.

Some similar items might be checked regarding the advisory committee, such as the identification of the officers and committee members and whether or not minutes of periodic meetings were kept. In addition, an evaluator might check to see that there were reports on file of the committee's recommendations and the actions taken.

EVALUATION OF THE TEACHER-COORDINATOR

It is said that a cooperative education coordinator can make or break a program. Certainly a coordinator who fails to fulfill the obligations of the job description can harm a program. Evaluation of the coordinator's achievements and activities will disclose how effectively the job is being done.

The investigation includes checking various relationships that occur within the school and in the community. Among those with whom the teacher-coordinator interacts at the school are the administration, faculty, student body, cooperative education students, and even the nonprofessional staff. In the out-of-school setting, the coordinator interacts with students' parents and the general public, civic organizations, and of course, employers and employer organizations.

The coordinator might be evaluated regarding the nature and

extent of the existing relationship between those various groups of people as they relate to the cooperative education program. Among the questions that would be asked in order to determine a coordinator's effectiveness are the following:

1. Is the coordinator fully credentialed to be a cooperative education coordinator, and does he or she make an effort to keep professionally current by attending conferences and professional meetings?
2. Are adequate records maintained regarding all aspects of the program?
3. Does the coordinator have a positive relationship with student-learners in the program and the school?
4. Does the coordinator insure that the related instruction provided to each student-learner is adequate for the student's needs and abilities?
5. Does the coordinator insure that student-learners in the program have adequate instruction and resource materials for related instruction to be informative and meaningful?
6. Does the coordinator assist student-learners to get social or remedial help from the qualified personnel at the school?
7. Does the coordinator supervise student-learners in the program according to the prescribed schedules and procedures?
8. Are people in the community made aware of the cooperative education program?
9. Does the coordinator maintain relationships with various civic and social groups in the community?
10. Are reports and associated paper work completed accurately and on time?
11. Are adequate records maintained regarding all aspects of the program?
12. Does the coordinator support the vocational youth organization and work with the program advisory committee for the continuation and improvement of the program.

EVALUATION OF PUBLIC RELATIONS

The nature and extent of public relations practices by the cooperative education coordinator directly influences the successfulness of the program. Evaluation should be concerned with the means that are used to provide publicity about the program; the various groups of people that receive information about the program; and the people that are recognized for their involvement with the program. In addition, the procedures should be reviewed that are used to inform parents of cooperative education students about the program.

Most coordinators use a variety of means to acquaint people with, and apprise them about, a cooperative education program. An evaluation process would check to see what means were used and what degree of effectiveness was achieved. Among the various forms of publicity that might be used would be media coverage, year-end progress reports, employer testimonials, success stories, school assembly programs, bulletin boards, school information booklets and brochures, PTA programs, open house programs, and career programs.

Teacher-coordinators provide information about their program to a variety of people, such as civic and service organizations, the Chamber of Commerce, school organizations, and social and professional organizations. Evaluation would determine the coordinator's involvement with these populations.

In addition to identifying the coordinator's involvement with those various groups, the means might be evaluated by which recognition is given for their time and effort. The diversity of recognition would be examined. Among the various means a coordinator could use are awards, letters of recognition, public announcements, press releases, and dinners or luncheons. Cooperative education students would get recognition for their outstanding achievement in many of the same ways. In addition, some outstanding students might be awarded a scholarship. The youth organization also provides a means of recognition for outstanding students and it is an important public tool.

Public relations with parents of students in a cooperative education program are of two types. The first involves providing information to parents whose children are considering joining a cooperative education program. Evaluation of this type of public relations would involve how the parents were informed about the program and what opportunities were given to the parents to ask questions or share concerns about the program. Many coordinators prepare printed material for parents. Others call or have an interview with the parents.

The other type of publicity parents receive is that of on-going information about the program and their child's progress in the program. Evaluation would be concerned with how parental contact was maintained and the nature and extent of the information provided.

EVALUATION OF STUDENTS WHILE IN THE PROGRAM

Evaluation of how the program meets the cooperative education students' needs provides, in some respects, an overview of the effectiveness of a cooperative education program. While several indicies might be used, such as the alumnae follow-up, one of the easiest ways to evaluate how well a program fills students' needs is to find answers to the following questions:

1. Do the students receive informative information about the program?
2. Are their questions answered in personal interviews?
3. Do they receive career education counseling?
4. Is the learning and work experience adapted for their personal needs and interests?
5. Do students receive meaningful related instruction to help them adapt to the world of work and to their particular trade?
6. Is there adequate support instruction and educational materials and media available for their use?
7. Is there a meaningful learning experience at their work station?
8. Is the work they do at the training station related to a training plan and is their related study coordinated with it?
9. Do they have an experienced person responsible for their work experience at the training station?
10. Are they supervised periodically by the program coordinator?
11. Are they encouraged to practice good safety procedures?

12. Are the periodic evaluations made on their progress shared with them so they can learn from the experience?
13. Do they participate in an active vocational youth organization?
14. Do they receive recognition for their achievement in the program?
15. Do they feel that others in the school and in the community have a sense of respect for the cooperative education program?

FOLLOW-UP SURVEYS

The evaluation process is not complete unless feedback from the individuals who are directly involved in the cooperative education process can be obtained. The use of follow-up instruments provides feedback for evaluation as well as accountability of the program. Follow-up studies can be used for planning, to identify manpower needs, and to modify or change program structure depending upon the responses made by the respondees.

The Center for Vocational Education at the Ohio State University lists in their Research and Development Series, Publication Number 106, *A Manual for Conducting Follow-up Surveys of Former Vocational Students,* the following overall objectives of the follow-up procedures:

1. To provide information for product evaluation, e.g. percent of graduates placed on jobs, levels of salaries and wages earned by graduates, percent who are satisfied on the job, etc.
2. To provide some process evaluation information on training programs and other school facilities, etc.
3. To provide comparable information on graduates from various vocational and technical training programs within a state (private school, adult education, and academic education programs) so as to set up norms against which future programs can be evaluated.
4. To provide information on placement and geographic mobility trends for manpower planning purposes.
5. To provide placement, job satisfaction, and wage information to guidance personnel for counseling purposes.

6. To provide relevant information for accountability and building up the image of vocational education in the community.
7. To provide information to fulfill placement-related USOE reporting requirements by the states.

Cooperative education teacher-coordinators should follow-up their graduates from the cooperative education programs several years after they have left school. In order to accomplish this, the teacher-coordinator must develop a system that will enable him/her to complete a follow-up study. The coordinator should develop a follow-up file on each student prior to graduation. That file should contain the following information:

a. The name and address of the student.
b. Names and addresses of relatives and close friends.
c. A code number showing the job title of the student and/or the actual job title.
d. A code identifying his/her rank in the graduation class.
e. Information on the student's career goals and any other necessary data that can be used as criteria in measuring success.

Figure 50

STUDENT-LEARNER DATA SHEET

STUDENT-LEARNER
PHOTO

Name _____

Address _____ Town _____ Zip _____

Birth Date _____ S.S. #_____ Grad. Code _____

Home Phone # _____ Grad. Date_____ Grade _____

Occupational Objective _____

Total Co-op Hours _____ Total Earnings _____

Employer _____-   Relative _____

Address _____   Address _____

Town _____ Zip _____   Town _____ Zip _____

Telephone # _____   Telephone # _____

Special Skills _____   Future Plans _____

The rationale for asking for the names and addresses of relatives and friends is to insure that you will be able to obtain the graduate's current address at the point in time when you are about to conduct your survey. Graduates will, of course, move on and leave no forwarding address and the information that can be obtained from relatives and friends will help you track down the student-learner. Another technique that has proven successful with many teacher-coordinators in the field is to have the existing class prepare a holiday card that can be sent to all alumni. The personalization of this kind of a technique could also include a request that the alumni members return a similar holiday card with their current address. This type of technique provides a great deal of follow-up information since students who send holiday cards normally enclose a little notation on what they are doing and where they are located.

The next step in preparing for a follow-up survey is to determine your follow-up interval schedule. Will it be one year, three years, five years? Once that decision is made the follow-up instrument should be planned and designed so that it includes information regarding the retention of jobs or employment in the related field, additional education or training, unemployment history, salary advancement, job duties, etc.

Once the instrument has been developed, it should be mailed to all graduates with a return date specified. If the student-learner does not return the questionnaire within the given time, one of two procedures can be followed: (1) Send out a form letter to the student-learner indicating that "it might have been a simple oversight but we have not yet received their questionnaire" or (2) Follow through with a telephone call if resources are available.

When the returns are in, the coordinator should make arrangements to tabulate the results, analyze the responses, and develop a report that can be used for public relations purposes, as well as for statistical data that can be reported to the school authorities and state and national agencies. The report, of course, will be general in nature; names of student-learners will not be disclosed.

Figure 51*

COOPERATIVE EDUCATION PROGRAM STUDENT EVALUATION FOLLOW-UP

One Year

Dear Cooperative Education Graduate:

In order that we might provide the most effective type of education and training for high school students, we are asking you to take a few minutes to evaluate the Cooperative Education Program at

_____

You can be sure that your help will be greatly appreciated.

PERSONAL DATA

Name _____
       First   M.I.   (Maiden)   Last

Sex: Male _____   Female _____

Present Address _____

Telephone Number _____

Program area in which you were enrolled in school (check the appropriate cooperative education program).

_____ 1. Cooperative Agriculture Education (CAE)

_____ 2. Distributive Education (DE)

_____ 3. Health Occupations Education (HOE)

_____ 4. Cooperative Home Economics (CHE)

_____ 5. Cooperative Industrial Education (CIE)

_____ 6. Cooperative Office Education (COE)

_____ 7. Work Experience and Career Exploration Program (WECEP)

EMPLOYMENT DATA

Current Employment Status:

Employed   Unemployed

_____ Full-time   _____ Seeking full time employment

_____ Part-time   _____ Seeking part time employment

_____ Self-employed   _____ Not seeking employment

Cooperative Education Program Employer:

Name of Company and Location _____

_____

_____

*C.I.E. Administrative Handbook, State of New Jersey, Department of Education, Division of Vocational Education, April 1978.

Figure 51 — (Cont'd)

Job Title _____

Work Experience (List your PRESENT position)

Date Started _____ Exact Title of Position _____

Name of Employer and Location _____

_____

Salary or earnings per year: (Check appropriate column.)

_____ Under $5,000   _____ $10,0001 — $12,500

_____ $5,001 — $ 7,500   _____ $12,501 — $15,000

_____ $7,501 — $10,000   _____ Over $15,000

How did you obtain this job? _____ coordinator _____ friend _____ family _____ school

_____ employment agency   _____ Other (Explain)

_____

How related is this job to the Cooperative Program you took in high school?

_____ Same   _____ Highly related   _____ Somewhat related   _____ Not related

Indicate the amount of help you received from the Cooperative Education Program. Mark only those items which apply to you.

	Much Help	Some Help	Little or No Help
a. To meet entrance requirements to specialized training institutions.			
b. To continue my education.			
c. To prepare for employment.			
d. To get along with people.			
e. To define my career goal.			

Did you belong to a vocational student organization such as:

_____ DECA _____ VICA _____ FBLA _____ FFA _____ FHA/HERO _____ (HCCNJ)HOSA
_____ Other (Explain) _____

If yes, how did it benefit you? _____

_____

Do you think you would have profited from participating in the work experience phase of cooperative education earlier in high school?   _____ Yes _____ No

If yes, explain _____

_____

Figure 51 — (Cont'd)

Rate the following:

	Excellent	Good	Average	Poor
Related Class				
Job Placement				
The Coordinator				
Your Employment Experience				
If applies, Youth Club Activity				
Overall Co-op Program				

How have you benefited by being a member of a Cooperative Education Program?

_____

_____

_____

List those courses you feel helped you the most, as well as those courses you feel you should have taken, but didn't, while in high school.

Courses		Helped Me Most	Should Have Taken
1.			
2.			
3.			
4.			
5.			
6.			

THANK YOU!

Figure 52*

COOPERATIVE EDUCATION PROGRAM STUDENT EVALUATION FOLLOW-UP

Five Year

Dear Cooperative Education Graduate:

In order that we might provide the most effective type of education and training for high school students, we are asking you to take a few minutes to evaluate the Cooperative Education Program at

_____

You can be sure that your help will be greatly appreciated.

PERSONAL DATA

Name _____
          First   M.I.   (Maden)   Last

Sex: Male _____   Female _____

Present Address _____

Telephone Number _____

Program area in which you were enrolled in school (check the appropriate cooperative education program).

_____ 1. Cooperative Agriculture Education (CAE)

_____ 2. Distributive Education (DE)

_____ 3. Health Occupations Education (HOE)

_____ 4. Cooperative Home Economics (CHE)

_____ 5. Cooperative Industrial Education (CIE)

_____ 6. Cooperative Office Education (COE)

_____ 7. Work Experience and Career Exploration Program (WECEP)

EMPLOYMENT DATA

Current Employment Status:

Employed	Unemployed
_____ Full-time	_____ Seeking full time employment
_____ Part-time	_____ Seeking part time employment
_____ Self-employed	_____ Not seeking employment

Cooperative Education Program Employer

Name of Company and Location _____

_____

Job Title _____

_____

*__C.I.E. Administrative Handbook.__ State of New Jersey, Department of Education, Division of Vocational Education, April 1978.

Figure 52 — (Cont'd)

Work Experience (List your PRESENT position)

Date Started _____   Exact Title of Position _____

Name of Employer and Location _____

Salary or earnings per year: (Check appropriate column.)

_____ Under $5,000   _____ $10,001 — $12,500

_____ $5,001 — $ 7,500   _____ $12,501 — $15,000

_____ $7,507 — $10,000   _____ Over $15,000

How did you obtain this job? _____ coordinator _____ friend _____ family _____ school

_____ employment agency   _____ Other (Explain)

_____

How related is this job to the Cooperative Program you took in high school?

_____Same   _____Highly related   _____Somewhat related   _____Not related

Indicate the amount of help you received from the Cooperative Education Program.   Mark only those items which apply to you.

	Much Help	Some Help	Little or No Help
a. To meet entrance requirements to specialized training institutions.	_____	_____	
b. To continue my education.	_____	_____	_____
c. To prepare for employment.	_____	_____	_____
d. To get along with people.	_____	_____	_____
e. To define my career goal.	_____	_____	_____

Did you belong to a vocational student organization such as:

_____DECA   _____VICA   _____FBLA   _____FFA   _____FHA/HERO   _____(HCCNJ)HOSA

_____Other (Explain) _____

If yes, how did it benefit you? _____

_____

Did you change your career goal?   _____Yes   _____No   If Yes, Why?

_____ No longer interested in that field

_____ Went to school to learn new career

_____ Took a new position in another field

_____ Employment opportunities limited in area of training

_____ Other (Explain)

Figure 52 — (Cont'd)

Check the appropriate columns in which the cooperative education teacher helped you in high school.

_____ In school problems   _____ In work related problems

_____ In family or personal problems

Would you recommend the Cooperative Program to other students?   _____ Yes   _____ No

Did you **originally** enroll in the Cooperative Program in high school to get: (Check one or more answers below.)

_____ Out of school earlier in the day   _____ Job experience

_____ Pay   _____ Other (Explain) _____

_____

Was your feeling, expressed above, the same at the end of your Co-op experience? (Please comment)

_____

_____

Education beyond high school: (Check the appropriate line(s) and fill in where necessary.)

Attending	Attended	Completed	Type of Education	Name of Institution	Name of Program
			Adult or evening school		
			Technical or business school		
			Licensing or certification Program		
			Apprenticeship program		
			Two-year college		
			Four-year college		
			Other		

Military Service:

Branch _____ Job Title _____ Length of Service _____

THANK YOU!

EVALUATIONS BY PARENTS AND EMPLOYERS

Unlike the follow-up evaluation study of graduates from a cooperative education program, which can be conducted at periodic intervals of one to five years or more, the evaluative instruments for an employer and/or parent should be conducted within one year after their participation in the program. In order to have any kind of intelligent responses that will benefit the program's improvement, it is essential that these two populations be surveyed as soon as possible after their participation. This immediate feedback is essential. To assist the teacher-coordinator in this endeavor, a sample instrument for an employer evaluation and a parental evaluation is provided.

Figure 53*

PARENTS' EVALUATION OF THE COOPERATIVE EDUCATION PROGRAM

Dear Parent:

In order that we might provide the most effective type of education and training for your children, we are asking you to take a few minutes to evaluate the Cooperative Education Program at _____

Please be assured that your help will be greatly appreciated.

Coordinator _____

Your Name _____   Student's Name _____

	Very Much	Much	Little	Very Little
1. Has your child's progress in the Cooperative Education Program given him/her a better chance for a promotion or salary increase?				
2. Has your child formed the habit of using his/her time and money wisely?				
3. Has your child made a noticeable improvement in self-control?				
4. Has your child developed good leadership and followership through this training?				
5. Was the training station suited to your child's interest and needs?				
6. Did your child's experience in this program increase his/her interest in school as a whole?				
7. Did the training help your child understand and get along better with people?				
8. Did your child become more interested in personal grooming as a result of the training program?				
9. Was there a noticeable increase in self-confidence shown by your child?				
10. Did you notice any personality change/development as a result of the training and experience gained from the program?				

11. On the basis of your observations, what suggestions would you make for improving the Cooperative Education Program? _____

_____

_____

12. Other Comments:

*New Jersey State Department of Education, Division of Vocational Education and Career Preparation.

Figure 54*

COOPERATIVE EDUCATION PROGRAM
PROGRAM EVALUATION BY EMPLOYER

Through periodic evaluation, we endeavor to improve our Cooperative Education Program. We would appreciate your completing this checklist and returning it in the enclosed envelope.

FROM YOUR OBSERVATION:	Very Much	Much	Little	Very Little	Additional Comments
1. How much did your business benefit from its participation in the Cooperative Education Program?					
2. Do you feel that the student-learner received vocational benefit from the supervised training?					
3. Did you notice any marked improvement in the student-learner during the training period?					
4. Is a co-op student generally more productive in work performance than a beginning worker without supervised work experience?					
5. Does a student-learner have a better attitude toward work and associates than an afterschool employee who has no school supervision?					
6. Did participation in the Co-op Program cause any burden on you and your business associates?					
7. At the end of the training period, did the student-learner measure up to your employment standards?					

8. Was the teacher-coordinator helpful? _____Yes _____No

9. Would you continue to participate in the Cooperative Education program? _____Yes _____No

10. Please make specific suggestions that will enable us to better serves the community. (Continue on reverse side if necessary.) _____

_____

_____

FIRM NAME: _____   SIGNATURE: _____

ADDRESS: _____   TITLE: _____

PROGRAM: _____   SCHOOL: _____

*New Jersey State Department of Education, Division of Vocational Education and Career Preparation.

BIBLIOGRAPHY

Adams, Kay Angona: Measuring rainbows.   *Cooperative Education Quarterly,* 10-11, May 1978.

Assessment Guidelines for State-Approved Cooperative Work Experience Diversified Occupations (CWE-DO) Programs in Local Public High Schools. Hartford, Connecticut State Department of Education, Division of Vocational Education, 1973.

C.I.E. — Administrative Handbook. Trenton, New Jersey State Department of Education, Division of Vocational Education and Career Preparation, 1971.

DiPianta, J.J.:   Follow-up of a work-experience program.   *Balance Sheet, 49:*404-405, May 1968.

Establish a Student Placement Service and Coordinator Follow-up Studies. Columbus, The Center for Vocational Education, Ohio State University, September 1977.

Evaluation of Work Experience, Cooperative Education, and Youth Manpower Programs — An Annotated Bibliography. Columbus, The Center for Vocational Education, Ohio State University, Series #28, October 1975.

Evaluative Criteria for the Education of Secondary Schools, 4th ed.   Washington, D.C., National Study of Secondary Schools Evaluation, 1969.

A Follow-up System for Vocational-Preparatory Students for the State of Washington.   Olympia, Wa, Division of Vocational Education, 1968.

Instruments and Procedures for the Evaluation of Vocational-Technical Education Institutions and Programs. Washington, D.C., National Study for Accreditation of Vocational/Technical Education, American Vocational Association, 1976.

Lyons, E.H. and Hunt, D.C.:   Cooperative education: evaluated.   *Journal of Engineering Education,* 436-444, May 1963.

A Manual for Conducting Follow-Up Surveys of Former Vocational Students.   Columbus, The Center for Vocational Education, The Ohio State University, Research and Development Series Number 106, 1975.

Nerden, Joseph: Statewide evaluation of vocational education.   *Contemporary Concepts in Vocational Education,* 402-407, 1971.

Perloff, Robert and Sussna, Edward: Toward an evaluation of cooperative education: A managerial perspective.   *The Journal of Cooperative Education,* 54-73, March 1978.

INDEX